# IN SEARCH OF ADVENTURE

**IN SEARCH OF ADVENTURE**
was funded by

**King George's Jubilee Trust**
**The Dulverton Trust**
**ARCO**

# IN SEARCH
# OF ADVENTURE

Editor
John Hunt

TALBOT
ADAIR
PRESS

Published by:
The Talbot Adair Press
Newlands, Pewley Hill
Guildford, Surrey GU1 3SN, England

Design by:   Graham Bingham

Cover by:    Bill Cameron-Johnson

Index by:    Dr. K. B. Everard

ISBN   0 9511835 4 0

Printed by:  Bourne Press, Bournemouth, England

# Foreword

From my own experiences during expeditions and exploration far afield I have found a deep sense of fulfilment and an enduring delight, both because of, and despite, the sometimes tough conditions of living which such journeys impose. I have long been convinced that the challenges presented by nature can be of profound significance for personal development. This is why I suggested that opportunities for adventure would be an appropriate theme for a consultation at St. George's House, Windsor Castle.

I am delighted that this proposal, which I made three years ago, should have been the seed which has now borne fruit in this report. I am very grateful to John Hunt and his colleagues for carrying this through.

Lord Shackleton    KG PC OBE

# ACKNOWLEDGEMENTS

We are deeply indebted to the Project Director, Roger Putnam, for applying his long experience, his energy and enthusiasm to the wide range of enquiries which have formed the basis of this report. With the able support of David Atiyah, who has sifted and analysed the vast volume of information which Roger Putnam has gathered from various parts of the United Kingdom, he has successfully undertaken a monumental task. We warmly thank Bill Cameron-Johnson for his skill in creating the imaginative cover design.

The paper which provided the foundation for this report was the work of Dr Martin Holdgate, CB, who had to withdraw from the Management Committee on his appointment as Director General of the International Union for the Conservation of Nature in Geneva. We owe a great deal to Dr Holdgate for his contribution to the St. George's House Consultation and during our early meetings.

We also wish to thank Rosalind Gilmore, who was the organiser of the St. George's House Consultation and a member of the initial steering group, whom we have consulted from time to time after she had to retire owing to her duties at Windsor Castle.

We owe a particular debt of gratitude to a number of organisations which have assisted our work. The Outward Bound Trust very kindly seconded Roger Putman to act as Project Director for the study. The Sports Council gave valuable support and advice, particularly in the design and preparation of the quiestionnaires. Berkshire County Council Education Service allowed us to conduct a wide-ranging survey of fifth year pupils within the Authority. British Nuclear Fuels plc and the Outward Bound Centre at Eskdale gave much-appreciated support with photocopying and administration of the study. The Duke of Edinburgh's Award office helped with the advance publicity for the launch of this report. We also greatly appreciated the hospitality of the Royal Geographical Society, the venue for most of our meetings.

We must also acknowledge gratefully the help of the many individuals and organisations who have contributed to the report by giving generously of their advice, by organising meetings on our behalf, by completing lengthy questionnaires, or by other practical assistance. This report would not have been completed without their active support.

Finally, the management group wishes to extend special thanks to the King George's Jubilee Trust, the Dulverton Trust and ARCO, who most generously provided funds for this study to be carried out.

# THE LORD HUNT OF LLANFAIR WATERDINE, K.G., C.B.E., D.S.O.

Lord Hunt is perhaps best known for leading the British Everest Expedition which made the first successful ascent of the summit in 1953.

But his distinguished career stretches well beyond his many expedition achievements and encompasses the Military, politics and service to youth — for which he was created a Life Peer in 1966. He was made a Knight of the Garter in 1979.

Educated at Marlborough College and the Royal Military College, Sandhurst, he was commissioned into the King's Royal Rifle Corps, serving initially in India and Burma. During his Military career, he was awarded the C.B.E. and the D.S.O., and the India Police Medal for services on secondment to the Police in Bengal.

In 1965, at the invitation of Prince Philip, he became the first Director of the Duke of Edinburgh's Award Scheme, which has involved more than two million young people in adventure activities and community work since it was founded.

His commitment to youth has been tireless. He has been Chairman of the Government Committee on Young Immigrants and the Youth Service (1968-9); of the Intermediate Treatment Fund (1980-86); and of the Parole Board of England and Wales (1967-74). He has been President of the Rainer Foundation (1970-85), the Council for Volunteers Overseas (1970-74), the National Association of Youth Clubs (1954-73) and the National Association of Probation Officers (1974-80).

During the Nigerian Civil War of 1968-70, Lord Hunt was adviser to the British Government on relief aid. He headed a Committee which advised the Government of Northern Ireland on the Police in Ulster in 1969.

Lord Hunt remains an active mountaineer and skier. He is a Past President of the National Ski Federation, the Alpine Club, the British Mountaineering Council, the Climbers' Club, and the Royal Geographical Society.

As Chairman of the Management Group which co-ordinated the study which formed the basis of this report — 'In Search of Adventure' — Lord Hunt has brought his wide ranging experience to bear in meeting the challenge of this important task.

# CONTENTS

## Table of Contents | Page No

# CONTENTS

# CONTENTS

# Introduction

A sense of adventure has its roots in the beginnings of the human race, and this innate spirit of quest has been manifested throughout our own nation's history. At times it has given rise to great achievements: the voyages of the Elizabethan adventurers, of Cook, Shackleton and Scott, and many others in more recent times. These deeds have been a source of inspiration to our people and, in particular, to our youth.

Since 1945, increasing numbers of young people, not content with learning of such events as these from their television screens or through the written word, have sought adventure personally, albeit on a modest scale. Many organisations have followed the lead of such bodies as the Scout Movement, the Outward Bound Trust and the Duke of Edinburgh's Award in providing for this mounting wave of enthusiasm. There is abundant testimony from these, and other, sources that such experience has enhanced self-confidence and initiative, widened perspectives and fostered co-operative attitudes.

In contrast to these positive indications of the continuing spirit of enterprise in today's youth, sadly, vandalism and hooligan behaviour, delinquency and crime, drug and alcohol abuse present a very different and negative side of some young people. Yet there is plenty of evidence that these young people, too, can find delight and fulfilment in an environment of open spaces, and that this experience can bring positive change in their attitudes and conduct.

Seldom have enterprise and personal responsibility been more needed, or has it been more important to encourage the will to work together. At a time of rapid and radical change - social, economic and political - it may well be that our own survival now, as it was at mankind's beginnings, depends on our success in cultivating those qualities in many more of our young people. Much, which in times past made for adventure, is now commonplace, made easy and accessible to many and, through the media, a matter of entertainment. This points to the need to cultivate a more enterprising and adventurous approach, as one component in programmes for the development of the young.

This was the message conveyed and illustrated so effectively by such pioneering educationists as Dr Kurt Hahn and Sir Jack Longland. It was brought home afresh to us, the presenters of this study, during a consultation held at St George's House, Windsor Castle in October 1986. The participants had studied the needs of young people at first hand, and many had practical experience in socially difficult areas, where the problems of deprived and disadvantaged youth are most severe.

The idea of such a consultation had been put forward by Lord Shackleton, a member of the Council of St George's House and a past-President of the Royal Geographical Society and was agreed by Sir George Bishop, President of the RGS and the Dean of Windsor, the Right Reverend Michael Mann. The premise was that more should be done through the medium of challenging outdoor activities, to encourage and enable many more young people, especially those living under deprived conditions in the inner cities, to discover and pursue the challenges presented by nature.

The evidence of those attending the consultation was so positive, so compelling, that the participants decided to pursue their enquiries and undertake further action. To this end, a small steering committee was formed under the chairmanship of Lord Hunt, who had chaired the consultation itself. In an initial memorandum, the steering committee set out to lay the foundations of a strategy which would:

* extend the range and scale of opportunities for participants especially in deprived areas;
* enhance the quality of the experience;
* make the organisation of these activities more effective; and
* improve awareness to young people and those who influence them, of what is on offer.

We do not claim that physical activities in a natural environment provide, by themselves, a panacea for our social problems. Much is being done, through changes in the education system, job training schemes and provision for other leisure activities and skills. These are all important aspects of preparing for adult life. But with ever-advancing technology, opportunities for less-skilled work are becoming fewer. For many people there is more leisure. It is vitally important to encourage all young people, whether or not they are fully employed, to be enterprising and adventurous, and to help them — through education, training and leisure provision, — to widen their interests.

We are in no doubt about the pleasure and benefit which experience of outdoor challenges gives to young people, especially those least likely to find such opportunities for themselves. We believe that our findings vindicate and reinforce the claims of many people with first-hand knowledge in this matter, that programmes based upon, or embracing, this element can be of immense benefit to young people and to society in general.

It is with that conviction that we offer this report to those in central and local government and to others working both in statutory and voluntary youth organisations, in schools and in the field of leisure provision. We hope that our recommendations will be the subject of debate and action by all who have at heart the interests of young people and the wider community.

Lord Hunt of Llanfair Waterdine, KG (Chairman), CBE, DSO

Professor John Adair,
Visiting Professor of Leadership Studies, University of Surrey

Professor Denys Brunsden,
Professor of Geography, King's College London

Dr. Richard Crane,
London Outdoor Activities Initiative

Dr. K.B. Everard,
Chairman, Development Training Advisory Group

Roger Orgill, MBE,
Chairman, National Association for Outdoor Education

Brian Ware, OBE,
Vice-President, Young Explorers' Trust (Secretary)

Nigel Winser,
Assistant Director, Royal Geographical Society

# PREFACE

## by the

## PROJECT DIRECTOR

This is a study of the present day use of outdoor environments for challenging and adventurous activities by young people. The study attempts to present a broad overview of the activities currently taking place in Britain, to identify some of the most interesting or significant programmes and to suggest ways forward and opportunities for the future.

## *Outline of Report*

The study is set out in three sections. The first chapter briefly examines the history of the development of Outdoor Education and Outdoor Adventure for the young.

The second section, from Chapter 2 to Chapter 8, presents an overview of the adventurous outdoor experiences available to young people. I investigated the work being carried out in four different age-bands; 8 to 11 years (junior school); 11 to 16 years (secondary school); 16 to 19 years (tertiary schooling or youth training); over 19 years (further and higher education or career training). I tried also to examine and to compare the differing perspectives of those who organise or provide adventure experiences for the young, and those who choose to sponsor or support such programmes, often as part of school or career training or education, and often also with a 'personal development' purpose.

The second section also includes observations about the range of opportunities for different groups of young people, the role of the major national bodies, the needs of specific groups such as ethnic minorities or the disabled, and the use of outdoor activity for young offenders or those at risk of getting into trouble.

The third section, from Chapter 9 onwards, identifies the main themes and implications arising from the study, and identifies the obstacles which hinder participation. These issues include the management and leadership of outdoor ventures, and also the impact of such activity on the physical and the human environment. This section contains proposals for the future which suggest how resources might be developed and used more effectively. The outline of a long-term strategy is presented, with specific practical recommendations.

# Defining the Scope of the Study

One of the main difficulties in carrying out the study has been to define the limits of the investigation, and this problem is linked to that of finding a terminology which is both clear and generally acceptable.

Experiences for young people out-of-doors appear to have four major themes, which are often linked and have different values. The first theme is the development of skills; these may be technical, intellectual or social. The second theme is that of the outdoor and the human environment; this may be studied from a scientific standpoint, or appreciated aesthetically, or may provide the subject of a practical project. The third theme involves the concept of service: to society, to the community in which the activity is taking place, or to enhance the physical environment. The fourth theme is that of personal development; it is primarily about the change and growth of the individual taking part in the activity.

Each of these themes presents a valid purpose for adventures in the outdoors, and it has become increasingly clear to me that no one of these themes can be pursued without some involvement with the others.

# Terminology

A number of expressions are used to describe practical outdoor work with young people. *Outdoor pursuits* and *outdoor activities* are the names usually given to the activities and physical skills which are learned. Both are almost synonymous with *outdoor sports*, although there is usually a less overtly competitive element than in the more conventional sports. Some argue that *outdoor pursuits* has a recreational connotation, and *outdoor activities* an educational implication. Both, at least in the popular imagination, have a strong physical basis and may well imply the presence of hazard to the participant.

Other comparable concepts are those of *field studies* or *environmental studies*. Both expressions suggest the extension of academic work into the outdoor environment. Such an extension provides a valuable balance to work in the classroom, and may lead to original discoveries in the relevant disciplines. Except in so far as the term *environmental studies* implies an aesthetic or creative purpose, the focus is essentially on cognitive learning.

Two other expressions, which are used increasingly, are *adventure training* and *adventure education.* This concept of adventure can encompass a wide range of experiences, not merely physical. In practice the expression *adventure training* is largely used by the uniformed services to imply a disciplined and progressive development of outdoor skills in challenging and risky situations. Most definitions of the word 'adventure' emphasise the elements of hazard and uncertainty of outcome. I consider that for this reason the 'adventure concept' is significantly different from those described earlier. *Adventure education* has an even wider implication, suggesting as it does a distinctive approach to the educational process, through the medium of a practical experience in which physical skills and environmental knowledge and awareness are harnessed to see the travellers safely through journeys or experiences in which outcomes are unpredictable and the quest itself may involve physical hardship or emotional stress.

Two other terms now in common use are *development training* and *personal and social development.* Whilst these make no specific reference to the education environment in which they occur, both are used as a description of outdoor experiences usually taking place away from the home neighbourhood. The educational implications of both expressions are broader than those referred to earlier, and suggest a process of change and development in the individual as a person, rather than a development of specific physical or intellectual abilities. This notion of holistic development, often summed up in earlier years as *character-training, character development* or even *attitude training,* is now central to much of the work that takes place involving young people out-of-doors. Much of the emphasis has shifted from externally-imposed training towards more self-motivated learning and self-development, and this is similar to moves taking place in education and training generally.

The most commonly used expression in this field, however, is *outdoor education.* This is carefully defined by the National Association for Outdoor Education as

> *"A means of approaching educational objectives through guided direct experience in the environment, using its resources as learning materials."*

Most *outdoor education* programmes will contain a combination of outdoor activities and environmental experiences and will involve a commitment to personal and social development as an important aim. Common to all these descriptive terms and their implicit meanings, is the element of adventure. For this reason, I have used the term *Outdoor Adventure,* as a generic term, which covers these activities which are central to the aims of the study.

The study has revealed the extent to which Outdoor Adventure is related to 'residential experience'. The opportunity to live away from home, school or work in a neutral setting with a group of companions, is perceived by many to be of great importance for personal and social development. The combination of this element of living away from home with a challenging set of practical activities provides a concentrated and very powerful learning experience.

The residential experience does not necessarily involve a fixed base; it may equally take the form of an expedition or extended journey. Many of those consulted in the study consider that the expedition provides a unique opportunity for learning and discovery, whether about oneself, others or the environment. Although residential experience and Outdoor Adventure are not synonymous, they are closely related and are seen as equally important elements in many outdoor education programmes.

For the purposes of the Outdoor Adventure study, I have adopted a broad definition which ignores the semantic niceties. 'Adventure', in which the notion of 'challenge' is included by virtue of this definition, has been interpreted in a broad sense. Thus the adventure may be of the mind, of the spirit, of the imagination, as well as a physical experience; it should entail uncertainty of outcome and a degree of hazard, and most importantly, the outcome should not be predetermined; it should depend on the efforts, the judgement and the commitment of the participants themselves. In other words, they should manage as far as possible their own project, within a suitable framework.

I have not included in the study any activity which takes place indoors. Where activities may take place both indoors and out, as in the case of rock-climbing, canoeing or horse-riding, no attempt has been made to investigate the indoor elements.

However, because much current development is taking place in built-up areas, I have included urban open space, fringe and derelict land within the definition of 'outdoors'. A broad view has also been taken of those specific sports and activities which may appropriately be included. Outdoor Adventure encompasses many differing activities, and although the popular perception is of the traditional adventure sports, such as mountaineering, sailing, canoeing and expeditioning, there are a number of sports gaining in popularity, which figure increasingly in outdoor programmes. The definition should therefore be wide enough to include newer pursuits such as trail-biking, para-gliding and survival exercises, as well as less physically demanding activities such as camping, 'earth awareness' experiences and farming. It may, in truth, be said that almost all human activity is, in some sense, adventurous for the young, particularly when practised for the first time, and it seems right to adopt deliberately a broad interpretation of the concept of Outdoor Adventure.

'Youth' too has been given a wider interpretation. The study focuses particularly upon the age group 11 to 19 years, but I have also examined work carried out with youngsters between the ages of 8 and 11, since the foundations of adventurous activity are often laid in the family or at primary school with children in this age group. I have also briefly examined provision for the 19 to 24 age group, since these are significant years of career training for many young adults, and the lack of family constraints often allows freedom to engage in particularly ambitious and worthwhile ventures in remote environments. This age group is also an important source of leaders for younger people venturing out of doors.

# *Method of Work*

The study has been conducted over a twelve-month period. An initial circulation of information to key individuals and national bodies indicated a high level of enthusiastic support. Subsequently, meetings were held with groupings of those most significantly involved in, or affected by, activities in this field including outdoor education teachers, industrial sponsors, the probation service and intermediate treatment groups, local authority recreation department officers, the voluntary sector and appropriate national professional bodies. In addition, visits were made to a number of programmes of particular interest, which may be breaking new ground or which present examples of excellent practice.

To provide a broader perspective, an extended questionnaire was sent to 950 individuals with an active or concerned interest in Outdoor Adventure. A total of 342 responses were received, which form a valuable source of information for the second section of this report. In order to assess awareness of, and attitudes to, outdoor activity among young people themselves, a questionnaire survey was also carried out among 400 15 to 16 year-old school pupils. Alongside the active investigations an attempt has been made to examine some of the written contributions in the field, with a view to exploring the nature and effectiveness of the learning processes involved in adventures out-of-doors.

Outdoor education links closely with many other disciplines of education or learning; indeed it epitomises the possibility of general cross-curricular education and 'learning by doing'. It is in its potential for an integrated and holistic approach to learning and personal development that the exceptional value of adventurous experience for young people, and indeed for adults as well, lies.

*"The adventure — and it is the test of a good adventure — goes on, the same for every generation. It can lose nothing by time or repetition. The first sight of the sea, of the desert, of an elephant, or of a mountain, remains the first sight for each new child, and evokes afresh the same response. The passion for discovery, for the mastery of unknown difficulty, stays always the same."*

Geoffrey Winthrop Young, "Oh High Hills"

# CHAPTER 1
## A HISTORICAL PERSPECTIVE

# *The Early Background: Developments before 1914*

1.1 Adventure education is founded in a variety of philosophical and historical antecedents. The foundations were laid in the nineteenth century, in part as a result of social changes, in part because of the practical requirements of an era of imperial responsibility, and in part through the vision of a considerable number of influential and innovative educators and others involved with young people.

1.2 The administrative requirements and the widespread extent of the British Empire called for many young people to journey to distant places. The traditions of sea-faring and the urge to wider exploration, often in the hope that trade would follow, together led young men either from choice or from necessity to visit every continent and every ocean. The nation depended for its raw materials, and increasingly for its food as well, on trading links with distant lands. The great explorations of the African continent by Livingstone, Burton and others and the celebrated grain races to Australia and around Cape Horn exemplified the adventurous journeys of these pioneering travellers.

1.3 The tradition of travel and exploration for largely practical ends was reinforced by a parallel drive to conduct scientific investigation and fieldwork in the remoter regions of the world. The great explorers, such as Captain James Cook in the eighteenth century and Charles Darwin in the nineteenth, established a tradition of scientific exploration which persists today. Even the Victorian passion for collecting, observing and classifying led to some remarkable journeys in distant and often dangerous places, which have their parallel in the fascinating achievements of the natural history film makers of our own times. Natural history became a fashionable interest of the educated classes in the eighteenth century; Britain became a home for an unequalled range of collections of early human artefacts and natural species, collected from every corner of the world. This interest in the natural world was reflected in the establishment of a multitude of natural history societies; in 1873 there were 169 such local societies and 104 field clubs across Britain, with an estimated membership of 50,000.

1.4 The nineteenth century also saw the beginnings of university fieldwork, for example in geology and in the emergence of 'local surveys'. Some schools founded their own Natural History societies; Belfast Academy in 1830, Marlborough in 1864 and Rugby in 1867. At Marlborough, fieldwork raised a storm of protest, for fear it would harm the school games!

1.5 The introduction of universal suffrage in 1867, giving every (male) citizen a direct responsibility for the selection of his parliamentary representation, led to changing ideas about the educational processes appropriate for such responsibilities. A number of progressive educators were not content with the narrow pedagogy of the time. Many drew their inspiration from Plato, from his ideas about balanced development, and his belief in the principle of freedom:

> *"Don't use compulsion, but let your children's lessons take the form of play. You will learn more about their natural abilities that way".*

*The Republic, Book 7*

1.6 Another important influence stems from the Romantic movement, heralded by Rousseau in the eighteenth century. Rousseau's conviction that happiness could only be achieved if man lived in a state of nature led him to formulate new principles for the education of the young, in which the child is allowed full scope for individual development in natural surroundings, shielded from the 'harmful influences' of civilisation. The Romantic writers and poets, including Wordsworth, Coleridge and Blake, saw and felt the world brilliantly afresh, finding inspiration in the natural landscapes of the Lake District and the Alps. They were much influenced by the legends and mythology of oriental and Homeric literature. They were active nature-lovers, sensitive to the power of the wild landscape and the spiritual relationship between man and nature. They exercised a strong influence upon many of the radical and progressive schoolmasters of the nineteenth and early twentieth centuries.

1.7 What became known as the New School Movement began 100 years ago, with the founding of the first of the English progressive schools at Abbotsholme, started by Cecil Reddie. To some extent, these schools represented a reaction to the prevailing forms of public school education, with their emphasis on chapel, classical studies and team games. At Abbotsholme, Bedales and the other progressive schools established in the first half of this century, the influence of the Romantic movement was evident; following Wordsworth, progressive educators regarded nature as the true educator. Children should be free to realize the spiritual and imaginative power that lay within them, through practical, direct experience of the surrounding environment.

1.8   Such progressive thinking, however, was almost totally irrelevant to the great majority of children in England and Wales, for whom education in any form until the end of the nineteenth century was minimal and traditional in style. The 1870 Education Act required for the first time that school should be placed within the reach of every child, with the primary task of improving literacy, and with few liberal or vocational elements, although provision was made for physical education and games. In 1891, all elementary education school fees were abolished. The Education Act of 1902 made county and county borough councils the local authorities for elementary, secondary and technical education. The Act brought under the new authorities both the Board schools established in 1870 and the voluntary schools previously established under the auspices of the Church. Public money was thus available for the first time to provide professional teachers and a proper level of efficiency on a nationwide basis. Although the 1902 Act did little to broaden the curriculum, it enabled teachers to work more effectively with smaller classes, and to develop a pattern of teaching which took greater account of the interests and needs of the children themselves.

1.9   In this they were helped by the pioneering work of Pestalozzi, who claimed that the best method of education was to link explanation of the physical world directly with the child's own experience, of Froebel and Montessori, all of whom contributed either in the nineteenth or in the early years of this century to the growth of freedom in education, and a broader view both of educational subject-matter and of pedagogical method.

1.10  At the same time that the system of education was being reshaped to meet the needs of the nation in an era of expansion and technological and political change, and of young people for whom the responsibilities of citizenship had been enlarged by the extension of the suffrage, a number of other significant developments took place. Organised youth groups were established, some of which have since played a major role in the development of Outdoor Adventure activity for young people. Notable among these were the Boys' Brigade, founded by Sir William Smith in 1883, (see 3.53) and the Boy Scouts, founded in 1908 by Baden Powell, after an experimental camp on Brownsea Island in 1907 (see 2.16, 3.49, 3.50, 6.63, 6.64, 9.21, 10.9). The growth of the Scout movement, and of the Guide movement subsequently (see 3.51, 3.52), both at home and overseas, was dramatic; by 1910 Scout membership had already reached 100,000 and twelve years later it exceeded one million.

1.11 The later years of the nineteenth century and the early years of the twentieth also saw an increasing trend towards recreation in the countryside. It became fashionable for the moneyed classes to visit and walk in the mountains, and to cruise or sail for pleasure. Even those less well-off were able to enjoy the countryside. The Cyclists' Touring Club was founded in 1878. In 1891, T.A. Leonard, who has been called 'the father of the open-air movement', founded the Co-operative Holidays Association. Some sought more exciting ventures; the exploits of the Victorian mountaineers, notably the first ascent of the Matterhorn, Slocum's circumnavigation of the world in the 1890's, and the epic polar journeys of Shackleton and Scott in the early 1900s, caught the public imagination. Polar exploration, mountaineering and sailing have a special place in the history of Outdoor Adventure, not least because of the amount and quality of fine descriptive and philosophical writing which they have inspired. The hazardous nature of these enterprises, and the freedom and independence from society which they epitomise, prompt fundamental existential questions about man and nature, life and death, freedom and responsibility. Such themes lie at the heart of outdoor, and indeed all, education.

# The Inter-War Years

1.12 The years before the first world war saw the establishment of education for all children in forms more closely relevant to their needs, and the increasing enjoyment of holidays and recreation in the countryside by the more affluent. The years between the wars saw relatively little advance in education provision. The Education Act of 1918 was the principal legislation enacted, raising the general school-leaving age to 14 years and abolishing fees for elementary schooling. However, classes remained large and, even by 1931, only one in five children received effective secondary education. University education remained the prerogative of a small minority, and traditional in its scope.

1.13 For much of this period the country was recovering from the effects of the massive national war effort, and coping with the depression of the 1920s and the slump of the

1930s. In this context it is perhaps not surprising that there were few advances made in educational provision. However, some progress was made in broadening opportunities for school pupils; by 1921, government legislation had empowered local education authorities to provide vacation schools, vacation classes and school camps. By 1928, fifteen education authorities were running school camps. The Hadow Report, published in 1926, set the framework for primary and secondary education which we see today, with the break occurring at 11 years (in England and Wales, but not in Scotland where the break occurs at 12), and with a proposed school-leaving age of 15 years (eventually implemented only in 1947). The report contained no mention of environmental studies as such, but recommended that teaching should be concerned with activity and experience as well as the transmission of facts and skills.

1.14 Partly as a result of this report, further moves were made in the late 1930s to establish opportunitiess for projects and excursions in the countryside, usually under the heading of nature study. Some relaxation of formal physical education requirements also took place, as illustrated by the provisions of the Physical Training and Recreation Act of 1937 and the Social and Physical Training Grant Regulations of 1939. The Act emphasised the need for the provision of camps and training facilities for outdoor activities, permitting grants to be made to voluntary organisations.

1.15 At the same time increasing numbers of 'camp schools' were established, mainly under the auspices of the National Camps Corporation; these were the forerunners of the outdoor centres established so widely in the years after the second world war (see 1.42, 6.39). However, there is little evidence that regular use was made of the outdoor environment as an educational medium, although important developments took place on other fronts.

1.16 In 1930, a significant development for young people wishing to visit the countryside took place with the foundation of the Youth Hostels Association (see 6.65). Together with other national bodies such as the Cyclists' Touring Club (founded in 1878) and the Ramblers Association (founded in 1935), this development indicates the acceleration of a movement by ordinary people into the countryside, assisted by the advent of paid holidays and the development of cheaper public transport, or for some by the ownership of motor vehicles. The very fact of unemployment enabled many young working-class jobless to leave their grimy towns for the clean air of the moors and fells. Access to such open country could not always be taken for granted, but the famous mass trespasses on the Derbyshire moors established the general presumption of access except at specific times of the year. The interest of the public in the countryside, and their increasing concern for its future, had already led to the founding of the National Trust in 1895, and of the Council for the Preservation of Rural England in 1928.

1.17 Two other developments in this period were noteworthy, foreshadowing the later popularisation of Outdoor Adventure for young people for 'personal development' purposes rather than for more narrowly environmental or fieldwork purposes. The first was the establishment in 1932 of the Public Schools' Exploring Society (later the British Schools' Exploring Society) by Surgeon Commander G. Murray Levick, who led eight expeditions to Finland, Lapland and Newfoundland before the outbreak of war. Although the Society has carried out a remarkable series of scientific investigations across the world, the primary purpose remains that of personal development, *"allowing young people to manage real experiences and to learn through doing"* (see 6.57 — 6.59).

1.18 A second development which was to have significant consequences was the decision of Kurt Hahn, formerly headmaster of the Salem school in Germany before his arrest by the Nazis in 1933, to go into exile in Scotland and to establish a similar school at Gordonstoun. Hahn, who has been described as 'a man of many good hunches', made a powerful contribution to the impetus to include challenging outdoor experience as part of an all-round educational experience. Many of his aphorisms have become well-known, notably his statement that the foremost task of education is *"to insure these qualities: an enterprising curiosity; an undefeatable spirit; tenacity in pursuit; readiness for self-denial; and, above all, compassion"*. His statement that *"it is the bounden duty of the educator to impel young people into experience"* remains controversial, but it is a key feature of the many educational initiatives which he inspired. At both Salem and Gordonstoun, Hahn was primarily interested in the kind of men his schools would produce rather than in narrowly academic accomplishment. Accordingly, Gordonstoun incorporated into its range of activities elements unfamiliar in conventional British public schools. Hahn supported involvement in the activities of the surrounding community, he encouraged all-round physical accomplishment, and he believed strongly in the value of expeditions on land and at sea.

1.19 In the years preceding the second world war, Hahn also developed his concept of the County Badge scheme for young people, which he hoped would be adopted throughout the country; this involved tests in athletics, swimming and life-saving, the pursuit of a creative project, and the completion of an expedition on land or water. Subsequently, a requirement for 'service' training was added, thus foreshadowing the Duke of Edinburgh's Award established 25 years later.

1.20 During the years between the wars, many enthusiastic mountaineers, sailors and other sportsmen formed clubs in order to pursue their chosen pastimes. Such clubs, particularly those associated with the universities, provided training and experience for those entering the teaching profession, who were then able to develop such activities in schools. In more recent years, the developing role and structure of the clubs has led them to take an increasing interest in the training of their younger members.

# The War Years and the Post-War Expansion

1.21 The second world war, unlike the first, gave impetus in a number of ways to the Outdoor Adventure concept. In the first place, a systematic attempt was made to train large numbers of servicemen in the skills of mountain and arctic warfare and survival in extreme conditions. In addition, non-traditional forms of leadership training and assessment were devised, which depended upon practical work in small units, such as the Highland Fieldcraft Training centre or the special services which were established to operate independently, often behind enemy lines. Furthermore, both the genuine successes and the myths of wartime adventure were recorded and dramatised, becoming part of the national folklore.

1.22 The war also accelerated radical social and educational rethinking, which led, at the conclusion of hostilities, to important changes in the nature and extent of the responsibilities assumed by the state for its citizens, and a major reform of the education system with the Education Act of 1944.

1.23 The year 1941 saw the establishment of the first Outward Bound school at Aberdovey, the result of the joint vision of Hahn and Laurence Holt, a shipping owner who believed firmly in the values of sail training. Courses of four weeks' duration were provided, principally for those intending a career at sea, but also including a wide cross-section of people from other backgrounds including, significantly, trainees from industry. The original purpose underlying the establishment of the Outward Bound school had been to provide a demonstration of the value of the County Badge scheme, but Outward Bound soon came to have a life and distinctive character of its own (see 1.27, 6.45, 8.22, 8.45 — 8.48). Courses were deliberately demanding, and included a variety of challenges for each participant, emphasising the development of individual qualities and attitudes rather than technical skills. The aim, unequivocally expressed, was 'character training'; at the naming of the ketch "Garibaldi" in 1943, Geoffrey Winthrop Young described the ethos of Outward Bound in its early days very clearly, and foreshadowed some of the initiatives taken in the years following the war:

> "To realise his better self, everyone must pass in youth through some test of adventure and hardship, and the adventure must be real... and yet it must be adjustable, so as not to over-tax adolescence. The forces of nature alone provide these natural adventures and tests of personality: the winds, the roughened surface of the sea, and the rough hill surface of the land. For centuries our people have been learning their manhood from our surrounding sea, from its uncertain adventure and stern discipline. And now at last, under the stresses of these great wars, we have been learning slowly whence we must draw those disciplines for manhood which our organised education in peace has never yet supplied."

> J.M. Hogan, "Impelled into Experiences"

1.24   The years following the war saw important developments, both on the wider social and educational front and also in the provision of outdoor experience for young people. Despite the hardships and shortages of the post-war period, an optimistic view prevailed, that change was both necessary and possible.

1.25   The 1944 Education Act made it the duty of every local authority *"to secure provision for their area of adequate facilities for leisure-time occupations in such organised cultural training and recreative activities as are suited to their requirements, for any person willing to profit by the facilities provided for that purpose"*. It was suggested that authorities should provide adequate facilities for recreation, social and physical training, and that they might establish camps, holiday classes and play centres, and might organise games, expeditions and other activities. Sections of the Act concerned with recreation were further reinforced by the proposal that *"a period of residence in a school camp or other boarding school in the country would contribute substantially to the health and width of outlook of any child from a town school, especially if the care of livestock, the growing of crops, the study of the countryside and the pursuit of other outdoor activities formed the bulk of the educational provision and were handled by specially qualified staff".*

1.26 Partly as a result of these proposals, Derbyshire became the first county to establish its own year-round residential outdoor school. The White Hall Centre for Open Country Pursuits was established in 1950, largely due to the inspiration of Jack Longland, director of education and a well-known mountaineer and supporter of Outward Bound and other experimental ventures.

1.27 The years after the war saw other important developments. In 1946 the Outward Bound Trust was established, with the intention of consolidating the pioneering work at Aberdovey and encouraging the establishment of more Outward Bound Schools. This led in due course to the founding of the Outward Bound Mountain Schools at Eskdale and Ullswater, and of the Outward Bound Sea School at Burghead (subsequently re-established as Outward Bound Loch Eil). In the early 1950s, the first Outward Bound courses specifically for girls were introduced, leading eventually to the establishment of the Outward Bound Girls' School at Rhowniar in mid-Wales.

1.28 In 1947, through the vision and the financial support of Francis Scott, and building directly on the successful war-time Senior Boy Training initiative of the National Association of Boys' Clubs, the first courses at Brathay Hall were held. A distinctive feature of these 26-day residential courses, developed in the 1950s, was the breadth of the educational experience. Outdoor activities among the Cumbrian fells and lakes blended with art and drama to foster self-discovery and the growth of self-confidence (see 6.43, 6.44, 8.72). The special place of fieldwork was early established at Brathay through the systematic surveying of the tarns of the Lake District, leading to the formation of the Brathay Exploration Group (see 6.60).

1.29 In Scotland, a similar development took place in 1948 at Glenmore Lodge, a former shooting lodge in the foothills of the Cairngorms, following a series of outdoor courses originally provided for the Air Training Corps in the Spey Valley. Residential courses lasting from one to four weeks were provided for colleges, universities, school groups and also for those seeking an active holiday. The centre was administered by the Central Council of Physical Recreation (later the Scottish Council of Physical Recreation) on behalf of the Scottish Education Department. Several courses each year were provided for students from Colleges of Physical Education in England as well as Scotland; these were some of the first attempts to include a residential outdoor training element into the preparation of P.E. teachers (see 6.23, 10.23).

1.30  The Central Council of Physical Recreation (see 6.32) was to play an important role in the development of outdoor opportunities for young people. Founded in 1939, it encouraged sport of every kind, and did much to foster the development of outdoor pursuits, particularly through the establishment of National Recreation Centres, at Bisham Abbey, Lilleshall and notably at Plas y Brenin in Snowdonia in 1956, which was to become one of the leading mountain training centres in Britain (see 6.23, 10.23). Shortly afterwards in 1959, the Scottish Council for Physical Recreation established a new purpose-built replacement centre for the original Glenmore Lodge, the origii.al building remaining in use for young people visiting the Cairngorms as a Youth Hostel, and being among the first to offer them specialised outdoor activity courses.

1.31  Other important developments in the post-war years, with a bearing on the development of Outdoor Adventure, were the Town and Country Planning legislation of 1947 and, more importantly, the National Parks and Access to the Countryside Act of 1949, which led to the establishment of the National Parks Commission (see 6.7, 6.11). The Act called for *"the preservation and enhancement of natural beauty and the provision of opportunities for open-air recreation and the study of nature"*. By 1957, ten National Parks had been established and positive steps had been taken under the new planning legislation to safeguard other areas of natural beauty and wild country.

1.32  Much significant progress in absorbing field studies and the earth and life sciences into the changing pattern of education also dates from the immediate post-war years. The establishment in 1949 of the Nature Conservancy Council gave impetus to this, for it was recognised that in addition to its conservation priorities, there were important educational aspects to its work. The report which preceded its establishment stated:

> *The true appreciation of scenery rests in part upon and is certainly enhanced by, some understanding of what might be likened to its bony structure — the forms and dispositions of the rocks and the variety of landscape which these induce, the shapes of the valleys and the summits, the flow of the streams, the cliffs and dunes and flats of the coast, and all the rich verdure with which they are clothed. These are things which can invigorate and refresh the mind and upon which a deep culture can be based."*

1.33 The report went on to call for a new look at the educational potential of field studies, suggesting, firstly, that such studies provided one of the best gateways to the teaching of science. Secondly, by opening the mind to enquiry and experimental activity, it would help equip students to come to terms with a world in which they would occupy changing places in a changing environment.

1.34 The development of field studies owes much to the Field Studies Council, an independent organisation founded in 1943 (see 4.26, 6.38). By 1948, it had opened four field centres, subsequently expanding to ten. These centres were open to people of any age; courses were designed primarily for sixth form students in biology, geography and geology. Teaching staff were encouraged to visit the centres with their pupils and were later able to plan and run their own field courses. Many university departments and teacher training colleges also used the centres, thus spreading their influence more widely.

1.35 The Geographical Association, which had been pioneering fieldwork as a vital part of the teaching of geography since its foundation in 1893, also became more active in the extension of field studies in the post-war period.

> *"Field studies make a departure from education based wholly on transmitted learning in that they provide abundant means by which students may learn through observation. Ideally, educational field work should continue through the whole of a child's school life. If it did so the curiosity of the child and his joy in the world of nature would never end abruptly as they so often do, but would lead in later youth to a critical interest in his environment and a capacity to gain reliable and usable knowledge from what he sees around him."*

> *G.A. Presidential address by G.E. Hutchings, 1962.*

1.36 From 1950 onwards there was a steady increase of interest in the use of the outdoor environment by young people. In part inspired by some of the outstanding adventures of the time, such as the ascent of Mount Everest in 1953, the crossing of the Antarctic ice-cap in 1957, and the single-handed circumnavigation of the globe by Francis Chichester in 1966/67, young people took to the hills and the lakes in increasing numbers. Such excursions were not confined to the well-to-do; young people of all backgrounds hitchhiked, cycled or went on their motor-bikes to the Peak District, North Wales, the Lakes and, increasingly, to the Alps. Many visited the Scottish Highlands, where the new ski industry was emerging. Most universities had flourishing outdoor and expedition clubs, and mounted increasingly ambitious expeditions to remote destinations.

1.37 In 1960, the Report of the Wolfenden Committee on Sport, established by the CCPR, recommended the creation of a National Sports Development Council, and the establishment of governing bodies for each sport, together with graded coaching schemes. The Sports Council was established in 1965, directly funded by government, and responsible both for widening participation and also enhancing standards of performance in the competitive sports (see 6.23 — 6.27, 10.22, 10.23). Also in 1960, the Albemarle Report on the Youth Service in England and Wales recognised the value of challenging activities such as expeditions, travel and mountaineering, and also low-key outdoor adventures closer to home.

1.38 The Newsom Report "Half our Future", appeared in 1963 and gave unequivocal support to the moves to provide outdoor and residential experiences to all young people, whatever their level of academic ability. The report pointed to the need for constructive outlets for physical energy and a wide range of activities to compensate for a 'cramping' environment, and commended the special value of cycling, camping, rock-climbing, fell walking, sailing and canoeing. The report strongly advocates the benefits of residential experiences for all pupils, and particularly, the academically less able.

1.39 As a result of these and other influences, the expansion of education provision generally, and increasing national prosperity, the period from 1960 to 1970 saw a substantial but unco-ordinated increase in the provision and availability of Outdoor Adventure opportunities for young people. Many local education authorities opened their own outdoor centres; charitable organisations such as Outward Bound and Brathay were fully subscribed and expanding their resources, and many new organisations came into being to meet the needs not only of school pupils, but also of young people commencing employment.

1.40 A particular feature of the post-war years in Britain was the extent to which employers in industry, commerce and the public sector encouraged apprentices or trainees to take part in outdoor ventures in the interests of personal development. It was increasingly widely recognised that training in technical or professional skills was not enough, and that attitudes and qualities of character were of equal importance in helping the young employees to make their most effective contribution in the workplace. Some companies in this period established their own outdoor centres, others supported the existing outdoor training organisations, and many encouraged young employees to take part in the Duke of Edinburgh's Award.

1.41 The Award Scheme was established in 1956 and rapidly caught the interest of young people. A flexible, readily accessible and inexpensive means of engaging in a wide variety of pursuits, the Award Scheme was encouraged in schools, youth clubs, voluntary organisations and by employers. It has been widely emulated in other countries. The outdoor elements of the Award are described in more detail elsewhere in this report (see 3.27, 4.18, 6.56).

1.42 Although in 1960 only two or three local authority residential outdoor education centres existed, there was a marked increase in the next two decades. An HMI survey, carried out twenty years later, established that there were some four hundred day and residential centres operated by education authorities, and that, in addition, huts, cottages, disused railway stations, village schools and camping facilities had been acquired by individual school and youth groups. There were also some 300 field study bases and over 500 outdoor pursuits centres and other residential accommodation provided by voluntary, private and commercial organisations. In addition, many authorities had established residential bases abroad, or encouraged educational cruises, ski tours and expeditions overseas.

1.43 Despite the dramatic expansion of provision for outdoor experience by local authorities, outdoor education was not generally recognised as part of the entitlement of every child. As a result, although some authorities made substantial efforts to give pupils these opportunities, others did little. Inspired by Sir Alec Clegg, Chief Education Officer and his deputy Jim Hogan (formerly Warden of Aberdovey) the West Riding of Yorkshire was one of the first to establish well-equipped outdoor centres and also encourage school-based environmental work and outdoor activities.

1.44 Perhaps the most comprehensive provision for outdoor education by any local education authority was that established by Edinburgh during the period 1960 — 1970. In addition to two substantial, well-equipped and fully-staffed outdoor centres at Benmore and Lagganlia, the authority established an outdoor centre in the city providing information, resources and an instructional base, as well as a number of specialist staff who were able to work with schools as necessary. Attached to this centre were a sailing base and a pony-trekking centre. The Education Department was also involved in the development of the Hillend Ski Centre, at that time the largest artificial ski-slope in Europe. Schools in the city were also encouraged to develop their own resources and staff skills for outdoor education. Considerable provision was made by the authority for in-service teacher training. Progression for young people was encouraged by good communication and positive encouragement throughout primary, secondary and tertiary education. The existence of Schools Associations for each of the major activities (sailing, skiing, canoeing, orienteering etc.) assisted further participation.

1.45 Other important developments in this period included the foundation of the Sail Training Association in 1956 and of the Ocean Youth Club in 1960, both with the purpose of providing experience under sail for young people. The first STA vessel, "Sir Winston Churchill", was launched in 1966 and the second, "Malcolm Miller" in 1967 (see 6.66 — 6.69).

1.46 The decade saw many other important developments in the provision of Outdoor Adventure outside the educational sphere. In 1960, Endeavour Training became an autonomous organisation, after operating for over 20 years under the aegis of the National Association of Youth Clubs. Under the inspiration of Dick Allcock, Endeavour pioneered the provision of flexible, student-centred training including outdoor experience as one important element in programmes of preparation for working life. Recognising the disadvantages of a permanent operational base, Endeavour chose to take its programmes to the customers, and thus anticipated many of the developments which were to occur twenty years later (see 6.49, 6.50).

1.47 The scale of expedition work in the remoter parts of the United Kingdom and overseas also increased during the decade. In 1962, the Schools' Hebridean Society began sending expeditions to Scotland, and in 1964, the Yorkshire Schools' Exploring Society was founded, to enable young people from the county schools to undertake more ambitious expeditions. Schools such as Braehead School in Fife, under the guidance of **Hamish Brown**, or Ampleforth, under Richard Gilbert, began as a regular practice to conduct expeditions for their pupils overseas. In 1969, Lt. Col. John Blashford-Snell founded the Scientific Exploration Society, which was to become a motivating force behind the great exploratory ventures "Operation Drake" and "Operation Raleigh", launched in the years that followed (see 6.61, 6.62). The scene was set for a considerable expansion, both of the scale of outdoor enterprise, and also of the conceptual basis and application of this whole field of activity.

# *1970 to the Present Day — Changing Needs and New Approaches*

1.48 It is not proposed to describe in detail the expansion of Outdoor Adventure for young people in recent years, since in large part this is covered in later chapters. However, some developments are so important that they should be highlighted.

1.49 The past 20 years have seen opportunities for indulging in every type of leisure activity expand at a remarkable rate. The development of sports facilities, including some for Outdoor Adventure pursuits, throughout the country; the establishment of country parks; the availability of all manner of games and sporting equipment; the introduction of new activities such as para-penting, moto-cross, fell-running and water skiing have all contributed to a growth of opportunity and choice which is unprecedented. At the same time, the cost of overseas travel, and the opportunities to visit the far corners of the world through the advent of mass air travel, have significantly expanded the horizons of the younger generation. Simpler pastimes have given way to more sophisticated ones, and yet the true educational opportunity presented by these changes has still not been fully grasped.

1.50 Recent years have seen a great increase in the number of private and commercial companies existing to service this expanding leisure, holiday and travel market. Multi-activity holidays for young children, trekking holidays through the foothills of the Himalayas or journeys by truck into the Sahara desert, all represent the growing commercial interest in this field. The commercial interest has also become evident in the supply of outdoor equipment; such is the variety of 'high-tech' gear available in the outdoor shops that it is easy to forget that Outdoor Adventure is of its essence a simple and elementary relationship of an individual with the environment.

1.51 The years since 1970 have also seen an increasing specialisation of provision and approach in Outdoor Adventure. As the merits of such experience have been recognised, so the need has arisen to clarify the learning processes and outcomes, and to relate them to the needs of each group of young people involved. The establishement of the Manpower Services Commission (now the Training Agency) and the introduction of residential or outdoor experience as part of the Youth Opportunities Programme, the Youth Training Scheme, and the Community Programmes of recent years, called for greater insight into these areas. At the same time, the development of education methods based on experiential learning and problem solving approaches, for instance through the Technical and Vocational Education Initiative (TVEI) and the Certificate of Pre-Vocational Education (CPVE), have done much to improve understanding of the true effects and value of Outdoor Adventure experience.

1.52 Perhaps as a result, it has become widely accepted that the traditional gateways to outdoor experiences, through field studies, skills acquisition, conservation work or residential and expedition opportunities are not separate, but inescapably connected. Whatever the specific nature of outdoor experience, all-round personal development of the individual has become increasingly recognised as the fundamental purpose, whether in formal or informal education.

1.53 Finally, recent years have seen the increasing professionalisation of the activities of the organisations and individuals working in this field. Provision for training, both in the technical skills and also in the human skills involved in Outdoor Adventure provision, has expanded considerably. A greater range of courses for aspiring tutors in this field has been developed in universities and colleges.

1.54 The emergence of professional bodies such as the National Association for Outdoor Education, the National Association for Environmental Education and the National Association of Field Studies Officers (see 6.36, 6.37) has begun to give a clearer shape to the various professional groupings involved. The establishment of the umbrella body for the Development Training Bodies (see 6.41), and of the various regional groupings of residential centres (see 6.42), establishes a more coherent framework and structure from which to address changing needs and the implementation of new legislation in education and employment, which together with recent European Community legislation signal radical changes in the 1990s.

# CHAPTER 2
## PROVISION FOR CHILDREN 8 — 11 YEARS

*"This is the only stage in the whole of education when the child is educated as a whole person."*

The Plowden Report, Children and their Primary Schools

This section is concerned with young children in the later part of their primary education at junior school. It also examines opportunities for Outdoor Adventure in their leisure time.

# General Considerations

2.1   The eight to eleven age-group is the youngest to be considered by the Outdoor Adventure study. By the age of eight, physical skills and co-ordination are well-developed, and the majority of children have the ability to use problem solving skills based on their own past experience. They are able to recognise problems, to consider possible solutions, and to select those which seem most effective. Most have achieved the ability to look after their own basic practical needs. After three years at infant school, they are used to a measure of independence from home, and have begun to develop the skills of living and working with others. At the same time they retain a strong capacity for imaginative and dramatic play. Their energy and curiosity are unbounded and so intent can be their concentration on so-called 'play' that it is evident that to them it represents much more than this; to them it becomes all-absorbing. They have not yet encountered the diverting pressures of puberty and adolescence.

2.2   Children of this age group, with this capacity for absorption in play activities, respond enthusiastically to the provision of appropriate outdoor experiences. The dividing line between play and adventure, which even for adults is hard to define, becomes almost indistinguishable.

# *Work in Primary Schools*

2.3 Many would claim that the primary stage of education is the most exciting. Curiosity and enthusiasm are at a maximum level, and the constraints of the curriculum are less pressing. This gives freedom for exploration and investigation outside the classroom, unbounded by the pressures for academic achievement. At the same time, interests and skills can be discovered which can be developed and expanded in later years both within and outside school.

2.4 The great majority of primary school staff, particularly since the radical changes in approach initiated by the Plowden Report, recognise the opportunity of these formative years and create appropriate programmes for their pupils. Practical and creative project work is much in evidence in these schools, and often skilful and imaginative use is made of the surrounding environment.

2.5 In most cases, even in the most densely populated urban areas, it is not necessary to travel far to find small but interesting outdoor locations where natural features can be explored and practical tasks attempted. Most of the ruined sites left after the 1939-1945 war have now been rebuilt (and these provided some of the most effective 'adventure playgrounds' for post-war urban children), but there are extensive areas in most cities, for instance in the derelict land of the Black Country or the surrounds of urban reservoirs, which provide rich and varied environments for outdoor experience. These pockets of 'urban wilderness', provided that access can be obtained, are particularly well-suited to half-day or full-day field trips which may combine simple scientific work with environmental awareness experiences and more physically adventurous pursuits.

2.6 An outstanding example of a small local resource is the 2¼ acre *Camley Street Natural Park* just north of London's Kings Cross main line station adjoining the Grand Union Canal. This example of 'countryside in miniature' was an abandoned coal-yard. Since 1983 it has evolved with enthusiastic backing from many sources into a unique outdoor resource for more than 5,000 schoolchildren each year. It is so popular with children and their teachers that it is fully booked months in advance.

*"Camley Street is not just a 'green oasis'. It has become a much loved place of its own. It is the*

*children's nature reserve; one where wildlife thrives, though it is often outnumbered by visitors. It is one of the few areas of central London where vandalism is almost non-existent, indicating local respect and involvement. The park's full-time teacher says 'Camley Street offers a unique opportunity for inner-city children to experience the natural world at first hand'".*

*London Wildlife Trust Newsletter*

2.7 Primary schoolchildren may also have the opportunity to visit more extensive areas of accessible countryside within the daily school programme. Some schools are situated within or close to open country, with access to farms, woodlands or moorland. More commonly, schools may have access to 'pocket parks' or country parks which can provide a range of adventurous experiences. For instance, the *Irchester Country Park* in Northamptonshire, formerly an ironstone quarry and close to the expanding urban areas of Wellingborough and Rushden, provides within its 81 hectares a variety of terrain and woodland, as well as an adventure playground and an information resource centre. This is one of a series of such country parks established in the county which are well used by local primary schools. The *Emberton Country Park* in Buckinghamshire, by contrast, incorporates a series of lakes created from the former gravel workings alongside the River Ouse. Here, there are good opportunities for introductory sailing and canoeing, as well as an artificial rock climbing face.

2.8 In some cases, education authorities have established their own local activity centres. The *Debdale Sailing Centre* was established by the City of Manchester Education Committee on a reservoir at Gorton, and this impressive facility is well-used by local primary schools for sailing and canoeing. In other cases, primary schools may make use of facilities or areas owned privately or by charitable trusts. The Ackers Trust development in the heart of the industrial West Midlands provides multiple opportunities for adventurous activities, including orienteering, artificial slope skiing, rock-climbing and BMX biking in a remarkably small area of formerly derelict industrial land.

2.9 Much of the work currently carried out at primary school level takes place on the basis of day visits from school, usually in class groups, and where the level of activity is necessarily elementary. The advantage of such work is that it can be integrated quite easily with normal school timetables, and can be supervised by class teachers who may not themselves have a high level of outdoor skill. In general, both boys and girls participate equally. Such activity can become a natural extension of work within the school, fitting easily into the framework of primary education.

2.10 Some education authorities have established outdoor centres within their own county, which may be used either for day visits or on a residential basis. The *Stanley Head Outdoor Centre* near Stoke-on-Trent is an impressive example; the centre provides courses for about 3,500 primary school pupils each year, and approximately one third of this work is for groups attending on a day-visit basis. Principal activities are walking, caving, rock-climbing, canoeing, rafting, writing and environmental studies, involving local history and geography, farming and industrial archaeology.

2.11 Although much Outdoor Adventure for these schoolchildren takes place close to the school, there are many examples of ambitious work carried out away from the home area in more distant places, involving the use of hostels, residential centres or camps. For example each fourth-year primary pupil at *Roose School* in Barrow-in-Furness has the opportunity to take part in a residential week or weekend at the Cumbria centre at *Denton House* in Keswick. The programme is tailor-made for the group, and thus integrates with the work being carried out in school. Almost every pupil takes advantage of this opportunity, and the experience is highly praised by both staff and youngsters. These fourth-year experiences are supplemented by one day visits to the *YMCA Centre* at Lakeside on Windermere for other outdoor and environmental work.

2.12 An alternative approach is illustrated by *Woodthorpe School* in Sutton Coldfield, where a four-year programme of outdoor experiences has been developed for 7 to 11 year-olds, with two sessions within the curriculum each week. The outdoor programme provides a cross-curricular experience which develops both individual and social competence. The programme develops bivouacing and camping skills, enabling pupils to carry out a final exercise involving an overnight camp. Almost all this work is carried out in the Birmingham area, and does not involve travel further afield.

2.13 These two approaches are combined at many primary schools, for instance in the work of the *Yarnfield Primary School* in Birmingham. Here, despite problems of transport and lack of staff cover, climbing days and visits to the *Ackers Trust Centre* on a day basis from the school are followed by school residential camps and by visits to local education authority or commercial outdoor centres for residential experience. School-based work includes mapping, orienteering and 'trust' games, the Ackers Trust provides rock-climbing and skiing, and the residential centre opportunities for canoeing, hillwalking and further rock-climbing.

> " *The culmination of much classroom work is the one-week residential course in the summer term at the Authority's moorland centre. Class teachers go with their own (primary) class groups accompanied by one other teacher, an ancillary helper and her husband and three students from the city art college, who undertake a photographic and display project based on the work of the children. When the pupils return to school the task of collation, recording, interpretation, elaboration and presentation of the material collected begins. Much will be illustrated through art and individual interpretations of events and scenes on the moor are completed using a range of media. A miscellany of drama, music and poetry is prepared together with a tape/slide sequence recording the events of the week. Perhaps the main reason for the high standards achieved by this school is the presence of a clear philosophy which ensures continuity and the progressive build-up of skills and attitudes. The headteacher believes that the children gain a deeper understanding of themselves and each other through sharing and taking responsibility...* "

(HMI survey "Learning Out of Doors")

2.14 The questionnaire survey indicates that the most commonly used activities for primary schoolchildren are country walking, orienteering and environmental studies. The most commonly expressed purposes for outdoor activity appear to be to develop creative imagination, appreciation of beauty and environmental awareness.

2.15 The result of any adventure programme should be that participants can operate independently of adults, and although this objective is rarely feasible with youngsters at primary school, nevertheless some interesting programmes have been attempted. For instance, 25 fourth-year pupils from *Castle Park Primary School* in Kendal, working in four groups, were able to complete a self-reliant journey across the Lake District over a period of several days, with a minimum of direct support from adults. They had a comprehensive preparation during the preceding months, in and out of school. The journey was organised as a 'treasure hunt', was shadowed by adults, and involved the use of different means of travel, i.e. bus, boat, on foot, and even railway! The staff organiser of this venture commented:

*"I feel that the greatest contribution that the scheme has made is to underline the elements of the curriculum in a practical way. To take one small example, the volume of maths problem solving has been quite phenomenal, and the vigour and enthusiasm of it outstrips any maths lesson. The same could be said for mapwork, sailing skills, stove operation, language work and so on."*

*(Adventure Education, Vol 2 No 2)*

# *Opportunities outside School*

2.16 Many opportunities for Outdoor Adventure are provided outside school by voluntary, charitable or commercial organisations. Two of the best known voluntary organisations are the Scouts and the Guides; there are over 250,000 cub scouts (aged between 8 and 10 years), and over 370,000 Brownies (aged between 7 and 10 years). Camping, outdoor pursuits and practical games play a significant part in their programmes of activity, and the cost of participation is low. Cub scouting is based on the themes of growing up, discovering, thinking, sharing and making friends. Working together in small groups is a key feature of cub scout programmes.

2.17 Another charitable organisation with camping as its key activity is *Forest School Camps, (FSC)* offering a range of holidays under canvas for young people from six to eighteen years. 60% of these are under 15, and 25% (approx 400 children per annum) are under 11. The camps provide practice in harmonious living together, development of self-reliance, rediscovery of the natural world, and enlarging horizons through travel. One of the benefits of the FSC experience is that children learn to manage themselves independently and to overcome their fears away from their parents. The flavour of the experience is caught in the following descriptions of a weekend course and a one-week course respectively:

*"We'll thrash through the Netherton Tunnel (3027 yards), — remember your torch! — we'll walk the Stourbridge and Staffs and Worcs canals, and use buses and trains for some bits. We'll see glass being blown and chains being made by hand. We'll boat it into the Dudley Canal (leggers please!) and see the hidden bits of Birmingham City centre before the train home"..."a hot sunny camp (even if it rains) but we'll be able to cool off in the river. There will be mudslides,*

*melodrama, magic, music, mask-making and much merriment. All this intermingled with story
telling and survival, tree-hugging, fire-lighting and woodcraft..."*

2.18 A fine example of community encouragement of Outdoor Adventure for young people is
provided by the *Ambleside Area Adventure Association (the 4 As)*, which offers
opportunities for a wide range of activities. These have included canoeing, cycling,
exploring nature, fell-running, fell-walking, geology, keep-fit, mountaineering, mountain
rescue, orienteering, outdoor photography, parachuting, pop-mobility, rock-climbing,
sail-boarding, sailing, skiing, survival, weight-training and winter mountaineering. Of
course, primary school age members do not necessarily engage in all these activities.
Membership of the Association is open to all, but a significant number of young people
join in the years between 8 and 11. The '4 As' has the advantage of operating in the heart
of the Lake District, and of having the resources of staff, students and equipment of the
Charlotte Mason College (see 4.82) to draw upon, but the broader aims are applicable in
all communities. They are:

> *"to provide facilities in the interests of social welfare for recreation and leisure time occupation
> with the object of improving the conditions of life for the inhabitants of Ambleside and its
> neighbourhood."*

This pioneering project is notable for the scale of community involvement and the
relative cheapness of membership and participation.

2.19 Valuable work has been achieved with primary schoolchildren in holiday time by the
*Cheshire County Council Countryside and Recreation Department.* Up to 1,000 youngsters
each year take part in adventure experiences in Manchester and other urban fringe areas
working with the Country Ranger Service. These initiatives have developed largely as a
result of the Countryside Commission policy statement "Enjoying the Countryside". The
main purpose is to enable schoolchildren to learn to use the countryside for outdoor
recreation safely and responsibly. Activities may include conservation work,
environmental awareness sessions, rock-climbing, abseiling, wayfaring, orienteering and
overnight expeditions, usually for the 7 to 13 age-group.

> *"How can any child resist an invitation to 'join the Rangers for a day of DISCOVERY,
> ADVENTURE, GAMES and FUN on the trail into unknown territory'. An expedition theme
> lends itself to many interpretations and gives the opportunity to incorporate the ingredients*

*necessary for a worthwhile, enjoyable, and justifiable experience. We include elements of risk taking, leadership, sharing, environmental awareness, fun and excitement. Obviously it helps to have an adventurous location, but expeditions could be held anywhere, even in a car-park with a little ingenuity. The format we follow is to have a definite BEGINNING — the TRAIL — leading to a CAMP for lunch — followed by various ACTIVITIES. We limit numbers to about twenty to enable us to give each person participating a quality experience. Expedition themes so far have been to "solve the mystery of the flying leaf-eaters" or to go on the trail of early Breton settlers, or simply an "invitation to lunch". Clues are found along the way, or food collected en route..."*

*(John Gittins — Assistant Director, Cheshire Countryside and Recreation Dept.)*

2.20 Many primary schoolchildren take part in outdoor exploration under the auspices of *Watch*, the junior wing of the *County Nature Conservation Trusts* and the *Royal Society for Nature Conservation*. Although the age limit for Watch membership is 18, the majority of members are aged between 7 and 13. Among activities for 1988 and 1989 by the Berkshire, Buckinghamshire and Oxfordshire Naturalists (BBONT) Watch group were Chiltern Hills discovery walks, farmland tours, pond dipping, reptile evenings, frog watching, hedgerow surveys, night watch activities, river and dragonfly studies, fungus forays and crayfishing. The activities of Watch groups are expanding nationally and for many children form a most important basis for sensitive use of the outdoor environment in later life.

2.21 *Newcastle Childrens' Adventure Group*, a charitable body on Tyneside also provides varied opportunities for Outdoor Adventure for urban youngsters. Up to 1,500 children between 8 and 13 take advantage of the programme each year, which involves 'taster' days of activity in the urban environment, and provides a drop-in base in the city centre. The organisers recognise the importance of such provision for 8 year-olds; this helps to provide relief for mothers in holiday time and an outlet for the strong adventurous instinct of this age group. Annual camps or residential visits to wild country areas provide an extended opportunity for more ambitious outdoor challenges.

2.22 A further example of a charitable organisation assisting Outdoor Adventure for the primary school age-group is provided by the *Adventure, Service, Challenge Scheme (ASC)*. Established in 1960 to meet the needs of urban unattached youth between 8 and 15 years, the scheme provides:

*"a structured scheme of activity for the young to provide them with a sense of achievement and progress, challenging activities and encouragement to give service to those in need."*

Some 25% (1,750 youngsters) are under 11 years of age. In its attempt to provide a wide range of experience for participants, it resembles the Duke of Edinburgh's Award Scheme; indeed it is seen by its organisers as an appropriate preliminary training before participation in the Award Scheme. Speaking of the Scheme, Dr. Robert Runcie, Archbishop of Canterbury, said:

*"I think there are four characteristics about this Scheme which you could apply to the creation of good communities anywhere. First of all there's the companionship it provides, and those gifts of acceptance, support and tolerance between people working on it which gives them a sense of security; and if you don't provide that anchor in life, no child will ever grow. The second thing is discipline, because companionship on its own can be quite soft. Thirdly, a community needs loyalty — communities, like individuals, only prosper if they are loved. Finally, well, I cannot do better than use the old-fashioned word 'vision', which gives the peculiar characteristics of this Scheme — adventure, exploring the unknown, giving service to others, and the challenge of meeting new opportunities. The ASC scheme binds those things together."*

# Commercial Providers of Outdoor Adventure

2.23 There is now a wide variety of commercial provision for Outdoor Adventure experience. Multi-activity summer courses for youngsters in the summer months proliferate each year, on the lines of American summer camps. Many are based in schools or colleges which would otherwise be closed in the summer holiday months. The examples of such opportunities which are described briefly here give merely an indication of what is available. Generally, the range of activities is wide, and youngsters can choose which they prefer; the emphasis is on enjoyment and variety. Many of these holiday courses provide an exciting experience away from home with the opportunity to sample such varied activities as kayaking, computing, farm visits and BMX biking. However the quality of such courses is uneven, as was highlighted in the 'Which' report of January 1986. The British Activity Holidays Association was established in 1987, partly as a result of this and other critical reports to enhance the general quality of provision.

2.24 *Rank Education Services Ltd. (Butlins)* make use of their holiday camp facilities for 'Schools Venture Weeks' in the spring and early summer months (March — May) each year. Fully residential courses are provided, principally for the 8 to 12 year age-group. These offer a wide variety of activities and games such as abseiling, boating, orienteering and swimming as well as coaching in the conventional team games and skills. In 1988, 172 schools took part in such Venture weeks, and Rank Enterprises claim that over the past 17 years some 500,000 youngsters have participated.

2.25 One of the largest providers of adventure holidays for children is *PGL*, which offers courses in 21 locations in Britain and some overseas. The emphasis is on exciting, practical activity rather than on expedition work; 'Pacesetter' holidays in South Wales offer a fixed programme at PGL's own centres; 'Adventure World' courses are largely based within the company's Boreatton Park estate; and the Superchoice programme, after an opportunity to sample diverse activities at elementary level, gives the opportunity for a wide choice of activity in the latter half of the week. Some 7% of the company's work is with the under 11 age-group, amounting to some 3,500 young people in all.

2.26 *Skern Lodge Outdoor Centre* in Devon offers purpose-designed school activity courses for junior schools. The set programme of activities in the magnificent North Devon coastal environment is designed with school staff beforehand, and is based on a half-day module. At the opposite end of the scale, *Lakeland Experience* in Cumbria has designed an outdoor programme in association with the Youth Hostels Association for groups aged 9 to 16, with a maximum course size of 16 participants. The distinctive feature of this programme is the close co-operation of the company with the Eskdale hostel, and the deliberate limitation placed on the size of the course to enable individual attention in the multi-activity programme.

2.27 All such commercial providers of 'adventure holidays' stress the educational value of their holidays, and indeed many have been established by experienced teachers. The director of *Adventure International Enterprises* at Bude, Cornwall, whose large and well equipped centre, formerly a hotel, can accommodate up to 400 participants, has set out his aims and objectives in a manner indistinguishable from those put forward by the teachers and others who proclaim the special merits of Outdoor Adventure as a part of regular education provision.

*"The aim of all this exploration of the world in primary schools is to use the natural curiosity of children to help them to discover how full of interest the world is, and to begin to learn how to look at it, what questions to ask about it, how and where to find the answers. That is what being educated is, and a child so educated need never be bored or have a dull moment."*

*John Blackie, (1969)*

## 2.28  *Summary*

(a) This is the stage when children's curiosity and enthusiasm are at a maximum, that play begins to develop into adventure, and important foundations are laid. (2.1, 2.2)

(b) Freedom for exploration and investigation outside the classroom encourages practical and creative project work designed to stimulate the imagination. The process starts in exploring the immediate surroundings and there is a need for children in urban areas to have opportunities to discover the natural environment of the countryside. (2.3 — 2.7)

(c) The basic skills of Outdoor Adventure may to advantage be introduced at this stage depending on access to outdoor pursuits facilities locally or in centres. (2.10 — 2.13)

(d) The contribution of voluntary organisations such as cub scouts, brownies or 'Watch' groups are particularly valuable in extending the adventure experience. (2.16 — 2.22)

(e) Adventure holidays, with the introduction to residential experience, provide a useful · and exciting culmination to this stage. (2.10, 2.11, 2.13, 2.23 — 2.27)

# CHAPTER 3
## PROVISION FOR YOUNG PEOPLE (11 — 16 YEARS)

*"The curriculum for a maintained school satisfies the requirements of this section (of the Act) if it is a balanced and broadly based curriculum which a) promotes the spiritual, moral, cultural, mental and physical development of pupils at the school and of society; and b) prepares such pupils for the opportunities, responsibilities and experiences of adult life."*

*Education Reform Act 1988.*

*"Those concerned with the secondary curriculum need to look more searchingly than ever before at its capacity to help pupils face the built-in uncertainties of the world they are entering at 16".*

*Curriculum 11-16: Working Papers by H.M. Inspectorate, 1977.*

This chapter examines some of the opportunities for Outdoor Adventure at present available to young people in the secondary school age group. It is at this stage of their development that most young people first encounter the more adventurous outdoor challenges, such as rock-climbing and white-water canoeing or overland journeys involving camping. They may do so as part of their school experience, or through participation in the many voluntary schemes which include outdoor activity.

# *General Considerations*

3.1 The eleven to sixteen age-group includes the period of puberty and early adolescence. This stage of development is of great importance in preparing for life as an adult, and for some young people the changes and adjustments entailed may be difficult and quite stressful.

3.2 Some of the developmental tasks of adolescents have been defined as follows (R.J. Havinghurst; Human Development and Education):

— *to achieve new and more mature relationships with agemates of both sexes;*
— *to accept one's physique and learn to use the body effectively;*
— *to achieve emotional independence from parents and other adults;*
— *to achieve assurance of economic independence;*

    *— to select and prepare for a vocation;*
    *— to prepare for marriage and family life;*
    *— to develop intellectual skills and concepts necessary for civic competence;*
    *— to achieve socially responsible behaviour;*
    *— to acquire a set of values and an ethical system to guide behaviour.*

3.3    Carrying through such demanding developmental tasks successfully calls for appropriate support and education, tailored to the needs of each individual, recognising that the timing and the rate of change vary greatly at puberty and during adolescence.

> *"To help them build up sound relationships with others, pupils need to be 'impelled into experience'. They should know what it is to exercise initiative and responsibility as well as to undergo tight discipline and control. In other words, they should have the opportunity to follow, to co-operate and to lead. Above all they need to develop that confidence which comes from a sense of achievement."*

*(Curriculum 11-16)*

# Work in Secondary Schools

3.4    In the past ten years there have been significant changes in the approach to education in secondary schools, which have implications for experience gained outdoors, and show it to be of increased value and relevance.

3.5    The introduction of GCSE, a uniform and yet flexible examination system for fifth-year pupils, has brought an increased emphasis on practical project work, problem solving approaches and learning by doing.

3.6    The introduction in Autumn 1989 of the national curriculum is a major development, clarifying those ten 'foundation subjects' which all pupils will study. The foundation subjects do not represent a complete curriculum in themselves; the whole curriculum will include aspects of personal and social education and a number of 'cross-curricular themes', one of which is environmental education. No mention is made of Outdoor Education in the new legislation; however, given the increased emphasis on practical work, it is clear that outdoor experience is relevant to several of the programmes of study and the contributory subjects, as well as a valuable setting for personal and social development.

3.7 The expansion of the Technical and Vocational Education Initiative (TVEI) for 14- to 18-year olds, with its encouragement for young people to take more responsibility for their own learning through self-discovery and enterprise, also emphasises the importance of enabling the young to solve the real-world problems they will meet at work and in adult life. Stronger emphasis will be placed on developing initiative, motivation and enterprise, as well as on problem-solving skills and other aspects of personal development. Some TVEI programmes include a residential experience, often using an outdoor centre. Experience-based learning lies at the heart of such residential experiences, and participants in some of the most effective examples may be given responsibility for the preparation, planning, and negotiating of the location and programme of activities, the journey, domestic and social responsibilities, as well as menus and equipment requirements.

3.8 A significant change taking place is the introduction of systems of pupil-profiling and records of achievement. The Record of Achievement should recognise achievement, motivate and enhance personal development and provide a recognised and valuable document for the pupil. As long ago as 1963, the Newsom report argued that

*"boys and girls who stay at school until they are 16 years of age may reasonably look for some record of achievement when they leave".*

The Newsom report also confirmed the conviction of many teachers that a wide range of activities developed in a residential context provides an abundance of opportunities to enhance and extend learning, and an almost unique environment to promote the social and personal development of young people and to bring teachers and students into closer contact. Such close contact is the key to effective profiling and appraisal.

3.9 It is evident that if records of achievement and profiles are to go beyond simple statements of academic achievement at school, it will be necessary to enable young people to demonstrate in practice their other competences and to develop effective means of assessing achievements in non-academic fields of work.

*"It does not seem reasonable that a young person's efforts, achievements and successes should*

*be summed up, after at least 11 years' schooling, by a collection of grades at examination. As well as 'what can he do?', an employer will want to know how well, how quickly, how independently he can do it."*

*National Council for Training and Development Report*

3.10    Valuable pilot work in profiling has already been conducted both in the maintained sector of education and also by a number of voluntary bodies using outdoor experience. An early example of a profiling exercise was conducted by the staff of the North Lewisham Support Centre, who organised a residential week of challenging outdoor activity at the Outward Bound Centre at Eskdale for a group of 4th and 5th year pupils with a long history of disruptive behaviour at school. They agreed to attend because they saw this as a way of making a fresh start and an opportunity to improve basic skills that had suffered as a result of their problems in mainstream education. The work included a wide variety of adventure activities and concluded with a two-day expedition to Scafell Pike. The staff involved spoke with great enthusiasm of the insights gained both by staff and by students as a result of this six-day experience. Each activity was profiled, covering a cross-section of skills. Students shared various aspects of the follow-up work, including letter-writing, descriptive writing, display work and preparing and mounting photographs.

*"I now know how much I can take from other people. I could learn to take more because I was often too short tempered. Once I did react and it was the right thing at the time, but generally it's not worth it because you lower yourself to their level. It ought to be a 2 week course... we were just getting to know each other and working well as a team."*

*Danny C.*

# Definition of Aims for Outdoor Education

3.11 Provision for Outdoor Adventure in secondary schools varies greatly between different schools and different authorities. Outdoor Education, and the use of the outdoors, are usually seen as vehicles for the delivery of the curriculum, rather than as curricular subjects in their own right. The value and priority attached to this approach vary greatly.

3.12 Many local education authorities are working towards a clear statement and definition of aims and purpose in their use of the outdoors, and are seeking to define clearly the goals and the learning processes characteristic of outdoor education, together with its relevance to personal and social development. The change of approach implicit in the move from a subject-based, educational process to a cross-curricular, experiential style is fundamental, and calls for a different and more open-ended way of working for teachers and schools.

3.13 The policy statements on Outdoor Education set out by Cumbria County Council, Devon County Council and Lothian Region are examples of the steps being taken to articulate the rationale for this approach to education. In the Lothian paper, the National Association for Outdoor Education definition of Outdoor Education is adopted;

> *"Outdoor Education is a means of approaching educational objectives through guided direct experience in the outdoor environment, using its resources as learning materials. This experience combines both a study of environmental aspects and topics and participation in those activities associated with the natural environment."*

The statement emphasises that Outdoor Education is not a subject, but an approach to education. Its role is then related to the four sets of aims formulated in the Munn Report (see Bibliography). These are: knowledge of self and of the physical and social environment; cognitive, psychomotor and interpersonal skills; affective development; and preparation for life, leisure and social competence. There follows a useful model scheme for incorporating outdoor experience into the school curriculum, together with an analysis of its relevance in different subject areas.

3.14 Devon County Council in its own draft statement on Outdoor Education sets out a widely-used model which demonstrates the interlinking components of this approach. Outdoor Education is seen as a synthesis of outdoor pursuits, outdoor studies and residential experience, and it is emphasised that Outdoor Education is *"a style, an approach or a strategy of learning through which educational objectives can be achieved"*. This approach is well illustrated by a number of examples, of which two are quoted:

> *"Jane is 12 years old and is making a model of her local town. When she first came to the school, Jane had little notion of appropriate behaviour when working and playing out of doors away from the structured environment of the school. During the past year Jane and her*

*companions have come to respect and enjoy the countryside fully and to apply sensible codes of behaviour. Her parents are delighted at the dramatic effect on her personal confidence and behaviour of a week's residential experience in one of the many field centres available to Devon schools. Here for the first time she has lived away from home, has learnt to work co-operatively with others in her group, and has been given real tasks to do and real decisions to make."*

*"15 year-old Paul has a GCSE project in geography and geology. This has involved field trips to a variety of sites for comparative studies and has included the use of local field study centres. He is hoping to be chosen for one of the school's Ten Tors teams and training for this has taken him to five week-ends on the moor including two overnight camping exercises. In this training he has learned to survive in wild country, to navigate to safety and to endure foul weather, personal fatigue and difficult walking conditions. Perhaps most importantly he has learnt about himself and his reliability as a member of a team. He now sees his teachers in a different light, as it is they who have given their time during the training sessions and have shared the discomforts of gale-force winds and driving rain. Somehow the relationships between school teachers and pupils have become more human."*

3.15 Another useful and clear illustration of the value and relevance of a well-designed outdoor programme is provided by the "Statement of aims of outdoor and residential education" drawn up and endorsed by a group of LEA advisory staff for Outdoor Education (see Bibliography).

3.16 Useful work has also been carried out to define the levels of achievement that can reasonably be expected at different age levels. A group of Outdoor Education advisers in the South West have proposed the following expectation for the age levels 11 years, 14 years and 16 years respectively:

## *Learning outcomes at age 11*

1 *The ability to find one's way safely in a locality, within a small group and with consideration for the environment.*

2 *To be able to participate at a practical level in the planning and carrying out of a short journey, be alert to potential hazards and to be able to act appropriately in accordance with safety procedures.*

3 *To understand and make use of a variety of plans and maps.*

4 *To have developed a concern for, and a respect of, the natural and built environment, leading to an awareness of the need to be involved in its care and protection.*

5  To have gained an awareness through first-hand experience of different environments, through observation, recording, investigation, communication and evaluation leading to a better understanding of people, places and their culture.
6  Through working in small groups to have shown a developing sensitivity to the views and reactions of others.
7  To have had experience of a measure of independence away from home overnight in the company of others.

## Learning outcomes at age 14

1  The ability to find one's way in an unfamiliar environment with the support of others.
2  The ability to plan, prepare and undertake a journey or visit with a minimum of adult supervision, consistent with safety and achievement and leading to a large measure of individual responsibility.
3  To illustrate application of recording, observation, investigative and evaluative skills in a variety of environments.
4  To illustrate responsible attitudes towards self, others and the environment.
5  Through an involvement in a number of outdoor activities to appreciate opportunities for personal participation for leisure in the community.

## Learning outcomes at age 16

1  The ability to plan, prepare and undertake safely a journey without direct supervision in an unfamiliar environment.
2  The competence to take purposeful roles within an extended residential experience.
3  The ability to apply a variety of subject skills and undertake practical investigations in outdoor environments.
4  The ability to work flexibly as a member of a team in leading and supporting roles as appropriate.
5  The ability to solve problems and make sound judgements about self and others in a variety of challenging situations.
6  Through first-hand experience of conservation issues to develop a sense of responsibility for the environment.
7  Through active involvement, to have an understanding of the wide range of physical and intellectual experiences and pursuits which the outdoors can offer individuals in their search for worthwhile leisure interests.
8  To understand how the body works in differing conditions, how it responds to various outdoor activities and environments, and what promotes its well-being.
9  To demonstrate the ability to reflect upon experiences; reviewing, recording and communicating the learning outcomes.

These learning outcomes are intended to assist teachers and others in planning an outdoor education curriculum.

# *Attitudes of Pupils*

3.17 The study of attitudes towards outdoor activities among a sample of 384 fifth-year pupils in Berkshire, revealed findings which are examined in more detail in Chapter 5. Their perception of adventurous sports was generally positive, and there was a high level of interest in trying such pursuits both among males and females. Awareness of opportunities available was limited. Less than 35% had heard of Outward Bound, Operation Raleigh, British Schools Exploring Society or the British Trust for Conservation Volunteers. 66% of the respondents were keen to receive additional information (see 5.62-5.69).

3.18 *The Outward Bound Trust* responded to the publication of the Newsom Report, and the proposal to raise the school-leaving age in the early 1970s by introducing a one-week course for fourth (and eventually fifth) year school pupils. The surveys of participant attitudes were revealing. Between 95% and 100% of participants enjoyed and found their experience valuable, and wished to repeat a similar experience. As in the Berkshire survey, water activities (in this case canoeing) were the most popular, and hill-walking the least popular activity. However, when asked to identify the "most rewarding" activity, the majority of participants identified the walk to a mountain summit.

# *Outdoor Education within the Curriculum*

3.19 Outdoor and adventure experiences may form part of the regular secondary school curriculum, although they generally take place outside school hours. At *Morecambe High School*, Outdoor Education has been a curriculum option for the fourth and fifth years. A syllabus has been established for each outdoor activity; these include the recognised pursuits, and also environmental studies and general adventure activities such as river running, boulder hopping, night walks, wide games, forest adventure activities and bivouacing. Progression is an important theme, to the point at which pupils can continue the activity safely at their own level. Much thought has been devoted to enabling this progression to take place in safety, and to clarifying the appropriate skills and roles of the teachers involved. The Head of the Outdoor Education department comments:

> *"Such progression requires taking the pupils from relatively safe situations where staff are nearly always at their side, to situations of greater risk, where staff supervision is not possible for long periods. They are now really 'on their own', carrying out and enjoying the activity safely and succeeding through their own acquired skills and experience, balancing out the risks involved. It is finding this balance which makes these activities adventurous, and is why people do them. It is this adventure which we are trying to get the pupils to enjoy through specialised outdoor pursuits."*

> *(Adventure Education, Vol 1 No 5 1984)*

3.20 The same goal, that of encouraging young pupils to take responsibility for themselves, is increasingly common in the work of outdoor educators in schools. In his description of work in an Essex secondary school with non-examination pupils staying on until 16, Chris Loynes indicates some of the problems this approach creates:

> *"It is our view that the only person that can undertake personal and spiritual development is the individual. Our intent is to provide the social and environmental stimuli to bring this about. The biggest step is to get individuals to take responsibility for their own learning. This is made even harder as we are fighting attitudes towards traditional schooling. The students expect to be spoon-fed and to ignore it if they want to. Through adventure activity and teamwork situations they are faced with situations they cannot ignore ... The challenge faced by the school running such a course is integrating this approach to learning into the broad curriculum and forming the links that will allow development to continue beyond the school and into the community."*

> *(Adventure Education Vol 1 No 3)*

3.21 It is possible for many secondary schools to make use of the surrounding area for adventurous activity on a one-day basis as part of the school curriculum, as do primary schools. The establishment of country parks close to or even within urban areas, particularly where the Park Ranger Service is supportive, enables introductory activity to take place on a flexible basis geared to the needs of the school group attending.

3.22 Such one-day programmes have been developed at the *Sankey Valley Park* in Warrington. They were initiated by a request from a local school for adventurous activities in an outdoor area with a 'wild' feel. The initial request was succeeded by others with further requirements to foster co-operation, team spirit and communication skills within groups. Activities are adapted to meet each group's demands. The general aims of the programmes are to enable groups to experience the challenge of demanding activity in a natural environment. By using the resource of the urban fringe parkland in an imaginative way, the same satisfaction and sense of personal achievement can be gained that is found in less accessible wild areas. Activities at Sankey Valley Park include canoeing, orienteering, ropes courses and initiative exercises, and as many as 450 young people participate during school time each year, in groups of up to twenty.

3.23 A similar close relationship exists between schools in the Wirral LEA and the Wirral Country Rangers. Approximately 1,000 pupils from primary and secondary schools in the area take part in different forms of outdoor programme both locally and also in more distant locations. Activities include canoeing, rock-climbing, expedition work and conservation work in association with the rangers. The rangers also organise two- or five-day programmes, and these are complemented by visits to the LEA centre 'Oaklands' and by the use of other commercial residential centres as appropriate.

3.24 It is clear that outdoor adventurous experiences cannot be built in to a school programme on a regular basis unless effective use of local open country can be developed. It is not practicable to travel more than a short distance for half- or even full-day activities. By using local parks, woodlands and rural footpaths, the *Aveley School* in Essex is able to provide outdoor experience for up to 250 14- to 16-year olds each year within the school timetable, and for a further 75 in clubs or out of school time. The aims are to introduce different activities so that they can attain demanding skills, develop social qualities, tolerance, co-operation and leadership, and gain satisfaction and enjoyment. Summer programmes are mainly water-based; winter programmes emphasise orienteering, abseiling and problem solving activities. The involvement of the school in Outdoor Education is considerably assisted by its strong link with the *Thurrock Outdoor Activities Association.*

3.25 One of the most comprehensive programmes of Outdoor Education is that established by *Lothian Education Department.* Here there is the great advantage of proximity to open country and excellent facilities such as the Hillend artificial ski slope. Specialist Outdoor Education teachers have been appointed in most secondary schools and the Advisory Service runs resources centres, residential centres and provides specialist instructors to work with schools on a peripatetic basis. Strong emphasis has been placed on linking the experiences gained at primary and secondary school and co-ordinating with post-school provision. A combination of school-based and residential experience at one of the authority's well-equipped centres allows for a balance of activities and skills, environmental studies, social development, community service and vocational preparation. Each major curriculum area is matched by a corresponding set of outdoor tasks. The principle has been established that all pupils should have the opportunity to participate in at least one residential outdoor course during their primary school career and again in the secondary school. As a result of the clear conviction of the values of Outdoor Education, over 60% of secondary pupils in the authority are able to experience adventure and challenge outdoors as part of their schooling.

3.26 *Cornwall County Education Authority* also enjoys the advantage of immediately accessible wild country and good opportunities for water-based adventure. The county has utilised these advantages in a cost-effective way by establishing several summer standing camps and a number of self-catering residential bases, to which school groups or classes can travel in term-time or the summer school holidays. Accompanying teachers or leaders plan their own group activities with the assistance of resident leaders. The largest standing camp at Porthpean, near St. Austell, can accommodate up to 200 pupils in 6 person tents, and provides a catering service in a large permanent dining hall as well as other permanent facilities including toilets, showers, first aid room, and resources room. Porthpean, and several other camps, can be used for outdoor activities (orienteering, canoeing, wind-surfing, sailing, rock-climbing and foot expeditions) and for environmental work and conservation projects. Cost is minimal, and the facilities are available also to out-of-county groups. The Porthpean camp is also the venue for an international gathering of young people each summer.

3.27 *Trinity School, Carlisle* actively promotes the involvement of young people in the Duke of Edinburgh's Award, across the whole range of ability. From 1984 to 1989 of the 203 pupils who have entered the Scheme, 194 have gained their bronze award, 96 the silver and 61 the gold. In 1988/89 eight staff were voluntarily involved. Ron Wright, Head of Outdoor Education at Trinity School, is convinced of the importance of this type of experience:

*"For most participants the most immediate outcome is the sense of achievement gained which will stay with them always. This sense of achievement associated with the Expedition section is always heightened if the participants have experienced adverse weather conditions or some other difficulty that made the challenge even more demanding. Nowhere in the classroom situation can the valuable learning experience of coping with the physical, mental and emotional stresses of an expedition, whilst at the same time focusing the mind on the difficult task of working together as a unit towards a common goal, be gained.*

*The experience gained will be of great benefit to the participants as they will be better prepared to deal with difficult situations in the future. They will be more aware of themselves and of how others react under stress and how to support them.*

*Initiative, perseverance and the ability to get on with others are all necessary for the success of an expedition. These are qualities that employers place a premium on and on many occasions pupils have either written to me or recalled just how much of an interview was taken up in discussing their experiences in the Award Scheme. College, Universities and other public bodies as well as employers perceive the Award Scheme and especially at Gold level as a character profile which sets prospective candidates apart from the rest."*

3.28 Most outdoor programmes in secondary schools involve some expedition work or camping away from the school, either at the linked residential centre, where such a facility exists, or as a separate venture carried out either at week-ends or during holiday periods. The extent of such activity, even more than in-school work, depends heavily on the willingness of staff to give up their own time, and the availability of appropriate resources. Expeditions are normally restricted to the British Isles, but some ambitious overseas ventures have been organised.

3.29 One such event is the Sahara expedition undertaken at two or three year intervals by senior pupils from *Shorefields School*, Liverpool. This is an inner-city community school, and in 1985 29 young people from Toxteth, including past and present Shorefields pupils with some young unemployed, travelled overland through Europe to Tunisia and Algeria. In the mountains they worked on an inventory of stone monuments, undertook lightweight expeditions, carried out a settlement study and trekked to visit cave painting sites. The expedition prospectus stated the aims of the venture for the members as follows:

*For the members*
— *to participate fully in the planning and execution of a major expedition;*
— *to survive together for ten weeks in physically demanding and unfamiliar surroundings;*

- *to travel adventurously but safely;*
- *to carry out a programme of adventurous activities and simple but original field projects;*
- *to experience independent survival away from the main group in an alien environment.*

There is no formal selection process, but Alasdair Kennedy, the teacher who has been the driving force behind these ventures, has been particularly anxious to attract disadvantaged youngsters to take part. The cost has been kept as low as possible — £300 for 10 weeks in 1988, mostly raised beforehand. The expeditions are the culminating experience of a continuing programme of urban 'taster' experiences which involve up to 300 young people from this inner-city school each year. On a similar earlier expedition, Mr Kennedy wrote of his expeditioners:

> *"While each youngster responded in a different way, all were able to rise to the challenge, and achieve a level of excellence which few people are privileged to attain. They were heaped with responsibility, and given the skills to enable them to cope. They were stretched and challenged in a multitude of ways, and they had to win through, for the success of the expedition depended on each individual. At times even survival itself depended on a group of inner-city youngsters who in normal circumstances would not even be allowed out of school without the right bit of paper... They learned technical skills and social skills. They learned a lot about the way in which people of all nationalities can work together. They learned to be self-sufficient. They learned a whole set of new values. Those of us whose business is education should look at what such projects can achieve, and look carefully at how the majority of youngsters can be exposed to such benefits."*

> *(A. Kennedy, Adventure Education Vol 1 No 2)*

3.30 Such ambitious expeditions are more frequently characteristic of schools in the independent sector, which have both the resources and the tradition to encourage such activities. However, the strong pressures to succeed academically in such schools may militate against the provision of adventurous activities within the school curriculum; outdoor work is often confined to holidays, with some week-end training. The schools established in the Hahn tradition, including Gordonstoun (the school of which Hahn was founding Headmaster), Rannoch School and others, have a strong tradition of outdoor work as part of a broad curriculum of experience beyond the academic.

3.31 At *Rannoch School* outdoor activities are part of the school curriculum, and over 200 pupils take part each year. The adventure work is primarily based on the Duke of Edinburgh's Award, with a strong emphasis on cross-country expeditions. Rannoch schoolteacher Roger Coates Smith believes that this programme enables a youngster to gain personal insights, develop awareness of others and of the environment, to provide a stepping stone to future activities and interests and experience a rewarding challenge. However he also counsels against the imposition of a too physically taxing regime if these goals are to be realised.

3.32 At *Uppingham School* up to 150 pupils each year take part in adventure experiences, of whom about 70% are male. Expeditions to all the major upland areas of Britain are a major feature, and some pupils progress to participation in further expeditions to Iceland. The work is reinforced by good links with the Young Explorers' Trust, the Brathay Exploration Group and the Duke of Edinburgh's Award. As is so often the case, it is the enthusiasm of one or two teachers that enables these out-of-school activities to take place.

3.33 Several ambitious journeys overseas have been organised from *Cawston College*, an independent boarding school in Norwich. Up to 100 pupils each year engage in a progressive programme of preparation and expedition work during term time, at weekends and during holidays. Weekend camps in Derbyshire, Snowdonia and the Lake District lead on to winter training sessions in Wales and Scotland, and ultimately to extended summer journeys to third world countries, where the different cultural environment provides a powerful learning experience. The organiser of these ventures, Tony Arthur, is keen that any pupil who is interested should be able to participate; there is no selection procedure.

> *"I like to get the weak and the inadequate to face up to their problems and overcome them through expeditioning".*

Tony Arthur has written very honestly of the difficulties of taking mixed ability groups to distant countries:

> *"If you are taking youth parties to the third world, it is vital to have leaders who can cope with all the problems it involves... The trouble is that on REAL expeditions the unexpected is always happening."*

3.34 Although there is a difference of view about the merits of this development, some attempts have been made to incorporate Outdoor Education into the mainstream curriculum as an examinable subject. A number of schools developed a CSE Mode 3 syllabus, and more recently the *London Borough of Havering* has produced a pioneering GCSE Mode 3 proposal, which represents a development of its earlier successful CSE model which had been commended by HMI. The GCSE assessment was made for the first time in 1988; over 80 pupils from five schools in East London were successful. The course integrates theoretical and practical aspects of outdoor education. Theoretical work accounts for 25% of the marks awarded, course work for 15%, and practical skills and their application 60%. Theoretical knowledge is tested in two written papers. Course work requires candidates to carry out a study of the five main elements of the course, namely campcraft, canoeing, mapwork/orienteering, rock-climbing and dinghy sailing. The practical assessment is conducted by the teacher, supported by an assessor, on two occasions for each activity offered. External monitoring and moderation is carried out by a Moderator appointed by the London and East Anglian Group of Examination Boards.

3.35 A consortium of schools in *Clwyd, North Wales*, has also developed a GCSE programme in Outdoor Education. This is a two-year course designed to provide pupils with an opportunity to gain understanding and expertise in the use of the outdoor environment. The course aims not only to introduce young people to outdoor activities, but also to educate for the proper use of the outdoor environment. Assessment objectives are as follows:

*"Both during and on completion of the course students should be able to demonstrate all or most of the following at a variety of levels:*

## Knowledge and Understanding

*2.1 To demonstrate knowledge and understanding of*

*(i)   the growing pressures on the outdoor environment, with special reference to a particular area or topic.*

*(ii)   the general skills, abilities and equipment needed to live and move safely and comfortably in the outdoors.*

*(iii)   three specialised outdoor pursuits.*

*2.2 To use appropriate terminology in demonstrating this knowledge.*

## *Skills and Processes*

> 2.3 *To collect, select, record and present information in a clear way.*
> 2.4 *To demonstrate a variety of general and specific practical and physical skills.*
> 2.5 *To demonstrate commitment and cooperation during practical sessions.*
> 2.6 *To apply knowledge, skills and understanding to the solution of problems both when working alone or co-operating as a member of a group.*
> 2.7 *To exhibit judgement based on sound argument when presented with problems relevant to the nature of Outdoor Education."*

Approximately half the marks are for knowledge and understanding, and half for skills and processes.

At *Prestatyn High School*, with a strong outdoor tradition, 90 pupils were involved in 1987/88 in the first 2 year GCSE programme. The course involved two double lessons each week and at least one full day out per term to Snowdonia or local venues.

# *Outdoor Education for Less Able Pupils*

3.36 Outdoor opportunities have been incorporated increasingly into school provision for less able pupils. The Newsom Report "Half our Future", addressing the needs of the less academically able pupils in secondary schools, emphasised the enormous value of appropriate extra-curricular activity, and in particular the part that successfully overcoming practical challenges can play in building confidence and self-esteem.

> *"The experience of living away from home for a short time, in a fairly small and intimate group, and in a novel environment ... is especially significant for our pupils. This is variously achieved, through school journeys, and expeditions, camps or residential courses of different types ... For the pupils who come from difficult home backgrounds and live in socially deprived neighbourhoods, these can be opportunities of special help."*
>
> *(The Newsom Report "Half our Future")*

This view remains as valid now as it was in 1963.

3.37 Appropriate outdoor experiences can also be of benefit to young people at school with special educational needs. The term 'special educational needs' is applied to a wide range of young people who have significant physical, sensory, intellectual or emotional disabilities and who require a combination of an adapted curriculum, teaching support and appropriate learning conditions to enable them to achieve their potential. Such support may be of a temporary nature, or cover the whole of their school career, depending upon the type and the severity of the disability. Increasingly, under present policies, the majority of these young people will be taught within mainstream education. A relatively small number will be catered for in small units, special schools or hostels.

3.38 Outdoor Education provides one of the most effective routes by which personal competence can be achieved, focusing as it does on the real environment, the physical and co-operative skills needed to cope with this, and providing at the same time a powerful opportunity for developing such youngsters' self-esteem. It is common that children with learning difficulties have low self-confidence and for many the outdoors may offer one of the few opportunities to hold their own with more academically gifted peers.

3.39 *Devon County Council Education Department* has set out a framework for Outdoor Education for pupils with special educational needs, defining the relevance of different activities and relating appropriate experiences to the needs of different categories of pupil, including those with severe learning difficulties, those with moderate learning difficulties, those with physical handicaps and those prone to emotional and behavioural disturbances. Great care has to be taken to design appropriate outdoor experiences for such young people; if the experience is unsuitable or the expectation too high, then the result may be damaging.

3.40 The *Special Education Unit at Ehenside School* in Cumbria has for many years included an outdoor component in its curriculum. This includes day visits, activities and walks, an annual visit with the 40-strong unit to a self-catering residential centre, and the opportunity for the 3rd year group to take part in an adventure course, usually with Outward Bound. Chris Bates, the teacher-in-charge of the Unit is convinced of the value of such experience:

> *"As part of the curriculum of Ehenside Special Education Unit, we endeavour to take all the pupils on a week's residential course each year. And we have taken groups of third year pupils to Outward Bound and to skiing courses in various parts of the UK. In order that these children can be integrated into the community in the future, they need to acquire life skills, which we feel they can only obtain by attending a residential course. Learning to look after oneself and adopt responsibility for each other within a group is a very important aspect of the 'growing up' process. These weeks help stimulate these children, giving them an opportunity to achieve success in many outdoor activities, which in turn boosts their confidence and maturity. We also feel that this experience stands them in good stead in their adult life, helping them to become better members of the community."*

3.41 *Foxfield School*, on the Wirral, is a Special School, providing a varied Outdoor Adventure programme for most of its pupils, who have severe learning difficulties. The school has access to a range of outdoor locations and habitats, which include the Dee estuary, shoreline, a country park, and areas of heathland. Most of these areas are suitable for walking, even with poorly-coordinated pupils. The school also uses four residential centres in the Wirral, North Wales and the Lake District. Peter Watson, teacher in charge of Outdoor Education at the school, believes that young people with severe learning difficulties can take part in all aspects of outdoor education at a level dependent on the severity of their disability:

> *"A vast majority of our pupils tend to lead a very sheltered and protected life. Opportunities to extend their range of experiences can be very stimulating. The outdoor programme complements much of the school curriculum and is often cross-curricular — language to describe something, creative experiences, social skills etc. The activities tend to be done in easy stages, so there is every chance of success."*

# *Outdoor provision by the Youth Service for the 11 to 16 Age-group*

3.42 Many young people have the opportunity for Outdoor Adventure through participation in youth clubs or youth centres. The Youth Service is concerned with young people between 11 and 21 years, with a particular emphasis on providing for those who are leaving school and beginning employment, training or YTS. However a great deal of significant work is carried out with those below 16 and still at school; informal activity in youth clubs presents a valuable contrast to the more formal school situation, and provides important preparation for life and work after school. The Thompson Report on the Youth Service (1982), with its strong emphasis on experiential learning and full participation in the organisation of activities, recognises the value of outdoor activities, particularly when conducted in a residential setting.

3.43 Youth Service provision of opportunities for Outdoor Adventure is examined in more detail in Chapter 4. One interesting example of such work is provided by the Norfolk Youth and Community Service; almost 400 young people in the 14 to 16 age group, of whom 70% are male, are involved in practical outdoor programmes which include canoeing, windsurfing and involvement in the Duke of Edinburgh's Award. Groups travel all over the British Isles, as well as to several European countries and are involved in environmental and conservation projects locally.

## Other Organisations which Complement Work in Schools

3.44 Much of the outdoor work which takes place in school time is supported by individuals or by voluntary and charitable bodies in the community outside. Individuals, often parents, may give informal assistance in 'club' activities after school hours. There are also many national organisations which contribute actively in co-operation with schools to provide challenging experiences for pupils.

3.45 The *Trident Trust*, through its 'Project Trident' programme, actively encourages participation in challenging activities, often as part of a residential experience. The Project enables young people, mainly 14- to 16-year old school pupils, to engage in work experience, community involvement and a personal challenge, which may involve a residential course at an LEA or charitable outdoor centre. Some groups may go on expeditions in the Lake District or in Scotland, perhaps with an archaeological or environmental slant. Bob Newman, Development Training Manager, firmly believes in the importance of the residential challenge:

*"the residential situation brings young people into contact with new adults and allows greater focus on issues related to self and others and living and working together. We value reviewing skills highly in this context. Adventure activities (including music, dance and drama) help to heighten the experience of extending individuals, working together and developing self-management."*

Up to 1,000 young people each year participate in a residential course through Project Trident, usually funded jointly by the Trident Trust, the education authority and the individual involved. Project bases have now been established in 43 different localities, mainly sponsored by local industry and commerce.

3.46 The *YMCA* provides substantial support to schools with outdoor programmes, notably at their *Lakeside (Windermere)* and *Fairthorne Manor (Hampshire)* residential centres. The Lakeside Centre, set in an estate of 240 acres with a half mile frontage to the lake, contains permanent residential facilities and also a tented base, operational from April to September. It can take a wide variety of groups. In addition to holiday courses for young people, a variety of activity and environmental experiences are provided for school parties. A particular emphasis has been placed at Lakeside on 'earth awareness' and 'acclimatisation' courses. Important features are the multi-activity days provided for primary schools in the South Lakeland area, specialised GCSE related field courses for secondary schools, and the opportunity for school groups to use the facilities for their own planned programmes.

3.47 The *Outward Bound Trust* during the past ten years has increased its provision for secondary school groups. In addition to the well-established three week courses for 14- to 16-year olds, which draw individual participants together from across the country to pursue a progressive programme of challenge activities in wild country, the Trust provides one-week courses for 4th and 5th year pupils taking part in school groups, intended to provide a broadening experience in a new and contrasting setting. Such courses attract approximately 500 young participants each year.

3.48 There are a number of well-established 'uniformed' youth organisations which provide adventurous experience in the outdoors for their members. Of these, probably the best known are the Scouts and the Guides, organisations which work with very large numbers of boys and girls in the 11 to 16 age-group.

3.49 Membership of the *Scouts* (age-group 10 ½ to 15 ½) is currently approximately 170,000 in some 12,000 scout groups. Scouting activities have traditionally included a strong emphasis on camping and the countryside, and these remain a central feature. However the Scout Association emphasises that activities of any nature, whether indoor or outdoor, are only a vehicle for the development of young people:

> *"Outdoor activities are a method, rather than aims and objectives in themselves. Of course, the challenge and adventure found outdoors can provide for exceptionally stimulating methods. Nonetheless our concern is how we can provide some development for many people rather than tremendous opportunities for a small number. We note that much valuable learning and personal development takes place in environments very near to the local community, as opposed to wild and rugged country. For us, life skills such as the ability to tolerate and care for others, to listen to others and value them as individuals, to reach corporate decisions and implement those decisions as a team, are the skills that will help cure the ills of society, will help individuals and communities to develop, and will lead to a greater understanding and relationship with the outdoors itself."*

> *(Executive Commissioner, The Scout Association)*

3.50 The activities undertaken by Scouts encompass the whole range of outdoor pursuits. Expedition work in independent groups is an important feature of Venture Scouting (see 6.63, 6.64), but the highlight of the year's programme for most scout troops is the annual camp, usually at a tented base, from which visits and practical activities take place. The specialised facilities available to Scouts are impressive. For instance, located in the now disused West India Dock in East London is the new Headquarters ship "Lord Amory", serving the Dockland Scout Project. 120 acres of protected water offer exceptional facilities for sailing and canoeing close to the centre of London, for Scouts, Guides and other youth groups. The project operates 70 canoes and over 60 other boats, and offers a comprehensive range of courses for young people and for aspiring leaders and instructors. In addition the HQ ship herself offers living facilities on board for up to 56 young people. Another vessel based in the Docks, the 50' motor vessel "Treshnish" provides weekend and longer periods of training in the Thames estuary, the River Medway and East Coast waters.

3.51 *The Guides* also regard outdoor experience as important and rewarding. With a membership of approximately 240,000 in the age group 10 to 15, they are the largest single-sex youth organisation in Britain. However the lack of qualified leaders and the concerns of parents about safety inhibit the provision of genuinely adventurous activity, and many Guides have not had the experience of camping. A research project to investigate attitudes to Guiding was carried out in 1987, and it showed that most Guides wanted to go to camp more often, and that in the main the activities they enjoyed most were of the adventurous and energetic kind. A popular way of engaging in such activities within Guiding is by using the Duke of Edinburgh's Award.

3.52 The research conducted by the Guides, and the investigations carried out by the Scout Association forward planning group, suggest that Outdoor Adventure will remain an attractive and highly valued aspect of the programmes of training for both organisations for the foreseeable future; the problem of training sufficient female leaders might be in part overcome by a closer co-operation in training between the two organisations.

3.53 Both the *Boys' Brigade*, with approximately 42,000 members between 11 and 16, and the *Girls' Brigade*, with approximately 13,000 in this age-group, also regard Outdoor Adventure as a valuable means of development for young people. Both organisations encourage participation in the Duke of Edinburgh's Award. In 1987/1988 the Girls' Brigade achieved over 570 awards, including 76 at Gold level. Boys' Brigade battalions initiate a wide variety of camps and other adventurous activities, and encourage the development of outdoor skills and qualifications. Some expeditions overseas are mounted, usually having a community service purpose. The Glasgow Battalion of the Brigade is responsible for the Dalguise Outdoor Centre near Dunkeld, where a range of residential courses is provided for the Brigade and other organisations.

3.54 Many young people are members of the *Air Training Corps, Army Cadet Force* or the *Sea Cadet Corps*, all organisations which make extensive use of the outdoors for adventure training. The purpose of such activity is to promote self-confidence, self-discipline, physical awareness, teamwork and leadership, and to provide the opportunity for excitement. The Newcastle-on-Tyne Cadet Training team provides one-day training sessions for up to 1,000 young people each year within the North-East, of whom the great majority fall within the 14 to 16 age-range. Activities are principally rock-climbing, abseiling, canoeing, hillwalking and obstacle courses. Participation is by young men only. However this is not true of the offshore cruises and other activities offered by the Sea Cadet Corps, which may take up to 25% female participants on its cruises aboard "Royalist".

# Further Provision

3.55 An educational charity which provides an unusual sailing experience for secondary schoolchildren is the *East Coast Sail Trust*, established in 1966. The Trust has restored a traditional East Coast spritsail barge, "Thalatta", for use by young people on five-day voyages in and beyond the Thames estuary. The former cargo space has been converted into living quarters with hammocks for 12 young sailors. The 300 young people who sail each year aboard "Thalatta" between April and October include children with learning difficulties or emotional and behavioural problems. The purpose of the expeditions is to broaden horizons by giving a glimpse of life in the era of sail, to look at life on the east coast today, and to learn to work together as a shipboard community.

3.56 *The Cirdan Trust*, based in Essex, also enables young people to gain experience of life aboard a traditional sailing vessel. The aim of the Trust is to enable young people from churches, schools and youth organisations to experience the excitement and adventure of cruising together in a large sailing craft, and to help them (and especially those from less fortunate backgrounds) to develop morally, physically and spiritually. Up to 700 young people have this opportunity each year during the operational season between March and November. The Trust has three vessels, a converted Baltic Trader capable of crossing the North Sea, a Thames barge suitable for coastal cruising, and a purpose-built yacht able to make longer journeys. Some Cirdan Trust cruises involve North Sea crossings to Holland.

3.57 There are a number of low-cost, mobile resource units available in certain areas. *MOBEX*, the Mobile Expedition Unit of the Young Explorers' Trust (see 6.55) is a mobile resource centre, a purpose-converted truck containing a wide range of outdoor equipment. Staffed by a full-time director, it can take the opportunity for Outdoor Adventure to the young people who have little or no access to such experience in their own schools or home areas. MOBEX provides city-based campcraft and outdoor skills training, preparatory to carrying out expeditions in wild country. The pioneering MOBEX unit has been working for the main part in the North West of England, with schools, youth clubs and clients from the probation service and the social services. Term-time work with secondary schools is limited by the lack of available voluntary support staff, but the flexibility of the resource enables adventurous challenges to be provided for many disadvantaged youngsters who would otherwise miss such opportunities.

3.58 A similar project is "*Operation Innervator*". This new venture, commencing in 1989, and sponsored by business and industry, plans to operate coaches equipped to take young people living in inner cities to areas of open country for Outdoor Adventure experiences. The coaches will carry equipment and be capable of use as mobile bases for outdoor activities.

3.59 Various police forces in Britain have initiated outdoor programmes from time to time with young people in the 11 to 16 age-group. Such initiatives have usually been attempted as part of a bridge-building operation with the local community, and occasionally specifically to provide for young people at risk. One of the most ambitious of these programmes has been that developed by the *Royal Ulster Constabulary* to improve community relations in the Province. Up to 12,000 young people are involved annually in this programme, for periods varying from one day to an extended expedition. Programmes may include cross-country rambles, weekend camps or longer summer camps. Alternatively, the longer experience may be an Outward Bound or similar extended course in England or Wales. Some 85% of those participating are drawn from the 11 to 16 age-group.

> "*We provide a physically and mentally challenging programme to cater for all sections of the community. The programme is aimed at personal development and social interaction.*"
>
> *(RUC Training Officer)*

The value of shared outdoor experience in the particular circumstances of Northern Ireland is examined more closely in Chapter 7 (7.20, 7.21).

## *Commercial Provision*

3.60 A large and growing range of commercial providers specialise in outdoor or adventurous holidays for this age-group, usually in the summer holidays. The majority of such courses are residential, often making use of schools or centres which are closed for the holiday period. There is also a developing tendency for boarding schools to open for such courses during the summer holidays, where they are sited appropriately. Such summer holiday courses may be compared with the long established American 'summer camp', offering a range of outdoor and other pursuits in a supervised setting. Such courses often provide excellent value for money, although the report published in "Which?" magazine in January 1986 questioned the staffing and safety of some of these holidays.

3.61 The largest commercial organisation is *PGL*, established in 1956 and already described in Chapter 2 (2.25). PGL offers a wide range of courses during the summer months, with a number of centres in South Wales and elsewhere. They have established bases in France, and were pioneering users of the River Ardeche for canoe journeys for school groups. The aspect of social education is not strongly emphasised, and the main focus remains on enjoyment and learning new skills. PGL and the numerous other commercial operators provide an adventurous experience for many thousands of young people each year both in Britain and overseas.

3.62 A major development in the past 15 years has been the large scale introduction of overseas or Scottish skiing visits for school parties. The growth of the winter sports industry has been a remarkable feature of outdoor holiday provision and a wide range of relatively cheap commercial packages are now offered to schools and local education authorities. These for the main part offer winter activities only, with little attention paid to cultural or environmental studies, or to personal and social education possibilities. Nevertheless increasing numbers of school groups take part in such visits, both within and outside term-time. The present scale of such visits is difficult to assess, but the extent of them is such as to suggest this as a major element in out-of-school activity of a challenging nature, with great potential for broadening horizons in what for most young people is a highly invigorating and exciting mountain setting. Skiing is now a regular part of sports and physical education provision for many Scottish children.

### 3.63 *Summary*

(a) This stage of development is very important for young people in their transition to adulthood. (3.1 — 3.3)

(b) Many current changes in secondary education seek to facilitate the development of young people by providing more practical and experience based opportunities for achievement. (3.4 — 3.10)

(c) Many local education authorities have developed excellent summaries of educational objectives, intended learning outcomes and principles of good practice, which give rise to cautious optimism for the future. (3.11 — 3.16)

(d) Young people are keen to experience Outdoor Adventure but lack information and awareness of opportunities. (3.17 — 3.18)

(e) There are many examples of effective programmes, both in the maintained sector and among voluntary and commercial organisations, where young people are able to progress safely in outdoor activities. (3.19 — 3.20, 3.25 — 3.29)

(f) The inclusion of Outdoor Education as an examination subject has been undertaken successfully in some areas. (3.34 — 3.35)

(g) Outdoor Education can play an important part in enhancing the confidence of children with learning difficulties or special needs. (3.36 — 3.41)

(h) There are wide-ranging opportunities for Outdoor Adventure for the 11 — 16 age-group provided through voluntary, charitable or commercial organisations. (3.44 — 3.61)

# CHAPTER 4
## PROVISION FOR YOUNG ADULTS (16 TO 19) AND ONWARDS

# *General Considerations*

4.1 Between the ages of 15 and 16 young people reach the end of their period of compulsory schooling and they face important choices in the transition to independent adult life. The 1982 report of the Review group on the Youth Service in England (The Thompson Report) suggested that young peoples' main needs were the acceptance of responsibility, in addition to the enjoyment of freedom.

> *"Young people say that above all they want to 'grow up' — they aspire to the stage next ahead of them. The stages in human development may be defined in terms of progress in relationships*
>
> — *with self,*
> — *with parents and other significant adults,*
> — *with friendship groups,*
> — *with a particular partner,*
> — *with colleagues in a school or work setting,*
> — *with a wider society, and*
> — *with an ultimate of some kind."*

4.2 Young people at the age of 16 are moving from a state of dependency to a state of independence or interdependence, and therefore a change in the nature of all these relationships is implied. The Thompson Report continues by indicating that such changes in relationships can only take place through experience:

> *"people achieve change by living through particular kinds of situation".*

Experiences which contain within themselves the potential for changing relationships are those:
— of being valued and accepted as a person,
— of measuring oneself against others,
— of making choices and seeing them through,

— of enduring and living with hard reality,
— of playing a part in a common enterprise,
— of being responsible to and for others,
— of receiving, giving and sharing ideas,
— of perceiving others' needs.

4.3 Whether young people remain in education at the age of 16, or become employed, or join a training scheme of some kind, it is essential that such experiential needs are met if they are to become effective citizens and achieve their full potential.

4.4 Young people in later adolescence develop the ability to view themselves and their actions more objectively and in perspective. This capacity for considered reflection enables learning to occur in a different way than for younger children. It is important that they should be encouraged to develop productive relationships with other young people and adults, deliberately seek new experience, receive praise, recognition and constructive criticism, and have the chance to develop the highest expectation of their own performance and capability. They need opportunities to develop self-confidence, respect and responsibility, to acquire new knowledge, skills and attitudes, and, most importantly, to have opportunities to reflect on and learn from experience.

4.5 Young people between 16 and 19 need to achieve independent status, and yet there are practical and cultural reasons preventing this. Preparation for working life, with the necessary training and vocational preparation, often entails dependence upon parents for some years after the period of compulsory schooling has finished. The difficulty of finding independent accommodation means that young people often continue to live in the family home. The young adult of 18 years is able to vote, may be married and even with his or her own children, yet still may remain dependent on the support of the family.

4.6 The time may come when all young people, on leaving compulsory education, will enter a period of further training of some sort, by remaining in formal education, by beginning specific career training, or by participating in a government-sponsored training scheme, such as the Youth Training Scheme (YTS). It is important in these changing circumstances that the learning and training 'package' should include a process of social and personal education which meets the specific needs of the 16 to 19 year age-group. In particular, the general aims of enhancing self-knowledge, giving control, choice, and responsibility, and learning to work more effectively with others should be tied to specific learning objectives.

4.7 Recently the inclusion of specific objectives in development training and personal and social education has been attempted more systematically; as individual expectations and the requirements of a changing society become clearer, such definition of objectives is of great importance. It is recognised that young people must be encouraged to take charge of this development and to assess the progress of their own learning.

4.8 Marked demographic changes are taking place at present, in Britain as elsewhere in Europe. Between 1975 and 1983 the 16 to 19 age-group increased in size significantly and in 1983 stood at 3.7 million. By 1993 there will be a reduction of over a million young people in this age-group, and although the number may rise again after that date it will not return to the former peak. The extent of these changes is still not generally realised; they present considerable problems in planning for future education and training needs. It may well be that youth unemployment, on the scale seen in the last 15 years, will continue to decline. The 16 to 19 age-group is the main source of recruitment for many commercial, manufacturing and public sector organisations. It appears likely that young people, a decreasing resource, will be very much in demand, but it is essential that they should have acquired the appropriate skills.

4.9 Some employers are well aware of this fundamental shift from a surplus to a shortage of young people entering employment. For instance the *Norwich Union* insurance group has introduced a high profile marketing campaign and flexible working arrangements, generous sponsorships and comprehensive training arrangements to induce young people to join the company. The *United Kingdom Central Council for Nursing* is considering opening up the profession, placing less reliance upon formal academic qualifications for entry, and taking action to reduce staff wastage and education wastage (those who qualify but do not practise as nurses).

4.10 Recent educational initiatives have encouraged the introduction of practical, work-related schemes and qualifications. One of these is the Certificate of Pre-Vocational Education, (CPVE), sometimes known as the '17 plus', a programme of general and vocational education, which can be followed either at school or college, on a full-time or part-time basis. CPVE comprises core studies (e.g. literacy and numeracy), vocational studies and additional studies. It enables young people between 16 and 17 to develop more relevant and more flexible skills, together with the experience, confidence and motivation to enable them to find appropriate employment. The core skills in CPVE are identified as:

> *a) Personal and career development*
>
> *b) Industrial, social and environmental studies*
>
> *c) Communication (developing the ability to communicate with people effectively in different circumstances)*
>
> *d) Social skills (increasing self-reliance and the ability to get on with people)*
>
> *e) Numeracy*
>
> *f) Science and technology*
>
> *g) Information technology*
>
> *h) Creative development (encouraging awareness of students' own creativity and developing their critical sense)*
>
> *i) Practical skills (developing the use of practical skills and their applications to real tasks)*
>
> *j) Problem solving (identifying and solving real life problems confidently)*

of which a), b), c), d), h), i), and j) are relevant to experience in outdoor education. The Certificate is awarded for one or two years' full-time study at schools or colleges. It concentrates on preparing young people for the adult world; the certificate and profile which are produced at the conclusion of the programme contain information about their capabilities and achievements.

4.11 The themes of 'capability' and 'achievement' are echoed in the 'Education for Capability' campaign initiated by the *Royal Society of Arts, (RSA)* in 1978. The aim of this campaign is to encourage and develop four capacities, especially among those in secondary or higher education.

> *"The great majority of learners — whether pupils at school, students at universities, polytechnics or colleges, or adults still wanting to learn - are destined for a productive life of practical action. They are going to do things, design things, make things, organise things, for the most part in co-operation with other people. They need to improve their competence, by the practice of skills and the use of knowledge; to cope better with their own lives and the problems that confront them and society; to develop their creative abilities; and above all to co-operate with other people. It is these four capacities that (are to be) encouraged and developed through Education for Capability."*
>
> *(Manifesto of the RSA Education for Capability campaign)*

The RSA Recognition Scheme highlights initiatives in the field of education and training which enhance capability. An early award was made to Brathay Hall Trust (see 6.43) for the excellence of its work in development training with young people.

# Options for Young Adults

4.12 There are broadly four options open to young people at the age of 16; they may stay on in education, join a youth training scheme, obtain permanent employment, or remain unemployed. Recent changes in benefits payment suggest that in future a smaller proportion of young people will remain unemployed but will choose instead, perhaps reluctantly, to join the Youth Training Scheme.

# Those Remaining in Education to 19 — Sixth Forms

4.13 The numbers of young people staying on at school or continuing full-time education at college is increasing. In 1975 25% of young people aged 17 were in full-time education and this rose to 33% in 1988. Approximately 25% of school leavers have joined Youth Training Schemes in the years from 1984 to 1988. Unemployment among 17 year-olds rose from 3% in 1975 to 17% in 1984, and (provisional) figures for 1988 indicate a fall back to 9%.

4.14 Even for those young people remaining in full-time education at their local comprehensive, the transfer to the sixth form is marked by a considerable shift in status and responsibility. Increasingly the sixth form in most schools has the atmosphere of a separate sixth form college, at which discipline is more relaxed and students are given responsibility for their own learning, timekeeping and dress. There is no compulsion to participate in physical or outdoor education as part of the curriculum, but opportunities may be available on the basis of club participation. Many young people become involved in outdoor activities on an informal basis at this time. In fact many young people in the sixth form choose voluntarily to undertake ambitious ventures; travelling overseas in vacations independently, taking part in adventure courses with organisations such as the Sail Training Association or Outward Bound, or involving themselves with conservation or environmental groups.

4.15 Approximately 25% of young people continuing into the sixth form do so by progressing to a Sixth Form College. A residential experience including challenging outdoor activities may be a particularly effective way of strengthening friendship in the new school, broadening horizons and increasing ability to take responsibility, particularly when shared with college staff. For these reasons *St Dominic's Sixth Form College* at Harrow provides an opportunity for all 'A' level candidates during their first year to experience a week either at a sailing base in France or at a residential base in Britain.

4.16 A well known international Sixth Form College is the *United World College* established at St. Donat's in South Wales. Here the educational philosophy is based on the thinking of Kurt Hahn, and the school programme includes Outdoor Adventure, often linked with community service. For instance, there are opportunities for students to practise mountain and sea rescue techniques, as well as to engage in various expeditions in the locality and overseas. The opportunities provided by Atlantic College are available to limited numbers of young people, but the school believes strongly in the cross-curricular nature and value of outdoor and environmental experience, and demonstrates the possibility of integrating such experience into the work of schools.

4.17 Three important avenues available for sixth form adventure experiences outdoors are provided through the Duke of Edinburgh's Award, through participation in expeditions sponsored by the school or other bodies, or through attending outdoor field or environmental study courses.

4.18 *The Duke of Edinburgh's Award* is described elsewhere (6.56) Many young people in the 16 to 19 age-group who remain at school as well as those outside will be engaged in the Scheme at Silver or Gold standard. At Silver standard, participants are required to carry out either an expedition or an exploration lasting for three days. At Gold standard a four day venture is required, in the form of an expedition, which has journeying as the main component, an exploration, which involves a practical investigation, or occasionally some other approved adventurous project which departs from these specified conditions.

4.19 Expeditions are normally carried out on foot, but they may involve travel by bicycle, canoe or on horseback. For Silver and Gold levels, the environment in which the venture is conducted must be unfamiliar to the young people. Gold ventures are required to take place in open or wild country, remote from habitation. Strict conditions are laid down as to the nature of the training required for these expeditions. An important feature of Award Scheme expeditions is that they are carried out by young people independently, without direct adult supervision.

4.20 Terry Lake is a Youth and Community worker based at *Conyers Comprehensive School* at Yarm near Stockton-on-Tees. Each year he assists over 300 young people, drawn from the school and the youth service, to experience Outdoor Adventure through the Award Scheme and through club activities. In 1988 a party of sixth form pupils from the school, in association with the Ocean Youth Club, sailed to the Jotunheim area of Norway to carry out mountain exploration there. During the course of this venture, twelve students gained Silver or Gold Awards. It is noteworthy that over half the participants in these adventure activities are girls; the Award Scheme is one of the few adventure opportunities in which female participation is as great as male.

4.21 Many schools encourage sixth form pupils to take part in overseas expeditions, either as members of a school party or through participation in one of the major county or national bodies set up to encourage such ventures. The principal national bodies involved with overseas expeditions for young people in the 16 to 19 age-group are the *Young Explorers' Trust*, the *British Schools' Exploring Society*, the *Brathay Exploration Group*, *Operation Raleigh*, and the *Scout Association.* These organisations are described in more detail in Chapter 6.

4.22 Many sixth form school pupils are assisted in participating in overseas expeditions through the work of local schools' exploring societies. *The Leicestershire Youth Exploration Group* supports educational and adventurous experiences and expeditions for young people between 16 and 21 years; they completed a five-week expedition in Kenya in 1988 involving bush-trekking, climbing on Mount Kenya and conservation in the parks and game reserves. *The Derbyshire Schools' Expedition Group* draws participants from schools and further education colleges, and administers expeditions both in the remoter parts of this country and overseas in locations including Iceland, Arctic Norway and the Pyrenees.

4.23 One of the longest established groups of this kind is the *Yorkshire Schools' Exploring Society.* Established in 1964 with the aim of organising larger expeditions which would be beyond the scope of individual schools, the Society has undertaken a series of ambitious ventures, to the Grand Canyon in 1985, to Peru in 1986, and to the Himalayas in 1987. In 1988 the Society organised its most enterprising project, taking 43 young people from 30 different Yorkshire schools to China, where in five groups they engaged in mountaineering and canoeing ventures and carried out a variety of fieldwork assignments in an area closed to western travellers until 1981. This was the most ambitious expedition for school pupils yet to be mounted in China. Each participant had to raise £1950 in order to participate, after completing a rigorous selection process. Many more young people in Yorkshire are keen to participate in such ventures; the limiting factors identified by the Chairman of the Society are lack of money and lack of administrative resources.

> *"The greatest benefits to young people are those intangibles which are difficult to describe and even more difficult to measure. This is why Outdoor Adventure programmes are held in such low esteem by 'orthodox' educationists — who believe if you can't measure the benefits then it can't be any good!"*

*(Don Robinson, Chairman YSES)*

4.24 Such ambitious ventures are normally beyond the means of the majority of individual schools in the maintained sector of education. However a number of public schools have undertaken comparable expeditions. For instance *Oakham School* strongly supports outdoor pursuits and has 300 participating in the Duke of Edinburgh's Award. There is also an Exploration Society which in recent years has mounted expeditions to Spitzbergen, the Sahara, Papua New Guinea, Norway and Kenya. Richard Gilbert, a teacher at *Ampleforth College* in Yorkshire has organised a series of expeditions for senior pupils to Iceland, Arctic Norway, the High Atlas in Morocco and to the Himalayas, where three pupils successfully ascended the peak Kolahoi (17,900 feet).

4.25 Many school pupils gain their first experience of the outdoor environment by taking part in fieldwork associated with the academic subjects which they are studying. Sixth form courses in subjects such as geography, biology or zoology may require a practical element of outdoor work to complement classroom studies. Such fieldwork may take place in local education authority residential centres, in youth hostels with appropriate facilities, or in suitably sited self-catering accommodation. A number of schools have their own small unstaffed outdoor centres, or in some cases have access to those of other organisations such as mountaineering club huts. Alternatively, they may use resources or courses provided by other organisations.

4.26 Established in 1946, the *Field Studies Council*, (see 6.38), has nine residential centres and one day centre, all well equipped and sited for outdoor field courses for school pupils engaged in GCSE, TVEI, CPVE and 'A' level courses. The Council believes that first-hand experience of the environment is an essential part of education, particularly for those studying environmental subjects at 'A' level. Much of the work of the centres is with the age group 16 to 19 years. The value of the residential aspect is also emphasised. The FSC also provides a wide range of open courses in addition to those courses tailored for the needs of school and university students.

# *Those remaining in Education to 19 — Colleges of Further Education*

4.27 A significant number of young people on leaving school enrol with a Further Education college to pursue an academic or vocational course. Further Education colleges may use the outdoor environment in the provision of a variety of courses. For example field visits form an increasingly important part of some specialised courses; history students, for instance, may approach their subject through practical analysis of the landscape.

4.28 Many Further Education courses contain a personal development module, and this may include a variety of opportunities to gain practical experience, sometimes using Outdoor Adventure activities. *South Devon College* has introduced an outdoor element into the curriculum of students following business and secretarial courses. Weekend courses which include canoeing, walking and group initiative tasks, have the aims of developing group cohesion, developing individual qualities of self-confidence and leadership, and establishing positive staff/student relationships.

4.29 In Further Education, outdoor education usually comes under the umbrella of the Physical Education, Social Studies or Recreation and Leisure departments. Some of those questioned in the study indicated the relatively low status that physical and outdoor education hold in many FE colleges. Outdoor education in FE colleges may form an integral part of a specific course; for instance, the BTEC National Diploma in Leisure Studies is designed to provide participants with a route into areas of the leisure industry such as management of leisure centres, hotels, outdoor or activity centres, or alternatively into employment in the countryside as, for example, country rangers or interpretive staff.

4.30 Alternatively, opportunities may be provided for students taking other courses to have experience of adventurous outdoor activities as a recreational or 'personal development' element of their course, perhaps on a weekly half-day basis. Such an arrangement requires convenient access to appropriate facilities or environments.

4.31 *The West Cumbria College* at Workington has designed a one-year Diploma course in Sport and Recreation of which about half is devoted to outdoor activities and the countryside. This course is highly practical, and includes three one-week placements at a variety of centres and leisure complexes, and also residential experience in huts and on expedition. Activities include mountaineering, canoeing, orienteering, windsurfing, sailing, and fellrunning. Students also gain experience of working with young children. The primary emphasis of the course is on developing leadership and decision-making, rather than developing high levels of personal skill. The college also offers the BTEC National Diploma in Leisure Studies, a two-year full-time course for 16 to 19-year olds and also mature students, with the emphasis on management and planning in the leisure industry. The course includes options in outdoor pursuits, tourism, and the countryside and provides a one-week mountain residential experience and two one-week expeditions, for which students themselves make all the arrangements, as well as a number of placements.

4.32 Students enrolling at colleges have widely differing experiences of, and attitudes to, Outdoor Adventure. Some have considerable previous experience; others none at all. Some seek excitement, others seek different company, others simply wish to leave home. Colleges have in recent years been required to deal with large numbers of young people taking part in YTS schemes or who are unemployed. Some of these young people have a history of failure, and would not choose to attend willingly a course of formal education. For some of these, Outdoor Adventure offers a significant route to achievement and success.

4.33 Two themes recur in establishing the case for outdoor education within further education: the need to educate for leisure, and the role of outdoor education in widening the curriculum and integrating the different aspects studied.

> *"Each young person should be helped to construct his or her own curriculum through a process of negotiation, not only with the immediate session in mind, but also planning carefully for the future and taking account of activities and interests pursued outwith the education system in leisure time."*

*(16 to 18s in Scotland: An Action Plan)*

4.34 *The Scottish Vocational Education Council (SCOTVEC)* was established in 1985 and is responsible for developing, administering and assessing the National Certificate. The National Certificate, open to over 16 year-olds, operates on a modular basis, giving a wide range of options relevant to career training or to personal interests. This flexible and vocationally relevant qualification may be taken by pupils in their post-sixteen school education, by students at FE Colleges or as part of YTS training. The Physical Education and Recreation practical performance modules contain seven certification activities within the category of outdoor pursuits. These are orienteering, hill-walking, Alpine skiing, sailing, Nordic skiing, windsurfing and canoeing. Learning outcomes are defined for each activity at introductory and four higher levels of achievement. At present over 500 schools and colleges in Scotland offer the SCOTVEC National Certificate, and this at present therefore probably represents the most widely available certificate course in Britain involving outdoor training for the over-16s.

# *Youth Work and Outdoor Adventure*

> *"What is behind the motivation of young people to engage or not in sport? Those who do participate do so for a whole variety of reasons, including fun, challenge, comradeship, status, physical fitness or relief from boredom. They do so because some significant other, perhaps a parent or youth worker, has offered encouragement by word or deed. Peer group pressure is yet another factor ."*

*(David Stead "Sport, Young People and the Youth Service." 1987)*

4.35 Many youth and community workers accept the value of an outdoor programme of activities in meeting the needs of young people. For instance, the *Liverpool Community Education Service* recognises and supports the valuable contribution which outdoor education can make in promoting the aims of the Youth Service and the development of young people.

> *"Not only recognised competitive sports and traditional and modern outdoor pursuits, but a wide range of artistic, cultural, historic, geographical, social, economic, political, environmental, recreational and other educational activities can be promoted in an outdoor setting. Much of the work done in the Youth Service could take on a new impetus through the development of an outdoors perspective."*

> *(Liverpool LEA Policy paper)*

4.36 The Liverpool LEA suggests that the guiding principles of such a development of outdoor work should be:

> — *Integration. The outdoors dimension should be an integral part of the structured learning process, and should not be merely an afterthought.*
> — *Participation. Young people should be involved in planning and decision–making, and facing the consequences of their decisions.*
> — *Development. There should be a progressive acquisition of skills and general competence, with associated development of self-image and scaling up of ambition.*
> — *Extending. The experience of young people should be extended, as expressed in the Thompson Report.*
> — *Challenge. Activities in the Youth Service "must offer young people interesting things to do, new things to test their prowess and adaptability, opportunities for fresh experience, things to exercise the mind and body."*
> *(Thompson Report)*
> — *Person-centred. The emphasis should be on the learning process and not on the task.*

4.37 On the basis of these guiding principles, the authority suggests there should be a planned element of outdoor experience in youth centre programmes, that realistic staff and other resources should be allocated, that specialist skills can be acquired through co-operative projects with other specialist agencies, that much valuable work can be carried out without exposure to high-risk environments, and that greater resources should be made available, together with provision of staff training where appropriate.

4.38 The provision of an outdoor element within the Youth Service is dependent above all else on the availability of suitable experienced and qualified staff, and the study suggests that to a greater extent even than in schools, there is a shortage of such adults. *The Gloucestershire Youth and Community Service* outdoor education team of seven staff, supported by teachers and both voluntary and professional youth workers, provides outdoor experience for some 800 young people each year, about half of which fall in the 16 to 19 age-group. A further 2,000 to 3,000 each year visit the *South Cerney Watersports Centre.* Outdoor provision includes 'taster' short courses in various outdoor pursuits, camping and expedition work, week-ends, week-long courses with the emphasis on skiing, hill-walking and canoeing, and specialist leader training courses leading either to local or national qualifications. The County provides a wide range of leader courses in the major activities, free of charge, for teachers and youth leaders. The programme of such courses for 1988/1989 shows a total of 45 such courses in canoeing, sailing, archery, mountain walking, rock-climbing, windsurfing, expedition training and assessment, development training and residential course organisation.

4.39 Alternatively, outdoor work in the Youth Service may be focused on environmental issues and action. The curriculum paper 'Outdoor Education in the Curriculum' prepared by *Cumbria County Council* suggests three areas of outdoor studies which may be appropriate to the Youth Service. These are:

— *Self reliance and survival — the skills of living and working outdoors.*
— *Conservation — practical work in the urban areas, wilderness or foreign environments, using national organisations.*
— *Man and his Environment — examination of the role and effect of the individual within the natural environment.*

4.40 In Cumbria such issues can be explored in conjunction with a number of well-established organisations with which practical co-operation may be possible, such as the *West Cumbria Groundwork Trust*, the *Cumbria Wildlife Trust*, the *National Trust* or the *British Trust for Conservation Volunteers.*

4.41 The Department of Education and Science highlights the value of outdoor pursuits, adventurous activities and experiences away from the home environment in the booklet

"Education Observed; Effective Youth Work", pointing to the value of such activities for social learning.

> *"One group began by simulating a rescue from a crevasse, using climbing equipment rigged in a tall tree. After this they were given pieces of equipment and charged with the task of assembling it to convey all the members of the team over a simulated electric fence. Both activities required initiative, teamwork, negotiation and leadership, and both proved very challenging to all the participants. The physical skills required were new to all, but they achieved their objectives.*
> *The group were then invited to consider their styles of working: which techniques had proved successful and which ones were rejected? How good was the communication between the members? Why had some pieces of equipment been used to build structures? And why had some others been rejected? How far was the opinion of all members of the team sought? Who took the initiative, and why?"*

*(Education Observed, DES Publications 1987)*

4.42 There are many examples of enterprising Outdoor Adventure programmes operating within the Youth Service. For instance, despite shortage of time and resources, a Senior Community Education worker with *Somerset County Council,* Dillon Hughes, is able to provide a variety of outdoor experiences for his client groups, the largest number falling within the 16 to 19 age-group. Courses vary from straightforward skills training to negotiated courses with young people who are either referrals from other agencies or long-term unemployed. Aims vary according to the group needs. There are three basic ground rules: firstly, whatever is done is participative; the group is encouraged to make decisions and take responsibility for themselves, and their group's well-being and safety; secondly, every programme must be developmental, and so increase skills, knowledge and experience; thirdly, each programme must be flexible, relating to the needs of the group.

4.43 *Somerset Community Education Service* is trying to develop opportunities for young people from rural areas whose isolation and lack of access to opportunities and facilities are felt to match those of young people in deprived urban areas. Although Outdoor Adventure is not seen as a 'miracle cure', nevertheless it can help as part of a process which looks at attitudes, values and promotes self-esteem. An important part of this process is the action planning session which follows each programme; participants are expected to plan realistic short-term, medium-term and long-term targets for themselves.

4.44 Similar approaches are adopted in many of the new initiatives on Merseyside. These have been significantly assisted by the formation of the *Merseyside Outdoor Activities Association*. This Association, sponsored by the Sports Council as part of the Demonstration Project (see 6.26, 6.27), provides a forum in which local youth organisations can communicate and share information and resources. For instance, the *Sefton Youth Service* uses adventure experiences to help develop values and attitudes and to provide challenge and teamwork experience. It is planned to provide taster experiences in sailing, canoeing, windsurfing, rock-climbing and caving, and to encourage participation in the Duke of Edinburgh's Award. Much of the activity in this early phase of the programme is based upon half-day activity.

4.45 Jeff Nelson, a youth worker at the *Anfield Youth Activities Centre* in Liverpool, provides approximately twelve days of outdoor experience each year for up to 250 local young people mainly aged 16 and over. This is another recently-initiated project, mainly involving single-day multi-activity events organised locally. Aims are to improve self-image, to improve social skills through sharing in planning and execution of the tasks, and to improve personal effectiveness by decision-making, facing consequences and learning skills.

4.46 Outdoor Adventure within the Youth and Community Service may be a particularly appropriate means by which to address the needs of particular sections of the community. Young people at risk, young women, or members of the ethnic minority communities may require special separate provision to be persuaded to participate. The study has indicated a widespread wish within the Youth Service to cater for the ethnic minorities, the disabled and young people 'at risk' in ways appropriate to their special needs. These needs are examined in Chapter 8.

# *Education Support Grants to the Youth Service*

4.47 An important opportunity for the voluntary and statutory Youth Service to develop vocationally-oriented youth work, including opportunities for Outdoor Adventure, has been provided under the DES Education Support Grants (ESGs) for Learning by Achievement. The sum of £5 million has been made available for the three-year period 1988 to 1991, providing a major boost to innovatory youth work.

4.48 'Learning by Achievement' ESGs are available in this period to support expenditure on new, vocationally-oriented youth service activities for 14 to 21 year-olds at risk in a number of mainly inner city areas. The target groups of young people are those performing unsatisfactorily at school, those over 16 not in YTS or who have dropped out, and those who have no jobs after YTS. Initiatives should enable young people *"to perform challenging tasks to high standards designed to increase their personal development and range of skills."* One eligible category includes those which enable *"participation in adventurous activities, involving the challenge of the natural environment with particular emphasis on teamwork."* The National Youth Bureau suggested a number of outdoor projects which might attract support under the 'Learning by Achievement' heading:

— The development of partnership projects between youth services, local voluntary youth organisations, and national outdoor education organisations to provide adventure training opportunities in both urban and upland environments,

— The development of training programmes that enable young people to obtain basic outdoor and development training skills and set up self-help neighbourhood outdoor adventure projects,

— The development of diversified adventure training programmes to support the creative use of such areas as conservation and environment programmes, narrow-boats and the creative arts.

4.49 In order to provide the opportunity for Outdoor Adventure under the Learning by Achievement programme, Youth Services in the approved areas have made substantial use of the adventure programmes provided by voluntary and charitable bodies such as *Endeavour Training, Operation Raleigh,* and the *Outward Bound Trust.*

# The Youth Training Scheme (YTS)

4.50 A significant proportion of young people leaving school at 16 now take part in the Youth Training Scheme, which aims to provide two years' foundation and vocational training, together with planned work experience. Since 1986, YTS has been extended to a two-year programme. The great majority of trainees undertake their training in association with an employer or group of employers. The programme allows young people to obtain an occupationally relevant qualification, and encourages the development of personal effectiveness; enhancing confidence and self-knowledge, being effective in learning and using skills, exercising mature judgement and taking initiative and responsibility, both individually and in a team.

4.51 Many YTS managing agents recognise that Outdoor Adventure activities, within the context of a 'personal development' residential course, are a particularly effective way of helping young people towards this goal. However, such residential experiences are not mandatory, and the Training Agency, whilst encouraging them, does not provide any additional funding for this aspect of YTS. In March 1989 a number of modifications were made to the mandatory requirements for YTS programmes placing more responsibility on the managing agents and employers to design their own programmes. The two-year requirement is now being modified, and there is no longer a compulsory 20-week period of off-the-job training. This may mean a narrowing of the original broad scope of the programme, and will place a further question mark over the future of residential personal development programmes as part of YTS.

4.52 The *Manpower Services Commission (MSC)*, now the *Training Agency (TA)*, in 1985 drew up a manual for the operation of residential experiences within YTS, which contained a code of practice for residential and outdoor training. The manual and the code of practice together provide an excellent handbook for any organisation providing Outdoor Adventure experiences. The brief but systematic and comprehensive description of the learning processes, the design of the event, and the practical considerations which arise, provides a great deal of very useful information.

4.53 The Code of Practice of the MSC suggests that learning objectives may include:

— *the development of personal qualities, e.g. self-awareness, self-confidence, trust in others, sensitivity and tolerance, respect for others, communication skills, decision-making, clarifying personal objectives, developing qualities of curiosity and imagination, creative thinking, and developing personal recreational skills;*
— *the development of group skills, e.g. teamwork understanding, leadership skills, and the knowledge of roles within groups.*

It is suggested that these objectives may be achieved by outdoor activities, indoor groupwork exercises, project or environmentally based studies, conservation and service programmes or by the living-together experience.

4.54 Much of the the value of outdoor programmes in the context of YTS lies in the residential dimension rather than the Outdoor Adventure dimension. Many of the participants on YTS programmes are poorly-motivated and easily deterred by what they may perceive as rigorous or too-demanding tasks. The active and physical image of outdoor pursuits has led some managing agents to avoid such experiences. Nevertheless many development training organisations have seen high levels of achievement from young people engaged in adventurous activities who have never ventured away from their home environment before. This experience is echoed by many of the managing agents who include such experience for all trainees. Because of constraints of time and cost, most YTS residential adventure programmes last for a maximum of five days, with travel to the residential base on the Monday and departure on the Friday. The short period of time has led to a careful analysis of appropriate learning objectives and programme design.

4.55 *The Post Office*, takes up to 3,500 young people each year on outdoor programmes for young employees, including YTS participants. For their residential and outdoor programmes, the Post Office makes use of commercial organisations who in their view offer good value for money, offer a choice of alternative activities, and provide a high quality experience which is regularly monitored by the Post Office.

4.56 *British Home Stores plc* have about 100 trainees annually, of which 80 per cent are female. The company uses a Christian residential centre for outdoor experience. The company seeks an experience with a variety of skills, involving teambuilding, leadership and personal development. Most trainees participate in abseiling, rockclimbing, caving, orienteering and expeditions. It is felt that these experiences help to develop maturity and greater confidence, particularly in communicating.

4.57 Some YTS managing agents recognise the value of longer residential experiences, and are prepared to build them into the YTS programme despite the additional costs involved. A major scaffolding company *SGB* has for several years incorporated a three-week Outward Bound course into their YTS training provision. This arrangement differs from the others cited in that the trainees take part in an open course, rather than a programme designed specifically for the group, as is the normal situation.

# *Young People in Employment*

4.58 Since the end of the second world war, many industrial and commercial organisations in Britain have sought to develop their young employees by providing non-technical training aimed at helping them to become more effective at work. At the same time a number of organisations have grown up specialising in assisting this process, which was often referred to in the past as 'character development', but is now increasingly described as 'development training'.

4.59 Development training is distinctively concerned with the systematic and purposeful development of the whole person. It enhances personal effectiveness by evoking a sense of purpose, a set of general coping skills and a degree of self-understanding.

> *"Development Training represents an attempt to get away from the idea that training is a finite process, to teach specific skills once and for all; or alternatively that training serves a remedial purpose. It combines the concept of development — change and growth achieved through learning from experience — with that of training — learning specific skills for clear and identifiable purposes."*

*('Residential Training in YTS', MSC, 1985)*

4.60 Development training experiences are particularly relevant for young people between 16 and 19, in a period of rapid maturation and in a new work environment. Such training focuses on three areas of personal growth, namely capability, awareness and values. It uses a common approach to all these, based on learning by doing. Learning is achieved by:

— experience (doing);
— review (looking back over experience to share and reinforce learning);
— transfer (relating learning from the outdoor experience to other situations).

The development training tutor must understand this process and have the skills to enable it to occur. It is of its nature a profound and at the same time intensely personal experience, and it follows that those staff involved require a high level of empathy and counselling ability.

4.61 From the many organisations that include a development element in their training for young employees, the following three examples give an insight into purposes and outcomes:

a) *The National Westminster Bank* each year sends large numbers of young employees to take part in Outdoor Adventure experiences. The purpose of this commitment is to encourage self-development and leadership in a non-organisational environment and to provide a balance for their development which will develop personal qualities and enable them to meet future challenges confidently. The Bank has in the past provided sponsorship for young employees on Operation Raleigh and Outward Bound courses, and has encouraged participation in the Duke of Edinburgh's Award.

b) *British Nuclear Fuels* has encouraged craft apprentices to take part in similar ventures. For instance, up to 120 apprentices from Sellafield have in recent years taken part in courses with Brathay, Outward Bound, City Challenge or at a local LEA outdoor centre.

c) *Cumbria Constabulary* makes it a requirement that all their police cadets should attend an adventure course, regarding this as a means of developing confidence, independence and responsibility for one's decisions, and building leadership skills. Considerable value is attached to meeting other young people from different backgrounds, and for this reason an 'open' course is used with a wide variety of participants.

4.62 An increasing number of companies prefer their young employees to take part in a course tailored to their specific requirements, and many of the traditional providers of 'open' development training experiences now meet their sponsors' requirements in this way. The advantages of a 'tailored' Outdoor Adventure programme are that it can be designed to meet the specific company requirements or organisation, and it may be easier to organise effective follow-up and progression; the disadvantage is that the participants' behaviour is affected by pre-course relationships and the value of mixing with a wide cross-section may be diminished.

4.63 In order to provide a development experience over which they can exercise control, some organisations initiate and manage their own outdoor programmes. For instance *British*

*Rail* has established a residential training and adventure centre near Darlington, staffed with company trainers who also have the required outdoor skills. This centre is used for British Rail trainees and on occasion provides outdoor courses for other organisations.

4.64 In recent years the value and relevance of Outdoor Adventure experience have been increasingly recognised by industrial and commercial concerns, not only for the development of young employees, but as a means of management development as well. In such work there is a requirement for a sophisticated tutorial involvement, with a clear rationale for each activity and a deeper understanding of the processes involved.

4.65 There are many outdoor and other organisations which provide Development Training for young employees. In several cases the outdoor component of the experience is a small part of a much more comprehensive training opportunity; increasingly other training organisations are recognising the value of Outdoor Adventure as an illustration or demonstration of some of general principles of good working practice. For instance, many of the business schools include an outdoor element in their programmes for young managers.

4.66 Five major national organisations concerned with young employees and including a substantial element of outdoor work in their programmes are the members of the Development Training Advisory Group (DTAG). These are *Brathay Hall Trust*, the *Outward Bound Trust*, the *YMCA, Endeavour Training*, and *Lindley Lodge*. Their work is described in Chapter 6 together with that of other centres with similar purposes. (see 6.42 - 6.53)

4.67 The tradition of Sail Training for young people is long-established in Britain. There has been a notable increase in the opportunities for young people to take to the water as part of their education or in search of Outdoor Adventure including an expansion of opportunities to experience more adventurous voyages in larger vessels. Much of the work of the members of the *Association of Sail Training Organisations*, takes place with young people in the age group 16 to 19 years, and is aimed at confidence building, teamwork training and personal development. These sail training organisations are described more fully in Chapter 6 (6.66 - 6.72).

4.68 Many young adults become independent members of sailing and other outdoor sports clubs, and thus discover adventure outside the context of an organised programme or course. However most outdoor sports clubs provide some training for novice members, or encourage participation in national coaching courses.

# *Ministry of Defence*

4.69 The armed services have long recognised the value of adventurous training as a medium for developing qualities such as fitness, self-reliance, initiative and endurance. Since the 1950s these activities have been included as a component of training programmes, and in schemes designed to foster the personal development of young servicemen. The only service to provide such opportunities for young women is the RAF, and the numbers are very small. Currently the Ministry of Defence promotes three forms of adventurous training.

—     Resource and Initiative training,
—     Unit Adventurous training,
—     Joint Service Adventurous training.

4.70 The Resource and Initiative element of the initial training programmes of most Apprentice and Junior Leader entrants to the services is designed *"to further the development of character, resourcefulness and leadership qualities using real situations in the outdoor environment" (Ministry of Defence; Statement of Aims).* For these 16 to 18-year old young men, outdoor training is an integral part of the overall training programme, and is normally carried out by physical education instructors. Activities are pitched at a basic level, but include light-weight camping, mountain navigation, rock-climbing, canoeing and skiing. Such training is usually operated from tented base camps, or from some of the smaller week-end training centres such as Halton camp in the Lake District. It is not at present possible to provide this training for all new entrants to the services, because of constraints on the time available and the lack of suitable bases, particularly in winter. Currently approximately 4,700 Royal Navy non-commissioned recruits, 8,000 Army junior soldiers and 1,500 RAF apprentices and direct entry technicians receive this form of training each year. Some use is also made of other organisations to provide part of this training; for instance during the winter months each year a considerable number of army Junior Leaders attend Outward Bound courses, and also take part in Ocean Youth Club or Sail Training Association cruises.

4.71 Part of the syllabus for junior entrants to the Army requires the provision of External Leadership training. The progression may include a combination of leadership and character-development exercises, often in the form of group problem solving tasks, together with stress training emphasising endurance, self-reliance and, where applicable, leadership development. Such training is largely based on survival in an outdoor environment. Certain activities are categorised as appropriate for external leadership training; these include hill and mountain walking, elementary rock-climbing, canoeing, introductory caving, survival skills, cross-country skiing and all aspects of fieldcraft.

4.72 Unit Adventurous training is the name given to the scheme whereby service personnel, many of them between 18 and 24, can continue to take part in Outdoor Adventure as a means of developing personal skills and leadership. Participants plan and carry out challenging expeditions in testing environments in Britain or overseas. A key feature of these enterprises is that they occur at the initiative of local leaders, and are authorised by local units within their budget allocation. Participation in the Unit Adventurous Training scheme is popular, and is seen by the Ministry of Defence as cost-effective and beneficial. In one recent training year, a total of 71,000 male personnel took part in 4,978 expeditions, which included canoeing throughout the UK, in France, Germany and the USA; rock-climbing in the UK, the Alps, the USA and Canada; offshore sailing in the Atlantic, the Baltic and the Mediterranean; the crossing of a South Australian desert by camel; sub-aqua diving in Lake Titicaca; mountaineering in Nepal, and jungle trekking in Brunei and Sarawak.

4.73 The Joint Service Adventurous Training, (JSAT), scheme provides a co-ordinated framework for provision of adventurous activities by the three services. These training opportunities are available to young servicemen, and therefore fall within the ambit of the study. The training is designed to develop fitness, self-reliance, physical courage, initiative, powers of endurance and interdependence. The Navy takes responsibility for most water activities, the Army for mountaineering and canoeing, and the RAF for gliding and parachuting. The majority of the courses provided under the JSAT lead to qualifications needed by potential expedition leaders and trainers. They are popular and generally heavily over-subscribed. In the training year 1987/88 there were 16,377 applicants for 9,666 places available within the scheme.

4.74 Additional arrangements for Outdoor Adventure training for young people planning a service career are available at Welbeck College, the Army sixth form college for young men intending to join the army technical corps. At Welbeck, 150 young men each year have opportunities for external leadership training on similar lines to the training provided for junior leaders and army apprentices. Some of this experience is provided by the college itself, and some by commercial providers. The College itself provides mainly week-end programmes including hill-walking, canoeing and rock-climbing, and arranges for other organisations to provide search and rescue training and winter activities.

# *Outdoor Adventure Opportunities for Over 19s*

4.75 The study has investigated on a limited basis the extent of Outdoor Adventure among those over 19. Most men and women in the 19 to 24 age-group have discovered their predominant leisure interests and their priorities of involvement. For many, sporting activities will have a primarily social purpose. However, a considerable amount of organised training in Outdoor Adventure continues to take place for many in this age-group, sometimes as a continuation of that carried out earlier, as in the armed forces or in some colleges of education, or as part of professional or career development. Outdoor Adventure involving over-19s is relevant to the study for the following reasons:

— It throws light on the opportunities for progression to more ambitious ventures,
— It highlights the scope for adventure and exploration for those with the freedom and resources to enable participation,
— There exists a considerable number of young adults in this age-group who are unemployed or disadvantaged, and who have missed the opportunities for Outdoor Adventure in earlier years.
— This age-group is a major source of leaders for any future expansion of provision.
— Work with this age-group has helped to clarify the learning processes involved in Outdoor Adventure generally.

4.76 A sizeable proportion of those finishing school at 18-plus continue into further education or into a professional programme of career preparation. They may become involved in outdoor experiences as a means of recreation or as an avenue of personal and professional development.

4.77 Most universities, polytechnics and colleges provide a rich variety of opportunities for all types of Outdoor Adventure through outdoor activity clubs, expedition or exploration groups, and other means. Such opportunities to extend horizons and strengths in all manner of ways and with new companions are important components of the university experience. Most colleges have their own outdoor clubs, and the standards of performance attained by young people in this stage of their lives can be very high.

4.78 The study also indicates the value that shared outdoor activities can have in broadening the experience of those who are frequently pursuing highly specialised academic courses. One college chaplain who organises a residential week for his students identifies the value of supplementing or challenging the highly intellectual and individualist pressures of university education, and the importance of encouraging learning in teamwork. This view has also been expressed by employers of newly-qualified graduates, who may have strong intellectual credentials, but lack the broader vision required for management responsibility in industry or commerce.

4.79 *The Cambridge University Explorers' and Travellers' Club,* one of the largest university groups associated with adventurous expeditions, illustrates the possibility for wider expeditions during those years spent at college, where extended vacations allow for ambitious journeys overseas. The Club has approximately 400 members, and some 120 of these each year engage in expeditions lasting on average two months. The purposes of such ventures, as expressed by the club president, are:

— To broaden outlooks on new cultures, landscapes and environments,
— To provide areas for exciting practical fieldwork,
— To provide opportunities for adventure, sport and rigorous environments,
— To provide interesting areas of work, related to the degree course undertaken.

4.80 Other universities and polytechnics provide first degree courses which contain an element of outdoor training and learning as part of the course content, directly related to the course of study itself. These for the main part are degree courses for those intending to become professional teachers, often specialising in physical education or environmental education. There are also degree courses in Leisure Studies and in Recreation and Community Studies, which may have an outdoor education component.

4.81 For instance, *Crewe and Alsager College of Higher Education* offers a four-year degree course leading to a BEd which provides 20 to 30 participants each year with a wide-ranging outdoor and environmental element; in addition the college provides outdoor education option courses for BTEC, and PGCE students. *The College of St. Mark and St. John* in Plymouth has developed outdoor education programmes which form part of the BEd and BA (Recreation and Community Studies) courses. An outdoor education supportive subject is planned for physical education students, to start in September 1989. These courses include both emphasis on technical skills and also examination of different problem-solving approaches. Several college staff involved with outdoor education have commented on the difficulty of finding time and commitment in large academic institutions for this type of flexible and experience-based learning.

4.82 *Charlotte Mason College* in Cumbria has developed a four-year BEd Honours course for intending primary teachers with a strong specialism in outdoor and environmental studies, including outdoor skills, environmental/ecological studies, and the examination of philosophical and educational values. This is supported by wide-ranging opportunities to work with young people directly in adventurous pursuits, both through appropriate teaching practice placements, and through involvement with the local adventure association, the 4 As. (See 2.18)

4.83 *Moray House College of Education* (Edinburgh) provides outdoor skills and leadership training for approximately 200 students each year, predominantly 19 and 20 year olds. These are in the main BEd students or pre-service recreation managers, but the College also organises in-service training in outdoor education for serving teachers.

4.84 Graduates in academic disciplines may choose to study for a Postgraduate Certificate in Education (PGCE) and there are a number of such courses which offer an outdoor education component. One of the best-known is the PGCE course provided for 16 participants at the *University College of North Wales* at Bangor. The course is concerned particularly with the extra educational dimension offerred by the outdoor environment, with personal and social development opportunities, and with placing the outdoor work in a 'whole-world' dimension. At the same time the course is integrated directly with academic elements. Adventurous experience is a prominent theme and element in the ten-month programme, and considerable practical experience with young people is incorporated.

4.85 Most of the major Development Training organisations work quite extensively with those between 19 and 24, since this is seen as a critical period of training and development for young people intending a career in industry or commerce. The use by a wide range of commercial organisations of Outdoor Adventure, either through their own in-house operations, or through the use of commercial or charitable providing organisations, has already been noted. (4.58 — 4.66)

4.86 Particular interest and attention has been paid in recent years to the opportunities for leadership training and management development provided by outdoor activities. Following pioneering work in this field by Brathay and by Outward Bound, a number of organisations were established specifically for this purpose. The Leadership Trust grew from early measures taken by Bulmers to develop young managers. Since then a large number of training organisations have been established with management development in the outdoors as their principal function. In his book "Outdoor Development for Managers" published in 1985, John Bank lists 24 such organisations; the number has increased substantially since that date.

4.87 Outdoor courses for managers have become highly sophisticated vehicles for learning, providing a combination of dramatic and intense practical tasks or exercises with subtle and often demanding reviews, debriefs or analysis. Interpersonal and team issues may be explored in considerable depth. The success of such courses is measured almost entirely in the extent to which the experience can be related accurately to the work situation experienced by the manager. For this reason, these specialised courses are of particular interest to those involved with young people out-of-doors. In view of the high cost of many courses for managers, and the scepticism with which they are still viewed by many, significant research efforts have been made to establish the effects of these experiences in the longer term. The outcome of these investigations will help to shed light on the general impact of Outdoor Adventure upon participants.

4.88 The services have, as previously described, ( 4.70 — 4.75) made considerable use of outdoor experience with young soldiers, sailors and airmen. Much of the leadership training provided has been 'in the field', often making use of outdoor activities. In fact, the general influence of services training on the level and quality of civilian provision has been considerable over the years. Not only has the 'action-centred leadership' model, which stems from the work of John Adair at Sandhurst, been widely adopted in civilian settings, but there has been a widespread transfer of good practice, as members of the pool of well trained ex-servicemen have become involved in adventurous activity with cadets and with many other youth organisations and training providers that have taken them into employment; in addition, many young people in custody have benefitted from such training.

4.89 The potential for further valuable contributions of this kind may to an extent be limited by the militaristic image of services' training; if the perceived difference in value systems in the armed services and the youth services could be surmounted, there is much that practitioners could learn from one another about the effective use of Outdoor Adventure for the development of personal effectiveness and leadership.

4.90 A substantial number of companies provide outdoor development for their junior managers. A typical example is provided by *United Biscuits*, who involve up to 100 employees each year on residential outdoor activity programmes, including most of their management trainees. Training needs are identified through appraisal and review systems; generally the purpose of these courses is to develop personal effectiveness and team skills by initiative and problem solving tasks. The action-centred leadership model is used extensively as a conceptual basis for the practical work. The company uses a combination of in-house courses and those provided by commercial and charitable organisations.

4.91 Not all organised outdoor experiences for the over-19s are work-related. For instance, a growing number of organisations provide intensive and disciplined outdoor courses, often with a survival training emphasis, for individual applicants. The growth of courses with an 'outdoor survival' theme has been an interesting recent phenomenon. In parallel, there are now far-ranging opportunities for adventurous treks or cross-country journeys, either on foot or by vehicle, offered by a wide range of commercial tour operators. The membership of such tours is generally quite young, and the experience may be undergone deliberately as an attempt to find adventure or to broaden horizons. Many such tour operators cater effectively to an increasing need. The work of such organisations as *Wilderness Expedition Skills Training (WEST)*, and *World Challenge* exemplify the two approaches.

4.92 The final example of work with over-19s is in essence a leader training scheme for those who may not be able to gain such experience through higher education, through costly overseas ventures, or through participation in organised residential courses. *BREMEX*

*(The Brent Mountain Expedition Training Scheme)* was initiated 25 years ago to help to develop among the young adults who participate the ability to enjoy challenge, to find a healthy and constructive way of life, and to achieve fulfilment. *"Underlying the whole concept of our expedition training scheme is the theme of an intelligent appreciation of nature as it is found in the wild, less accesible places; the enjoyment of scenes and horizons and experiences in such settings; a respect for nature in its many forms; and the ability to explore these areas and to take part in the various associated skills with a high degree of competence."*

*(BREMEX Tutorial notes.)*

4.93 Originally supported by Brent Youth and Community Service, BREMEX provides a service for those who would otherwise have little opportunity for training in outdoor skills and leadership. Up to 100 participate each year, roughly one third being female. In addition to expeditions carried out throughout the British Isles, mainly in the mountain areas, sub-groups have travelled overseas on expeditions to the Alps, the Pyrenees, the Andes and the Himalayas. The scheme is operated at low cost, and exclusively with voluntary staff.

## 4.94 *Summary*

(a) On leaving compulsory education young people face a range of choices in the course of moving to a state of greater independence. It is essential that their needs for new experience should be met if they are to become effective citizens and achieve their potential abilities. (4.1 — 4.3)

(b) It is important that from the age of 16 onwards, young people should develop productive relationships with other people, including adults. (4.4)

(c) Despite their desire for independence, social circumstances often impose constraints. (4.5)

(d) In these circumstances, training programmes assume special importance. (4.6, 4.10, 4.11, 4.59 — 4.65)

(e) In this connection, a hopeful factor is that, for demographic reasons, youth employment prospects should improve. (4.7 — 4.8)

(f) For those who are able to continue in tertiary education the problems are less acute, and prospects are better. (4.13 — 4.16, 4.27 — 4.33)

(g) A number of schools and organisations make provision for Outdoor Adventure programmes for the 16+ age range, (4.17 — 4.20) including expeditions overseas (4.20 — 4.21) both in educational establishments and the Youth Service. (4.35 — 4.46)

(h) Other organisations provide openings for field study work. (4.25).

(i) Education Support Grants are available in some urban areas to encourage and enable these opportunities. (4.47 — 4.48)

(j) 'Development Training' approaches are increasingly used both for young employees and within the Youth Training Scheme. (4.50 — 4.54)

(k) The Ministry of Defence has done much to encourage Outdoor Adventure within the Services and has significantly influenced and assisted civilian programmes. (4.69 — 4.74, 4.88 — 4.89)

(l) Outdoor experiences are increasingly provided to assist the professional or career development of junior managers.

# CHAPTER 5
## THE QUESTIONNAIRE SURVEYS

# *Introduction*

5.1  The only way of reaching large numbers of those involved in Outdoor Adventure was by using a written questionnaire. The questionnaire was designed to elucidate current activity, problems and practice throughout the country. It was not a comprehensive study covering all work taking place, but a sample of facts and views from as many different sectors of the field of Outdoor Adventure as possible. The questionnaire served an additional purpose in stimulating thought and raising awareness among those consulted.

5.2  The main questionnaire was targetted at three different groups, namely:

Users — Those who make use of Outdoor Adventure programmes or events provided by others,

Providers — Those who provide, tutor or operate Outdoor Adventure programmes or events,

Others — Those who fall into neither of these categories, but who have a 'concerned and supportive interest' in Outdoor Adventure.

The questionnaires for the first two groups were broadly similar but the questionnaire for the third category allowed a more open-ended form of response. In reality, the boundary between the providers and the users was not as clear as had been anticipated and it was hard to separate the two groups. It was difficult to identify groups or individuals involved in this field as users only. This summary of the findings of the questionnaires, therefore, does not make the anticipated clear distinction between the responses of users and providers since there is a broad area of overlap.

5.3  In identifying 950 individuals involved in Outdoor Adventure experiences for young people, the widest possible spread of backgrounds was sought, but some areas are more fully covered than others. It was emphasised that respondents should answer the questionnaire as individuals, drawing on their own knowledge, experience, preferences and ideals. In practice, this worked well and in addition to expressing their own ideas forcibly, many also sent policy statements put out by the organisations with which they were involved.

5.4  A total of 342 questionnaires (36%) were returned within an extended deadline, necessitated by the postal strike. The majority of the responses were from the providers and most of the information and conclusions have been drawn from these. Providers responded with enthusiasm; they represented all sectors of the Outdoor Adventure field including commercial, charitable, local authority and the armed services.

5.5  The results produced by the questionnaire have not been set out in full. Some of the questions have been reproduced verbatim below where appropriate. The information collected provides a large bank of data, which has been drawn upon throughout the report, and not merely in this section.

5.6  75% of respondents were involved with Outdoor Adventure experiences both directly by dealing with groups of young people, and also in a management capacity with responsibility for managing other leaders and in helping with policy making. This reflects, to a great extent, the prominent positions that they hold within their organisations.

# SECTION 1: The Responses of Providers and Users

In this section the results of questions to providers are summarised, together with the parallel results from users where appropriate.

5.7  **Question 1:**
*Describe your educational or developmental aims in providing adventure and challenge experiences for young people*

The predominant educational aim of Outdoor Adventure activities for both providers and users was personal and social development. Increasing environmental awareness showed strongly, particularly among those employed by local education authorities.

5.8 Use by the armed services of outdoor programmes was aimed to develop leadership skills and teamwork.

5.9 Developing outdoor skills as an end in itself, did not feature strongly, except among those involved in Higher Education; notably those training the trainers. Having fun, achieving success and developing recreational interests were other popular aims given by providers.

5.10 Industrial and commercial users of outdoor programmes gave aims with a rather different emphasis, more specifically related to work and its environment. Developing personal effectiveness, initiative, problem solving skills and feelings of group identity featured strongly. Probation and Social Service workers use outdoor programmes tailored to their own situation, to help young offenders in rehabilitation and to widen their horizons. To quote directly from one questionnaire: *"to show young people there is life beyond London SW11"*.

5.11 **Question 2:**
*Give details of the types of adventure programmes you provide*

The majority (60%) of programmes currently used by respondents are of a multi-activity type, although the range of activities covered varies widely from programme to programme.

5.12 Expeditions, mainly on foot, both within Britain and overseas are widely used, including those required by the Duke of Edinburgh's Award.

5.13 Development training programmes, field study courses, sail training voyages, adult leader training courses and environmental programmes are all well represented in this survey.

5.14 Lengths of programmes are related to their aims. One-week courses are the most common programmes within education, three-week courses are popular for personal development, weekend courses for developing leisure interests, overseas events and expeditions for teamwork and single outdoor activity days for enjoyment.

5.15 **Question 3:**

*Conservation and Environmental aspects of Courses*

Over 60% of providers include environmental or conservation work within their programmes, either directly through caring for the local environment and community, or through working in conjunction with other organisations (eg. British Trust for Conservation Volunteers, Nature Conservancy Council, National Trust, Forestry Commission, National Park Rangers).

5.16 **Question 4:**

*Mix of clients and selection of students*

The majority of providers work with a wide variety of client groups, although secondary school children and those in 16 — 19 education were most strongly represented. There was a widely expressed wish to work more frequently with disadvantaged youngsters or those at risk.

5.17 Student selection for programmes varies considerably. Many are chosen as a result of their own expressed personal interest, although a large number of centres or organisations operate through client organisations making block bookings. In these cases the centres have little involvement with students prior to arrival. An application and interview procedure is followed for some of the longer programmes, notably some overseas expeditions.

5.18 **Question 5:**

*Periods of Operation*

Of this sample, 80% of providers operate throughout the year, with most of the rest operating an extended 8, 9 or 10 month season, excluding the worst of the winter.

5.19 **Question 6:**

*Numbers of students and length of programmes*

Quantifying the national numbers of individuals involved annually is not an easy task. The questionnaires covered the provision of programmes for 420,000 young people each year, involving approximately 2 million person-days. The majority of these people had courses lasting 7 days or less, with a 5 day course being the most frequent. At the other end of the scale, 3,500 young people experienced programmes lasting a month or longer. Some of those responding to the questionnaire were unable to give figures relating to numbers.

5.20 There was a marginal bias towards boys participating (56%), though this single figure may be misleading. Apart from those operating in an all-female environment, there were no providers where girls were in a strong majority. Indeed, unless they are attending a local education authority centre through school, the figures suggest that girls attending an open course often find themselves outnumbered two to one by boys.

5.21 Many providers operate across a wide age range, although the largest volume of work lies with the 14-15 and 16-18 age ranges. Significant work is also being carried out with primary schoolchildren.

5.22 **Question 7:**
*Benefits*

In response to being asked to indicate relative levels of importance in developing different personal attributes, from a given list, there were some clear results.

---

**Table 1.1: What do young people gain? (Providers' perceptions)**

---

*High scores indicate greater importance*

10  Self-confidence, Teamwork
 9  Relationships, Self-awareness, Enthusiasm for life, Personal adaptability, Social awareness, Communication skills, Positive self-esteem
 8  Independence, Environmental awareness, Problem solving skills, Empathy
 7  Emotional Maturity
 6  Leadership, Interest in outdoor activities, Enthusiasm for work, Appreciation of beauty
 5  Outdoor skills, Creative imagination, Physical co-ordination
 4  Respect for ethnic minorities, Stamina, Awareness of handicap
 3  Intellectual capability
 2  Spiritual insights

---

5.23 In comparison, users showed greater interest in developing teamwork and communication skills, and less interest in environmental awareness, enthusiasm for life, appreciation of beauty and an interest in outdoor activities.

5.24 Developing intellectual ability, enthusiasm for work, leadership and independence were seen to increase in importance with older age groups. Developing appreciation of beauty, creative imagination and environmental awareness were seen as decreasing in importance with age. Building environmental awareness was seen as particularly important among those working with primary schoolchildren.

5.25 Attempting to connect attributes with particular activities was very difficult for many people. A typical comment was,

> *"it's not the activity, it's the approach. Any activity can be used to develop any particular attribute."*

Rock-climbing and kayaking were seen to be particularly strong activities for developing the personal attributes of self-confidence, positive self-esteem and self-awareness. Problem solving exercises were seen as strong in developing teamwork, communication skills and relationships. It was evident that expeditions were perceived as being suitable for developing attributes right across the spectrum, from personal to group skills. Much expedition work also has a strong environmental purpose or component.

5.26 There was no strong preference expressed about developing relationships between young people and their peers, adults, or the opposite sex.

5.27 **Question 8:**
*Use of Activities*

Providers were asked to indicate the relative scale of use of activities they included in their programmes. Overall, the highest levels of activity were found to be: mountain walking (summer), camping and expeditions on foot followed by; backpacking, country walking, orienteering, and flat-water canoeing. Other activities figuring prominently were; single-pitch rock-climbing, abseiling and initiative exercises.
A wide range of less conventional outdoor activities are also commonplace, of which bivouacing, gorgewalking and rafting are the best examples.

5.28 The recent growth in the number of artificial ski slopes is considerable and is reflected in the questionnaire. One third of providers indicated they include some artificial skiing in their programmes.

5.29 Among creative activities, photography, drawing and writing were the most common, although 40% of providers admit to making no attempt to include any creative element in their programmes. 'Earth awareness' or 'acclimatisation' activities were found in varying degrees in 55% of programmes. Despite this, by no means everybody is familiar with these ideas. Some form of community service is included in half the programmes.

5.30 As expected, different activities were used more frequently with different age groups. For the young (8-15 years), orienteering, country walking and environmental studies were seen as particularly suitable, while for those over 16 there was more emphasis on camping, backpacking, mountain walking and rock climbing. Some activities, for example, canoeing (flat-water), were seen as equally suitable for all ages.

5.31 Less than half indicated that they included First Aid within their programmes on a regular basis.

5.32 Three different, but related, purposes were identified for which expeditions are used:
(a) as a different environment in which further to develop skills and to enable young people to experience travel in the outdoors;
(b) to develop personal attributes of self-confidence, independence and leadership;
(c) to develop social attributes of teamwork and relationships.

5.33 There was a widespread view that expeditions have the strongest all-round benefits for young people.

5.34 A broad range of academic subjects is studied using the outdoor environment as a classroom, mainly biology and geography and their related subjects.

5.35 **Question 9:**
*Reviewing the Experience*

There was general agreement between users and providers that the periods in their courses spent reviewing activities were of particular importance. Group discussions, in one form or another, emerged as the most common method for reviewing, although naturally different methods suit different age groups. For example, with primary school-children, it was popular for the children to write a diary and draw a picture.

5.36 **Question 10:** *Learning Models*

A large number of respondents appeared not to use a clear conceptual framework or relevant learning models for their work.

5.37 **Question 11:** *Which outdoor areas (including urban) do you primarily use?*

| Table 1.2: Geographical Areas Used | |
| --- | --- |
| Lake District | 68 |
| North Wales | 61 |
| Scotland | 58 |
| Peak District | 36 |
| Urban areas | 26 |
| Yorkshire/Northumbria | 25 |
| Devon/Cornwall | 16 |
| Coastal waters and Estuaries | 13 |
| Northern Ireland | 9 |

Of the major upland areas of Britain, North Wales and the Lake District are the areas most heavily used. The Highlands of Scotland are also a popular area but the difference in scale generates a different set of issues and problems

The Alps and, to a lesser extent, the Pyrenees, are the most popular areas abroad, followed by other areas of France, Norway and Iceland. When choosing a destination abroad, one respondent summarised his ideas succinctly: *"anywhere remote, yet accessible and cheap to get to"*.

## 5.38 Question 12:

*What impact do the adventure experiences you are involved with have:*

*(a) on the Environment?*

There is evidence of some ignorance or complacency related to the impact courses have on the environment. Nearly a third of those replying felt their programmes had little or no impact. Erosion of footpaths, ghylls, crags and campsites, was acknowledged by many as an inevitable consequence of their programmes, but this was balanced by the positive impact achieved through increases in the levels of environmental awareness of their students. Most sailing programmes emphasise the importance of not polluting the marine environment. Most land programmes emphasise the importance of carrying out all rubbish.

5.39 *(b) on the Local Community?*
Providers believed generally that the impact of courses on local communities was beneficial overall; the boost to the local economy outweighing the infringement imposed on quiet rural communities. Users expressed little concern or awareness of the impact the programmes they used had either on local communities or the environment.

5.40 **Question 13:**
*What steps do you take to avoid inconvenience to the local community or damage to the environment?*

(a) Three different measures emerged as making up the best policy to minimise the impact of programmes:
    (i)   through the education of the young people, raising of their environmental awareness, and insistence on following strict codes of conduct, eg. the Country Code.
    (ii)  through closer liaison with environmental groups and authorities and maintaining good public relations with the local community, especially local landowners.
    (iii) through careful control exercised over the use of sensitive areas, the numbers taking part, by varying sites and routes wherever possible, including if necessary prohibiting the use of certain areas completely.

(b) Adequate staff training and, where necessary, maintaining careful supervision over students, particularly during evenings, were also seen as crucial measures.

5.41 **Question 14:**
*What evidence do you have for the effectiveness of your programmes?*

This was widely expressed in the form of feedback, both from the students themselves, and their parents, teachers, sponsors or employers. However, most respondents have made little effort to research the impact and effect of adventure programmes in a scientific or controlled manner. The demand for courses and in particular the high percentage of rebookings from regular customers is cited as an indication of effectiveness. Many commercial users are in no doubt as to the value of adventure programmes:

> *"young people exposed to this type of experience have tended to advance more rapidly within the organisation".*

## 5.42 Question 15:

*What do you think might be the most effective way of making the benefits of your programmes more widely available to greater numbers of young people?*

The responses have been collected under broad categories, the numbers refer to the number of respondents in each category.

---

**Table 1.3 How to increase availability?**

---

* Through an expansion of resources, properly funded to include more centres, expanding existing operations and employing more professional staff. (73 responses)
* Through increased, improved, carefully planned publicity to ensure full advantage is taken of what is currently available. (50 responses)
* Through generating wider national and political recognition of outdoor education, its value and its place within the school curriculum. (43 responses)
* By improving staff training opportunities and improving arrangements for volunteers and teachers to take part. (21 responses)
* By finding ways of making courses more readily available to young people who can't afford them. (15 responses)
* By encouraging more organisations to 'do it themselves' rather than using programmes laid on by others. (10 responses)

---

5.43 **Question 16:**
*Working with Young Offenders*

About a third of providers indicated that they are actively involved with helping young offenders, although in many cases this reflects their willingness to accept specialist groups for a course or individuals on open courses. Hard evidence that Outdoor Adventure programmes are effective in rehabilitating young offenders is limited. Reduced re-offending rates are quoted by some organisations involved with long-term programmes; those providing short, one-off experiences usually are not able to judge the effectiveness of their programmes in this context. (This is covered in more detail in Chapter 8).

5.44 **Question 17:**
*Follow-up Activity and Advice*

(a) Most providers (75%) make some provision to follow up their programmes, mainly in the form of advice about further courses available or encouragement to join local clubs. Some teachers respond to demand by organising further opportunities for outdoor pursuits within schools.
(b) At a different level, where appropriate, encouragement is given to assist young people in becoming assistant or voluntary instructors.
(c) Opportunities for wider challenges or adventures overseas are less easily obtained. Only about a third indicated this information was available, ranging from more demanding courses to expeditions with organisations like the British Schools' Exploring Society and Operation Raleigh.

5.45 **Question 18:**
*Links with others*

(a) An attempt was made to quantify links or affiliations which providers had with other outdoor organisations. Although there is wide variation, the most typical picture is of organisations having a few local and regional links, several with national bodies, but very few internationally. Many voluntary bodies would value stronger links with other organisations working in the field.

(b) There was support for improving communications, both regionally and nationally, and a variety of different suggestions were put forward — which are considered later in the report.

(c) Access to a source of comprehensive, up-to-date information organised on a regional basis would be helpful to many providers, especially those not operating from their own centre. Suggestions included information on:

— organisations operating and the activities they use;
— available sources of transport and equipment for hire;
— details of suitable sites for activities and advice on access;
— accommodation, both at home and abroad;
— lists of available qualified staff.

5.46 **Question 19:**
*What are the major difficulties you experience at present in carrying out your work?*

The responses have been collected under broad categories, the numbers refer to the number of respondents in each category.

| **Table 1.4 Current Major Difficulties** |
| --- |
| 76   A lack of money or financial insecurity. |
| 53   A shortage of suitably qualified staff, together with a variety of staff-related problems (the cost of staff training, the new conditions of service etc.) |
| 39   A lack of time, particularly among those operating on a voluntary basis in their spare time. |
| 34   A lack of policy and commitment from authorities, principally local education authorities. |
| 30   A lack of transport and vehicles. |
| 26   A lack of resources; equipment, accommodation, storage. |
| 21   Problems with access, especially to rivers. |
| 11   Insurance. |

Insufficient time allocated for outdoor education on school timetables clearly frustrates many enthusiastic teachers.

5.47 **Question 20:**
*What are your prime requirements when recruiting staff and are they easily met?*

(a) Overall, for providers, outdoor skills and human skills (ie. group work and counselling skills) were seen as of comparable importance although different situations present different requirements. Over 50% admitted that their own requirements were not easily met when they were looking for new staff.

(b) Despite this, it was generally felt that levels of outdoor and human skills among staff on appointment were good. Their personal qualities were judged very good.

(c) In staff training, slightly greater attention is given to the training of outdoor skills than to group work skills.

(d) Parallel questions were asked of the sample of users with different results. They were most interested in the staff running their programmes possessing a high level of human skills. Broadly, in assessing current staff, they had high praise for their level of outdoor skills and expressed satisfaction with levels of human skills. Staff were seen as least strong in their conceptual grasp of the educational values of Outdoor Adventure activity.

5.48 **Question 21:**
*To what extent are volunteer staff used in the running of your adventure programmes?*

(a) Over 50% of those replying to the questionnaire indicated that volunteer staff played an important role in the running of their programmes. At the other end of the scale, 10% stressed they would never, or were not allowed to, use volunteers. (There were some inconsistencies in the interpretation of the expression 'volunteer staff').

**(b)Table 1.5 Summary of views on using volunteer staff**

| *Advantages* | *Disadvantages* |
|---|---|
| Enthusiasm and commitment (62) | Lack of qualifications, skill (27) |
| Bring different outlook, fresh ideas (26) | Lack of professional accountability (23) |
| Essential — no money to pay staff (25) | Needs large commitment to training and monitoring (21) |
| Works well if competent, monitored and not exploited (24) | They have other commitments (17) |
| Cost effective (19) | There is a high turnover (16) |
| Improves student:staff ratio (19) | Lack of dedication and reliability (14) |
| They are our instructors in the future, an investment (7) | They don't understand the underlying philosophy of the work (7) |
| | They're no substitute for permanent trained, experienced staff (4) |
| | They volunteer to do what they want, when they want (3) |

*(numbers refer to number of respondents)*

(c) A distrust of volunteers occurs among the professional ranks, and in its strongest form was expressed as:

> *"Unpaid volunteers prevent proper rewards for professionals: this outweighs all the advantages of volunteers."*

# SECTION 2: Responses from Users Alone

The questions in this section were asked only to users.

**5.49  Question 1:**

*What do you think are the strengths or shortcomings of the present overall range of programmes available?*

Views were generally complimentary, although many drew attention to the wide variation in quality between different providers. The cost of commercial courses was the biggest single complaint. The additional cost and time required for travel to centres operating in remote rural areas were also significant factors.

**5.50  Question 2:**

*How do you find out about the range of providers or agencies who offer outdoor experiences?*

Recommendations by others featured most strongly, followed by personal experiences and publicity material, especially in professional magazines.

**5.51  Question 3:**

*Why did you choose the programmes you are using at present?*

Reasons given varied widely, the principal ones being: cost, quality of service, location and 'content most suitable for our demands'.

**5.52  Question 4:**

*Availability and uptake of experiences*

(a) Assessing the availability of Outdoor Adventure experiences for young people in Britain today is very difficult. While some organisations use these programmes as an integral part of their employment or youth training programmes, others make them available to only a select few each year while yet a third category make no use at all of the outdoors environment for training. Cost was perceived as the single factor which most prevents larger numbers of young people having the opportunity to take part in an organised Outdoor Adventure experience.

(b) Half the users in the sample indicated that programmes were available to everyone in their organisation, although this cannot be taken as reflecting the picture nationally.

(c) Given the opportunity of places on programmes, an attempt was made to examine the percentage of young people who take up this opportunity. Again, there is a wide variation, from 5% to 100%, and it would not be fair to draw any firm conclusions from these figures.

(d) Among those reporting a low rate of uptake of places, the image of outdoor programmes involving high-risk activities and 'roughing it' in the countryside, almost in a military style survival exercise manner, was seen as the main reason which discourages young people.

# SECTION 3: The responses from those who have a supportive interest in outdoor adventure

The majority of the 64 individuals who responded in this category had themselves considerable experience of challenging activity in the outdoors and in many cases are now responsible for national schemes of training or coaching for young people, either in an outdoor sport or in connection with the conservation movement. The most common responses are summarised here.

5.53 **Question 1:**
*What do you perceive to be the main benefits or otherwise to grow from Outdoor Adventure and challenge experiences for young people, to young people themselves, to the organisations sponsoring them, and to society as a whole?*

(a) The main benefits perceived to accrue to young people were those of social awareness and social skills, increased self-confidence, ability to work in teams, self-reliance and independence and self-awareness. Through living and working together in a new environment, away from the usual constraints, young people are able to rise to challenges, achieve success, broaden their horizons and develop into more rounded human beings.

(b) It was felt that sponsoring organisations and individuals benefited through the satisfaction of a positive contribution to the development of young people, by developing desirable qualities among employees, and by enhancing their public image, through being seen to be involved in the development of youth. Schools which sponsor outdoor adventurous activity claim that it helps to develop more educationally rounded individuals and they indicate the value of education outside the classroom.

(c) Society as a whole was seen to benefit through the development of responsible, healthy young people with greater environmental awareness and better prepared to take their place in today's complex society and to cope with the demands of the future.

5.54 **Question 2:**

*What special benefits or otherwise may derive from expedition work overseas for young people?*

(a) It was generally felt that such opportunities broadened horizons and widened cultural experiences, encouraging a sense of belonging to the wider world and contributing to international understanding. By travel beyond their national boundaries, young people gain a new perspective on their own country and culture.

(b) Overseas expeditions were seen as having greater value if they enabled young people to work with members of the indigenous population and to provide some form of service to the community which was visited. The importance and value of developing awareness of other cultures and the needs of the developing world were strongly emphasised here, but a note of caution was expressed by one respondent:

> "I am not as convinced as I should be about expeditions overseas. Too many of these are over-priced, over-written up, jaunts abroad drawing on too small a field of participants who are known to each other before they start. The bigger the mix of participants' backgrounds, the better the expedition will be."

5.55 **Question 3:**

*How would a significant increase in outdoor challenge activity in the UK or overseas affect you?*

There was general support for an expansion of activity, although concern was expressed over the resultant increase in environmental pressure. A number of respondents expressed the hope that any expansion should include the involvement of more disabled young people. Any increase in activity should be properly resourced.

5.56 **Question 4:**

*Please describe your views on the problems or disadvantages posed by programmes of Outdoor Adventure.*

(a) Several respondents underlined the dilemma presented by the need to balance adventurous experience with proper standards of safety. In this respect the problems are those of management, and these were also reflected in the concerns expressed about the leadership of adventure activities: on the one hand a concern about incompetent leadership, related to the requirement to train leaders adequately, and on the other hand a wish not to move into a narrowly professional approach.

(b) Other problems presented by Outdoor Adventure programmes included those of accountability and insurance, as well as concern for environmental damage caused by such programmes. Some conflict was evident between those who recognised the value of activities as an end in themselves and those who saw them as a medium for social or curricular ends.

(c) The high cost of many such ventures was seen as a disadvantage, restricting access to many of those who would most benefit from the experience:

> *"the young people most needing this sort of experience come from homes which can least afford it".*

5.57 **Question 5:**

*How might the provision of outdoor challenge programmes be increased effectively and economically?*

Suggestions included a major fund-raising and publicity campaign, much improved communication among those working in the field, and influencing and educating those with power or money as to the real value of these experiences. It was felt that 'outdoor challenge' programmes should be incorporated within the school curriculum, and should be expanded closer to home in urban areas or on urban fringe sites. Many more sympathetic and trained leaders were required. Existing resources, such as some LEA centres which close during school holidays, may be used more productively. Above all, increased provision will require increased resources of both people and of finance.

**5.58 Question 6:**

*What do you identify as the main obstacles in the path of such expansion?*

Over half the respondents indicated that finance presented the major problem, inhibiting the provision of staff and training, resources, equipment and travel. The shortage of suitably qualified, experienced and dedicated leaders was highlighted. The development of less personal and more bureaucratic management systems was also cited. It was felt that the image of 'outdoor challenge' activity was unhelpful. There was a lack of recognition of the value of these activities among the people who carry power. Once again, the increasing problems of liability, insurance etc. were seen as preventing expansion.

**5.59 Question 7:**

*What new issues of responsibility and risk might arise in the event of major expansion and how might they be dealt with?*

(a) The major concerns related to issues of safety, increased risk and insurance provision. There was a concern that an expansion might lead to more accidents with consequent bad publicity and an adverse public perception.

(b) The second major concern related to the quality of staff and the lack of suitably qualified and experienced people available. It was thought important to maintain standards and not sacrifice quality for quantity, making more provision for training at appropriate levels. To address these issues, the most strongly held view was that the provision of training for potential leaders should be increased.

(c) There should be greater co-operation eg. between voluntary and professional groups, and much better co-ordination and communication. By drawing together voluntary, commercial and other organisations, existing available resources could be used more effectively.

(d) The multiplicity of national bodies with an interest in outdoor education leads to confusion and duplication. Several respondents suggested that overall control or guidance is needed, perhaps through a wider national body which would draw together and co-ordinate the work of existing organisations.

5.60 **Question 8:**

*What concerns do you have about the environmental impact of any such expansion? How might they be overcome?*

(a) A considerable number of respondents expressed concern about the increase in direct erosion due to over-use, especially in certain areas. A number of respondents were not unduly concerned, provided that any expansion was properly planned. The importance of this planning requirement is generally recognised. In particular, it is suggested that future expansion should take place outside the existing 'honey-pot' areas. There was little concern expressed for the impact upon urban environments. It was generally felt that any expansion should be within the context of a broad approach to outdoor education including concern for the environment:

> *"a positive experience in the environment should lead to a positive response to the environment. Respect should be taught along with the skills".*

(b) Other specific suggestions involved: creating a greater awareness of the environment generally including among political party leaders; some form of monitoring or control of use of particular sites; the importance of appropriate challenges and locations for each group.

5.61 **Question 9:**

*What concerns do you have about the quality of adult guidance or leadership of any such expansion and how might they be overcome?*

It was indicated widely and emphatically that there was a pressing need for more properly trained, selected and qualified leaders and that there should be a much greater provision for training in all the skills involved. Leaders require a wide range of competences, and strong personal qualities. Too rapid a pace of expansion of outdoor challenge experiences might entail outstripping adequate leadership resources. There needed to be an expansion of high-quality and better structured training programmes.

# SECTION 4: Survey of Young People

5.62 A survey was conducted of all fifth-year school pupils in three schools within Berkshire, to investigate current levels of participation in, and awareness of, outdoor activities. Replies were received from a total of 382 pupils.

The three schools were chosen to reflect different catchment areas; the Downs School in Compton, a rural school; Meadway School in Reading, an urban comprehensive; Easthampstead Park School in Wokingham, a large suburban comprehensive.

Caution is needed in drawing conclusions from the survey. Small variations between two schools, for example, may be due to several reasons and it would be imprudent to draw firm conclusions. Large variations, over 15%, however, are statistically significant, and worthy of comment. An explanation may be apparent; for example a particular school may be making greater use of a resource close to the school; or it may reflect a national trend.

The results included below are a summary of the findings, since there is not room to include all the tables in full. All the figures in the tables in this section are percentages of all the pupils responding.

5.63 **Question 1:**

*Activities*

With the exception of hillwalking and camping — both popular activities for family involvement — the schools themselves came out as the most frequent channel through which pupils have been involved in outdoor activities.

**Table 4.1: Attitudes to Activities**

|  | Have tried | Want to try | Don't want to try |
|---|---|---|---|
| Hillwalking | 46 | 11 | 43 |
| Rock-climbing | 25 | 39 | 35 |
| Camping | 71 | 18 | 12 |
| Expeditions | 37 | 22 | 40 |
| Orienteering | 39 | 22 | 40 |
| Canoeing | 47 | 31 | 22 |
| Sailing | 27 | 50 | 24 |
| Windsurfing | 26 | 53 | 21 |
| Skiing | 39 | 47 | 14 |
| Caving | 14 | 36 | 50 |

(a) As the table shows, camping is the single activity which most pupils have experienced, followed by hillwalking and canoeing.

(b) The difference in enthusiasm to try hillwalking and skiing is clear. Of those who have not been skiing 77% are keen to try, compared with only 21% for hillwalking.

(c) Overall, 8% of all pupils had no experience of *any* of the 10 outdoor activities listed in the questionnaire.

(d) Participation levels between pupils from different schools are similar, although there are variations for individual activities. These show no particular pattern. For example, only 12% of the pupils from Easthampstead have been rock-climbing, compared with 49% from The Downs School.

(e) Between boys and girls, trends are again varied. Overall, boys have been the more active, notably in watersports (sailing, windsurfing and canoeing) and skiing. 50% more boys than girls have experienced these activities. The girls score higher only in hillwalking (54% girls, 40% boys).

(f) Comparing enthusiasm to try new activities between the three schools, Meadway exhibits the greatest enthusiasm. Over 80% of the pupils from this school are keen to try camping and skiing. Between the sexes enthusiasm is comparable, except for rock-climbing and caving in both of which boys scored 20% higher and camping, in which girls scored 10% higher.

5.64 **Question 2:**

*Feelings*

| Table 4.2: Pupils Feelings about Outdoor Activities | | | |
|---|---|---|---|
| Fun | 75 | Strenuous | 15 |
| Good exercise | 69 | Dangerous | 15 |
| Exciting | 68 | Safe | 11 |
| They're different | 38 | Boring | 4 |
| | | Waste of time | 3 |

As the table shows, there was broad enthusiasm. Pupils from Easthampstead scored around 20% lower for 'exciting', 'good exercise' and 'fun'. Between the sexes, the boys scored more strongly on 'exciting' and 'dangerous'. Only 10% of girls considered outdoor activities dangerous. There was no evidence to suggest girls thought of these activities as more strenuous than boys.

5.65 **Question 3:**

*Reasons for non-involvement*

When asked why they were not more involved in outdoor activities a consistent 70% of pupils replied that they were 'too busy'. A third replied that these activities were too expensive, a figure which varied considerably between schools (Downs 44%, Meadway

128

31%, Easthampstead 26%). A third also blamed a lack of information, (Downs 32%, Meadway 45%, Easthampstead 25%). Very few gave the risk and danger element as a reason. Apathy scored low; 12%, though marginally higher amongst girls (boys 9%, girls 15%).

**5.66  Question 4:**

*Organisations*

Levels of awareness and use of various outdoor organisations and activity centres, both local and national were examined.

**Table 4.3: Summary of Responses to Question 4**

|  | *Am aware of* | *Have been involved with* | *Would like to join* |
|---|---|---|---|
| Duke of Edinburgh's Award | 91 | 10 | 25 |
| Operation Raleigh | 34 | 1 | 10 |
| Outward Bound | 32 | 1 | 11 |
| British Schools Exploring Society | 28 | 0 | 8 |
| Scouts and Guides | 97 | 23 | n/a |
| Youth Hostels Association | 76 | 11 | 16 |
| PGL Adventure Holidays | 55 | 6 | 29 |
| British Trust for Conservation Volunteers | 28 | 0 | 6 |
| Rhos-y-Gwaliau (Berkshire LEA Centre) | 19 | 3 | 6 |
| Pangbourne Canoe Centre | 60 | 10 | 23 |
| John Nike Ski Centre | 74 | 34 | 26 |

(a) The Scouts, Guides and the Duke of Edinburgh's Award have all achieved an awareness level of over 90% among young people. As with activities, enthusiasm to join organisations was highest among those involved with activities perceived as fun; the local ski centre, the local canoe centre and PGL.

(b) Some individual figures stand out. The Meadway School has a higher proportion of Scouts and Guides (33%) but virtually no YHA members compared with 21% in The Downs School. The pupils of Easthampstead Park School make great use of the John Nike Ski Centre, due to its proximity to the school. By contrast, only 5% of its pupils have joined the Award scheme compared with 15% for both the other two schools. Levels of involvement were comparable between boys and girls.

(c) Enthusiasm to join or become involved with organisations show variations. Meadway School comes out as the school most keen to join. Some 41% of its pupils expressed a wish to join the Award scheme, and 21% were keen to be involved with Outward Bound. More interest was shown by girls to join the Award scheme and the YHA; boys were keener on Operation Raleigh and Outward Bound. A high percentage, 74% of all pupils, from The Downs School, indicated they did not want to become involved with the Award scheme.

(d) Awareness of all organisations is generally higher among boys than girls. More than twice as many boys (46%) have heard of Operation Raleigh as girls (21%). Awareness at Easthampstead Park School shows variations when compared with the other two schools; 20% higher for PGL and Operation Raleigh; 10-15% lower for the Award scheme.

5.67 **Question 5:**
*Information*

A consistent 66% of pupils indicated that they would like more information about adventure holidays and expeditions, both within Britain and overseas.

5.68 **Question 6:**
*Reasons hindering uptake*

Over half, (53%) considered themselves 'too busy' to go on an adventure holiday or expedition, but 'too expensive' (41%) and 'don't know how' (39%) were also strong reasons given. Again apathy was not a major reason (13%). Between schools, expense figures more strongly in The Downs School, while Meadway scored higher with 'don't know how'.

## 5.69 *Summary of Findings*

(a) The young people in this survey were in general enthusiastic about outdoor activities and would welcome more information. Currently many consider themselves too busy to get more involved. Schools are the main channel through which young people take part in outdoor activities. Skiing, canoeing, sailing and windsurfing are the most appealing activities, PGL Adventure Holidays has a similar popular image. Hillwalking does not appeal to many young people.

(b) The Duke of Edinburgh's Award and the Scouting/Guiding movements are almost universally known. Rhos-y-Gwaliau, the LEA Outdoor Centre, was the least known organisation; 81% of the young people had never heard of it.

(c) Boys are more active in watersports and skiing, girls in hillwalking. The girls' enthusiasm to try activities matches the boys', except in rock-climbing and caving. Levels of involvement in outdoor organisations between boys and girls are comparable, although boys, in general, have a higher awareness of what is available.

(d) The cost of participation was a more significant factor among pupils from the rural school, while those in the urban catchment area were the most enthusiastic to get involved.

# CHAPTER 6
## THE PROVISION OF RESOURCES

6.1 Outdoor Adventure requires an appropriate arena. The essential resource for outdoor activities is accessible open space or water. Such open space may be close to, or even within, urban areas. It includes woodland, farmland, parkland or even derelict quarrying or industrial sites. The accessible water may take the form of natural lakes, rivers or the sea; or man-made canals or reservoirs. Underground exploration requires mines, or cave systems, and those participating in air activities such as gliding or parachuting require accessible air space or air corridors.

6.2 Each arena is subject to many pressures; for instance those of conflicting use; those of economic exploitation; and those imposed by legislation. Here are three examples of these pressures;

   a) Most areas of woodland are under conflicting pressure, they are a commercial resource, a special environmental habitat, a visual amenity and a venue for outdoor adventure and recreation.
   b) Farmland exists primarily to provide food for the nation on an economic basis. The needs of outdoor recreation are normally secondary.
   c) Access to disused mines and quarries may entail risk, placing obligations and responsibilities upon the owners, which can result in restriction of access.

## Public Bodies

6.3 Access to open spaces or water cannot be taken for granted. Nevertheless there are many public bodies which exist to promote access, and these are described briefly in this chapter, together with the part they play in assisting Outdoor Adventure for young people. Also described are the various professional groups and agencies which facilitate such work.

# *The Countryside Commission*

6.4   The Countryside Commission is established by Parliament to conserve and promote access to and enjoyment of the countryside in England and Wales. The Commission is concerned with all types of natural environment, mountains and moorlands, wetlands or lowlands, heritage coastlines, or the countryside close to the towns.

6.5   Being an advisory and promotional body, the Commission does not own or manage land or facilities. It achieves its objectives by collaboration with others; public authorities, farmers, landowners or voluntary bodies.

6.6   The Commission is able to provide a substantial amount of information on the use of the countryside, based upon its own researches. These show that at present about 30% of the population make use of the countryside for walking or other informal sports. Other research suggests that a majority of the population benefit less than they might from the countryside; they are unaware of what it offers, or lack the knowledge or confidence to enjoy it. The Commission is committed to improving this situation.

6.7   The Countryside Commission also actively promotes and funds local initiatives to make countryside experience more readily available to the public. For instance, it has actively supported the establishment of some 200 country parks and 1,500 miles of long distance walking routes throughout England and Wales. The Commission also provides advice and support to the Authorities which manage the ten National Parks in England and Wales, designated in the 1950s and the Broads Authority, designated in 1987, advising the government on funding and other matters affecting the running of the Parks.

6.8   The Countryside Commission also supports other initiatives, for instance the establishment of local recreation paths and the encouragement of measures to enable the disabled to visit the countryside.

6.9   In 1980 the report, prepared by the Dartington Amenity Research Trust, entitled "Groups in the Countryside" was published by the Commission. It focused on the demand for outdoor group activities in the countryside of England and Wales, and also on the specific issue of the impact of such activities on local communities and the environment within the National Parks. (See 11.10)

# The Countryside Commission for Scotland

6.10 The Countryside Commission for Scotland has a similar role to that of the Countryside Commission. It exists to conserve the Scottish landscape, and to improve facilities for the enjoyment of the countryside, having regard for the well being of rural communities. It has identified National Scenic Areas, covering 13% of the Scottish landscape; it has assisted in the establishment of 35 country parks and grant aids Ranger services in Regional Parks, Country Parks and on long-distance routes, of which three have been designated.

# The National Parks

6.11 The ten individual National Park Authorities in England and Wales and the Broads Authority significantly assist the provision of Outdoor Adventure experiences for the young. They provide information through visitor centres; residential courses for party leaders, as at Losehill Hall in the Peak National Park; liaison with school and youth services through appointed officers; and Ranger services, whose purpose is to manage and maintain the environment of the Parks and also to provide education and interpretive assistance for visiting parties. There are at present no national parks in Scotland, although the Countryside Commission for Scotland is at present reviewing the management of popular areas and examining the possibility of establishing them.

# Forestry Commission

6.12 The Forestry Commission, established in 1919, is currently responsible for almost three million acres of countryside in England and Wales, which represents 43 per cent of the total area under forestry in Great Britain and Northern Ireland. The Commission, in addition to its task of producing timber, has the duty under the Countryside Acts to have regard to the desirability of conserving the natural beauty and amenity of the countryside.

6.13 The Forestry Commission uses its powers to provide recreational opportunities and facilities for the general public consistent with its commercial objectives, and it manages its woodland to take account of the needs of conservation. The Commission has a continuing policy of developing its forests for informal recreation and quiet pursuits. Most visitors come for the day, to walk or picnic, but activities such as horse riding, sailing, field archery and orienteering also take place. The greater emphasis upon the recreational use and the amenity value of the forest is welcome as is the recognition by the Forestry Commission of the value of the forests for educational purposes and the study of natural history. Where there is a commercial objective, charges may be made.

## The Regional Water Authorities

6.14 The Regional Water Authorities own numerous reservoirs, widely used for canoeing and sailing and also some 445,000 acres of land, mainly in the upland moorland areas of Britain. The Water Act (1973) required Regional Water Authorities to make the best use of water, and land associated with water, for recreation purposes; as a result there has been a significant development of access to these areas in the past 15 years, with the opening up of some previously unused reservoirs for recreational purposes, as at Thirlmere in the Lake District. There is legislation currently in preparation which proposes the privatisation of water supply. One clause which may affect opportunities for Outdoor Adventure establishes that

> *"nothing in the Act shall require recreational facilities made available by a relevant body to be made available free of charge."*

Concern has been expressed by environmental and recreational bodies, who fear that existing access may be curtailed. It remains to be seen whether the new Act will include satisfactory safeguards in this respect.

## British Waterways Board

6.15 The British Waterways Board owns or is the navigation authority for a network of canals, rivers and reservoirs which form a leisure and tourism resource unique in Britain. These waterways extend to almost 2,000 miles and include 90 reservoirs. They provide a rich, natural habitat for plants and wildlife and support a variety of leisure and educational activities. The canals have particular significance in that they are to be found at the centre of some of our largest conurbations, as in the Birmingham or Manchester areas. This gives potential access to water for large numbers of young people close to home and thus presents a special opportunity for outdoor activity at low cost. Inland waterways are particularly appropriate for canoeing, and reservoirs for sailing and rowing.

6.16 The British Waterways Board has made an agreement with the British Canoe Union whereby the BCU membership fee includes payment for a canoe licence for the waterways. In addition, canal tow-paths present valuable long-distance walking routes, in some instances suitable for cycling as well. Residential experience may be gained through the use of narrow boats on canals for small groups. This means of transport allows for lengthy expeditions to be carried out through varied environments, offering particularly rewarding opportunities for environmental studies. The British Waterways Board recognises that public use and enjoyment of the waterways should be enhanced, including where practicable, provision for the disabled.

# The National Trust (NT) and the National Trust for Scotland (NTS)

6.17 The National Trust owns a total of 540,000 acres of land in England and Wales and 470 miles of coastline. The National Trust for Scotland owns 100,000 acres in Scotland.These land holdings include extensive areas of the National Parks in England and Wales and parts of the most scenic areas in Scotland, such as Glencoe and Ben Attow. The Trusts see their duty, above all else, as to conserve the landscape for the enjoyment of visitors, and this policy may at times places a limit on use for outdoor recreation or education. Where the National Trust has acquired farmland in the National Parks, camping has usually been restricted to certain authorised sites, and high level camping has been carefully monitored. At the same time, the National Trust has provided opportunities for young people to stay in the National Parks at its own residential facilities, such as Acorn camps, and also to work on conservation projects on its land.

# The Ministry of Defence (MoD)

6.18 The Ministry of Defence provides large scale resources for Outdoor Adventure training, primarily by supporting training programmes for servicemen, junior leaders, army apprentices, and junior soldiers. (See 4.94 to 4.98). In addition to the four Joint Service Mountain Training Centres, which provide external leadership training and outdoor skills, there are a number of training camps or centres in wild country, often within or close to MoD training areas, mainly used by Territorial Army groups at weekends and by junior soldiers and apprentices mid-week.

6.19 Work with civilians at present takes place mainly through the Cadet Training Teams, which support the work of the Combined Cadet Forces, the ACF, the ATC and the Sea Cadet Corps, enabling young people to experience military activities and various 'adventure training' opportunities. In the 1960s and 1970s the Army Youth Teams became a valuable training resource for young people ; among other tasks they visited schools and youth organisations, providing a range of challenging activities. The proposal to re-establish these Youth Teams as an aid to recruiting in the 1990s could provide a valuable additional resource.

6.20 The MoD owns large tracts of open country in South Wales, the Pennines, Wiltshire, Northumberland, Pembrokeshire and on Dartmoor, to which access is usually restricted, except for authorised activities, notwithstanding the fact that much of this land lies within the boundaries of National Parks. The Ministry also owns mountain huts in the Cairngorms and in Germany.

# *The Department of Education and Science (DES)*

6.21 The DES plays an important part in encouraging and developing provision for outdoor education and environmental education. A series of discussion papers from Her Majesty's Inspectorate have highlighted the cross-curricular value of outdoor education and environmental education and have encouraged the development of thinking about the place of such activity in the personal and social development of young people. A recently published paper, the thirteenth in the "Curriculum Matters" series, proposes ways of fostering environmental education; it establishes objectives and considers content, planning, teaching styles and assessment of pupils. It stresses that environmental education is not a subject in its own right, but that it draws on and contributes to concepts, skills and knowledge underpinning a range of subjects or areas of learning and experience.

6.22 The Department has clarified educational objectives and has developed codes of practice for outdoor education. In addition, funding has been made available to many of the voluntary bodies who provide opportunities for Outdoor Adventure to cover the cost of headquarters administration or of initiatives taken with specific groups or areas. Educational support grants have enabled some authorities to provide adventure experiences for significant numbers of their young people. The DES has also provided a valuable liaison between the maintained and the voluntary sectors through regular conferences and consultation committees. The DES has also fostered safety and good practice through the publication of safety booklets and bulletins.

# The Sports Councils

6.23 The Sports Councils for England, Scotland, Wales and Northern Ireland are charged, through Royal Charter, with the task of developing and improving the knowledge and practice of sport and recreation in the interests of social welfare and the enjoyment of leisure amongst the public at large in Great Britain and to encourage the attainment of high standards in conjunction with the governing bodies of sport and physical recreation. The Councils' principal aims are those of increasing participation and the pursuit of excellence. The Councils support the work of such national centres as Plas y Brenin, Plas Menai, Inverclyde and Glenmore Lodge.

6.24 The English Sports Council has recently eased constraints on access and opportunity and has encouraged partnership working, joint provision and dual-use policies. The Council works closely with national governing bodies of sport and a variety of national and regional agencies, together with national and local government departments. In its strategy review "Sport in the Community into the 90s", the Council has identified two principal target groups — young people and women. The strategy review stresses that priority should be given to encouraging provision for active sports in the countryside and to working jointly with other agencies and organisations to improve access to recreation especially in the urban fringe.

6.25 The Sports Council's Action Sport programme, launched in 1986 in partnership with the Manpower Services Commission, aims to draw into recreational activities socially disadvantaged people through the deployment of sports leaders. Action Sport is particularly targetted upon low and non-participant groups; women, ethnic minorities, unemployed and disabled people. The leaders' role is to establish contact and communication with them through outreach work. Once needs have been established, and barriers preventing participation identified, the leaders can arrange appropriate activities, working on a local or neighbourhood basis. All Action Sport schemes are run in partnership with local bodies and local authorities, many of whom continue these programmes when three-year Sports Council funding stops.

6.26 In June 1983 the Sports Council established a 'demonstration project' in Outdoor Adventure activities, the principal aim of which was to raise levels of participation among those living in the inner cities and urban areas. The demonstration project has promoted the use of canals, lakes and dockland waters for canoeing and sailing, and of parks and woodlands for orienteering, camping and adventure exercises. Journeying on foot, bicycle and horseback has been encouraged, using newly-developed linear routes and trails, and attention has been drawn to the use of ski-slopes and climbing walls. Information on access, participation and leadership opportunities has promoted the use of local countryside.

6.27 Strong efforts have been made by the Council to foster a co-ordinated approach in the provision of opportunities, by drawing together voluntary, statutory, and other providers in local networks. Importance has been attached to continuity and to developing and improving communications and creating links between neighbourhood, regional and national ventures involving Outdoor Adventure and expeditions.

# Local Authorities

6.28 Most local authorities make resources available for Outdoor Adventure through their education and youth service and also through recreation and leisure departments. The scope of provision through the education and youth service is described in chapters 2 to 5 of this report, but the increasing scale of provision by local authorities for local outdoor experience should also be recognised. Local authorities have actively encouraged the establishment of country parks and also recreation paths in their areas in recent years, and have helped with the effective use of such resources by establishing Ranger services having both a conservation and interpretive role. There is a developing and beneficial relationship in the work carried out with schoolchildren through joint ventures between schools and local Ranger services, as in Cheshire and Lancashire.

Access to such local outdoor opportunities, supported by Ranger services in this way, seems to be an important key both to initiating elementary outdoor work and also inculcating a proper approach to the countryside.

# The Training Agency

6.29 The Training Agency, formerly the Manpower Services Commission (MSC), has made an important contribution in recent years both to the development of training effectiveness in outdoor and residential work and also by funding, in the early years of the Youth Training Scheme (YTS), the opportunity for residential experience for young people as part of the scheme. The MSC booklet "Residential Experience in the Youth Training Scheme" remains one of the most useful guides to the provision of effective personal and social development courses for young people yet published, and it makes extended references to Outdoor Adventure activities in this context. In particular it emphasises the importance of developing effective methods of transferring the lessons acquired out-of-doors to the work situation.

# The National Bodies for Sport

6.30 Each major outdoor sport has its own national body, which exercises appropriate responsibilities towards the ethos of the sport, the participants, and where appropriate the environment. Most national bodies permit individual membership, although normally membership is through an affiliated club. Significant numbers of young people are associated with the national bodies, particularly those who take part in sport or Outdoor Adventure privately, perhaps through a club, or through a family interest.

6.31 The national bodies such as the *Royal Yachting Association,* the *British Canoe Union,* the *British Caving Association,* the *British Mountaineering Council* and the *British Orienteering Federation,* provide a supporting service to member clubs, training opportunities for participants and leaders, and insurance arrangements, and may negotiate access agreements where appropriate. Each national body has its own systems of training and coaching awards, providing assessment of technical skills for leaders and instructors.

# The Central Council for Physical Recreation (CCPR)

6.32 The CCPR is a joint forum for the national bodies for sport, and it has established an Outdoor Pursuits Forum in which relevant issues can be identified and discussed. The CCPR has taken the lead in establishing the Basic Expedition Training Award, a useful addition to the range of leader training schemes, providing a first qualification for adults working with young people out-of-doors. The work of the foregoing providers is complemented by that of a multitude of other national or local groups, four categories of which are described in the following paragraphs.

# Organisations Concerned with Conservation

6.33 There are many organisations concerned with conservation of the physical or natural environment which involve young people in their work. *The Royal Society for Nature Conservation* heads an active network of 48 local Wildlife Trusts and over 50 Urban Wildlife groups. The collective membership of these groups is over 180,000, with 30,000 junior members belonging to the 'Watch' club, mainly in the age group 7 to 13 years.

6.34 *The British Trust for Conservation Volunteers (BTCV)* has pioneered constructive work in the countryside and initiates a multitude of practical conservation projects, most of them involving young people as the major participants, throughout the British Isles. BTCV groups take part in urban programmes close to home and residential visits to more distant areas where specific projects can be undertaken in conjunction with organisations in the areas visited.

6.35 The *Groundwork Trusts* also promote environmental action for the benefit of the local community. The original Operation Groundwork was established in 1981 and the Groundwork Foundation was formed in 1985. There are 13 local Groundwork Trusts with 12 others currently being established. Central to the Groundwork concept is the involvement of young people in environmental projects, either as visitors or as Groundwork young volunteers. In 1986-87 it is estimated that over 17,000 young people were actively involved in Groundwork initiatives. These provided important new educational resources for schools, and restoration project work carried out by young people has established strong links with the community. A key feature of the work of

Groundwork Trusts is the partnership established between the local Trusts, private enterprise and the local authority, supported by much voluntary local effort.

# *Organisations Concerned with Outdoor Education*

6.36 *The National Association for Outdoor Education* is the national body concerned to promote the effective and safe use of the outdoors for educational purposes. The Association has done much to encourage safe practice in the outdoors and to examine the special application of outdoor education to groups with particular requirements such as the disabled. The Association includes within its membership a wide range of individuals from all sectors of the outdoor education field.

6.37 *The National Association for Environmental Education* exists to promote in schools, universities and elsewhere, a recognition of the inter-relatedness of man, his culture, and his bio-physical surroundings. The Association holds conferences and courses intended to give practice in using the environment in education, to foster concern for environmental qualities and to adopt an appropriate code of behaviour.

6.38 *The Field Studies Council* exists to promote environmental understanding through education, research and information. Its activities include the provision of educational courses for all age groups at nine residential centres and one day centre in England and Wales in those subjects whose essential teaching material is out-of-doors. Courses are provided both for specialists and of a more general nature, and school and university groups are encouraged to attend. The Field Studies Council centres support the environmental education work carried out in schools. Appropriate topics are chosen to complement the school curriculum. The underlying philosophy is that young people *"should acquire knowledge and skills relevant to adult life and employment in a fast-changing world".*

6.39 *The Association of Heads of Outdoor Education Centres* is an association of individuals responsible for the work of 90 established outdoor centres. The major aims of these centres, as presented in a survey carried out in 1976 were as follows; personal development 35 per cent, social development 30 per cent, environmental appreciation 20 per cent, academic improvement 11 per cent, other values 3 per cent. The majority of the centres represented in the association provide staffed residential facilities and outdoor equipment, available for use by visiting parties from local education authorities. The membership also includes the Directors or Wardens of an increasing number of commercial or charitable centres, many established comparatively recently.

6.40 A number of subject-teaching associations also encourage the appropriate use of the outdoor environment as part of educational experience at all levels, from primary school to university. For instance, the *Geographical Association* represents over 7,000 geography lecturers, teachers and students, and produces various specialist publications and papers which suggest effective means of developing fieldwork out-of-doors. The Association strongly supports such fieldwork, in the belief that geography should be taught through activity and first-hand experience, and that fieldwork away from the school or college environment is invaluable.

# *Organisations Concerned with Development Training*

6.41 *The Development Training Advisory Group (DTAG)* is an informal grouping of five of the major charitable providers of Development Training for young people. (See 4.58 — 4.66). The members of DTAG are the *Outward Bound Trust,* the *YMCA, Endeavour Training Ltd.,* the *Brathay Hall Trust,* and *Lindley Educational Trust* (described below). Each of these organisations offers a wide range of courses of differing lengths for groups of young people from a wide variety of backgrounds. They provide a mixture of open Outdoor Adventure courses and courses designed to meet the needs of particular sponsors. About 30,000 young people each year take part in DTAG courses. The collective concern of the membership of DTAG is to assist nationally in providing a service for encouraging the development of young people so as to enable them to contribute more constructively to their work, home, community and society.

6.42 There are also a number of local groupings of residential and outdoor experience providers in different areas. For instance the *Cumbria Association of Residential Providers,* the *Welsh Association of Residential Providers,* the *Derbyshire Association for Residential Education* and the *Organisation of Scottish Providers of Residential Experience (OSPRE)* all exist to further the concept of development training in the residential setting and to develop and uphold standards and quality of training in their different areas. The Training Agency has, through these groupings, actively encouraged the provision of in-service training courses for tutors involved in outdoor and development training.

6.43 *Brathay Hall Trust* was founded in 1946. The Trust operates from a large residential base on the shores of Windermere. Originally Brathay's work lay almost exclusively in providing young people in industry with the opportunity of widening their horizons through new experience and challenge. Now the central purpose of the Trust is to provide and develop the potential of development training for young and mature people. Much of Brathay's work is with men and women in regular employment. Open and contract courses are run for clients from industry, commerce and the public sector, who take up places for their employees at all levels of responsibility, from those just starting work to those with professional or managerial roles.

6.44 Brathay also has a significant commitment to development training work with young people not in regular employment. The Community Development Programme gives financial support to community initiatives in several inner cities and other urban areas, either in conjunction with the Youth and Community Service or through voluntary organisations. Brathay has established itself as a pioneer of new applications of development training, with a capacity for research, development and the training of trainers. Brathay Training Services is an accredited training centre (Training Agency).

6.45 *The Outward Bound Trust*, established in 1946, has five major outdoor centres, which provide intensive outdoor development training programmes year-round for a wide variety of user groups or individual participants. Such courses are up to three weeks in length, and give a progressively increasing level of challenge and responsibility to the participants. In addition, the City Challenge programme provides courses based on the theme of community service; again the aim is that of personal development, but taking place through work with the disadvantaged or disabled. More recently the Trust has developed an outreach programme in urban areas, designed to draw unemployed or otherwise disadvantaged youth into Outward Bound and help them forward in their lives.

6.46 Outward Bound has provided active courses for over 250,000 young people between 15 and 20 years; the Trust is now called upon increasingly to design contract or tailor-made courses for young employees, in addition to its longstanding programmes of open courses, and works with many disabled or disadvantaged groups.

6.47 *The YMCA* is one of the largest voluntary organisations in the world, and has a strong commitment to developing the potential of young people from all backgrounds. The major training agency associated with YMCA is *Y Training Services*, an independent agency providing a wide variety of courses for those at work of all ages or in the Youth Training Scheme. The YMCA has two major residential outdoor centres at Lakeside in Cumbria and at Fairthorne Manor in Hampshire. Both centres run a wide variety of courses, mainly for young people. Most of the courses with a development training emphasis are designed on a contract basis for individual organisations. The YMCA centres are able to provide for a variety of participating groups in different styles of accommodation. At Lakeside there is a strong environmental ethic, and the centre has done much to develop new ways of experiencing and learning about the outdoor environment. The centre also provides a range of imaginative courses for younger children, either in the form of adventure holidays or in association with schools, related to curriculum needs. Some 10,000 young people each year visit Lakeside, drawn from every social and working background.

6.48 There are a number of other locally-managed YMCA centres in Britain, several of which are appropriately situated as bases for Outdoor Adventure activities. In addition, the *Glen River National Centre* in Newcastle, Northern Ireland has a permanent tutorial staff and provides development training opportunities using the outdoors. Programmes are organised for schools and industry, and to assist community relations in Northern Ireland.

6.49 *Endeavour Training* is a national organisation which, unlike it partners in DTAG, does not have its own permanent outdoor bases, but when residential experience is required makes use of those operated by other organisations. Endeavour provides a training and development service for young people at work or on YTS courses. The training is designed specifically for the organisation involved, and makes use of both indoor and outdoor exercises. Much of the work is carried out in-company. Approximately 1,500 young people each year participate in Endeavour courses.

6.50 Endeavour Training has always recognised the importance of developing follow-up work or opportunities, which are provided through the National Endeavour Training Association and the creation and development of local groups to initiate activities and social projects, and to provide residential programmes and courses for the under-privileged. Endeavour has also formed the John Hunt Exploration Group, which encourages young people to experience overseas expeditions in some of the remote areas of the world.

6.51 *The Lindley Educational Trust* operates two residential centres in Derbyshire and

Yorkshire, where five-, seven- and twelve-day open courses are provided for young people at work or on YTS, as well as courses designed for individual organisations. Approximately 5,000 trainees each year take part in these events. Lindley lays a strong emphasis on negotiating carefully the rationale and content of the course with the client beforehand. Some formal theory is presented in workshop sessions before the introduction of practical action tasks which illustrate the topics or subject-matter. Outdoor exercises are used quite extensively; they are related carefully to problems and objectives in the work environment.

6.52 The five members of DTAG are not the only providers of development training opportunities for young people out-of-doors. Increasing numbers of LEA centres have expanded the scope of their work to include YTS or other work-related courses, as at the *Middle Head Outdoor Pursuits Centre* in North Yorkshire, or the *Derwent Hill Centre* in Cumbria. There are many other independent centres, run either under the auspices of charitable bodies or as commercial undertakings, which work with employment trainees. For instance, the *River Dart Country Park* residential centre in Devon works most extensively with YTS and other work-related groups, most commonly providing one-week problem solving and activity courses. *The Bowles Outdoor Centre* in Sussex provides personal development experiences, with a strong involvement with YTS, emphasising the importance of appropriate reviewing of experience and action planning. *The Industrial Society* also organises courses for young people, some of which include an Outdoor Adventure element.

6.53 Another grouping of organisations which have a development training interest is the *British Christian Outdoor Centres,* an informal association of outdoor centres with an avowedly Christian ethos. Founded seven years ago, largely through the initiative of the Abernethy and Lakeside (YMCA) centres, this group of approximately thirty centres meets annually for the exchange of information and ideas. Some of the organisations involved have an evangelistic purpose; others do not claim this, but base their work firmly upon a Christian foundation. In addition to land-based centres, such as *The Ranch Adventure Centre* (under the auspices of the Northamptonshire Association of Boys Clubs), *The Christian Mountain Centre, Carnoch Outdoor Centre* and Lindley, the group includes a number of water-based organisations including *Fellowship Afloat* and the *T.S. "Morning Star".* Most of these organisations and centres work with a wide range of groups of different ages.

# *Organisations Concerned with Expeditions*

6.54 From its beginnings *The Royal Geographical Society (RGS)* has supported and sponsored British exploration overseas. The Society screens and approves applications from large numbers of expeditions each year, mainly from colleges and universities. The Society together with YET (see below) administers the *Expedition Advisory Centre (EAC)*, which provides a specialised information and training service for those planning a scientific or adventurous expedition overseas. The EAC currently receives at least 8,000 enquiries each year and helps over 450 expeditions, many of which involve young people.

6.55 The *Young Explorers Trust (YET)* is the Association of British Youth Exploration Societies, established to increase opportunities for young people to take part in interesting and worthwhile ventures in remote areas, both in this country and abroad, and has a regional network which exists to link members and unattached youngsters. In association with the RGS, the Young Explorers Trust gives grant aid to a number of expeditions each year. In addition The Young Explorers Trust has developed a pilot mobile unit, MOBEX, which consists of a mobile expedition unit with the necessary transport and equipment to train inner-city groups in expedition skills. Currently *MOBEX* operates principally in the North-West. The Young Explorers Trust also publishes a magazine, YETMAG, containing a wide variety of information about expeditions planned or completed.

6.56 *The Duke of Edinburgh's Award*, founded in 1956, has become a major and highly influential scheme, enabling a large number of young people either on an individual basis or as members of a school, youth or work group, to experience a wide variety of challenges including those of exploration and expeditions. The scheme provides a programme of leisure activities for young people between the ages of 14 and 25 who work towards three Awards, bronze, silver and gold. The scheme is widely established in schools, youth organisations, companies and through Award Scheme regional centres. In order to gain an Award, young people must qualify in four sections of the Scheme, namely service, expeditions, skills, and physical recreation. About half the secondary schools in Great Britain now operate the Award. (3.27, 4.18 — 4.20, 8.12)

6.57 *The British Schools' Exploring Society (BSES)* provides opportunities for young people from schools and other walks of life to take part in exploratory projects in remote regions led by staff from the universities and teaching and medical professions. Young men and women between 16 and 20 experience the challenge of adventure in remote and hostile environments, and the chance to carry out scientific work in the field. BSES expeditions have recently included visits to Kenya, Papua New Guinea, Greenland, Canada, the Yukon and the Himalayas.

6.58  In 1988 the Society mounted a major expedition to the Western Himalayas, involving 77 British and 24 Indian young people, with 31 adults. In addition in 1988 a party of 84 young people visited Greenland. In 1989 BSES is mounting three expeditions to Northern Norway, involving a study of the geomorphology and glaciology of the Lyngen peninsula, investigating the glaciers of Oksfjordjokolen, kayaking the coastal waters in the Troms area. In addition in 1989/1990 an overwintering expedition will be mounted in south-east Alaska. Approximately 150 young people in total will have had the opportunity to take part in the 1989 ventures.

6.59  Participation in BSES expeditions is by selection; applicants should have some previous outdoor experience and be able to raise the personal contribution of £1,400 approximately which is required. The Society has recently taken a special interest in encouraging the disabled to participate, subject to their ability to cope with difficult terrain. Derek Jackson, former chairman of BSES, regards the quality of expedition leadership as of paramount importance in the organisation of such overseas ventures:

> "Leadership is the key to the success of the enterprise. Leaders must have appropriate qualities and knowledge of the world. They require an understanding of the process of development, must have political and diplomatic awareness and should not view the outdoors simply as a moral or physical gymnasium."

The outstanding safety record of BSES, operating often in remote and hazardous environments, must be largely attributable to this quality of leadership.

6.60  *The Brathay Exploration Group* was founded in 1947, originating in a project to chart the previously unsounded mountain tarns of the Lake District, where its headquarters have remained. The annual programme of Brathay expeditions developed steadily in scope offering a progressive experience from training expeditions in the Lake District, through varied projects in outlying parts of the British Isles, to major expeditions to countries as far apart as Iceland, Greenland, Poland, Tunisia, Kenya, Jamaica and China. Since the

1960s, in a typical year, there were more than fifteen expeditions with up to 300 members taking part. Brathay expeditions did much to influence the growth of youth exploration, notably by demonstrating the value and excitement of involving young people in tasks of real exploration in remote and demanding environments. The inspiration came from leaders who were all volunteers and who brought strong commitment, new ideas, varied skills and fresh approaches. A strong tradition grew up for former members to return as leaders, and this is now reinforced by good leader training opportunities. Brathay expeditions are small, normally less than twenty in number, and aim to retain a high degree of mobility and adaptability. Members have been recruited from a wide cross-section of young people, including in overseas expeditions, a significant element from the host country.

6.61 *Operation Raleigh* is the name given to a world-wide series of expeditions designed to provide young men and women between the ages of 17 and 25 years with opportunities to seek challenge, develop skills and encounter different cultures. Each expedition involves scientific research, community projects and adventurous activities shared with young people from different nations, backgrounds and beliefs. Expeditions are subsidised, and may cost each participant between £400 and £2,200. They last between ten and twelve weeks, in terrain ranging from high mountains to tropical rain forest. On their return to Britain, participants are encouraged to become involved in community projects; some return to become assistant leaders for a second phase of the venture. Research work carried out includes investigations into the destruction of the rain forests, soil erosion, the damage to coral reefs and the dangers to threatened species.

6.62 Up to the end of 1988, an estimated 2,600 young people from the UK had completed an expedition with Operation Raleigh, as well as 1,400 from overseas. They had been assisted by more than 1,250 staff. 46 land-based expeditions have been carried out in 28 countries, and 20 sea-based expeditions. Expeditions in 1989 are taking place in the Caribbean, Cameroon, Kenya, Australia, Chile, and Zimbabwe.

6.63 *The Scouting movement* has long had a tradition of travel and practical experience overseas, as well as enabling scouts from across the world to meet and to share friendship and adventure. International awareness is a part of the Venture Scout Award, and involves learning about other people, their culture and values, and becoming a more caring member of a multi-cultural society. Scout expeditions overseas have become increasingly common in the last 20 years, almost all having as a prime purpose the implementation of a development project in the country visited. For instance, in 1985 four Venture Scout units from Hampshire, Edinburgh, Wallington and Jersey visited Sri Lanka to assist with water sanitation and health projects. In the same year there were at least six expeditions by Scout groups to Africa, all engaged in community service projects as well as Outdoor Adventure.

6.64 The Scout Association (see 3.50) estimates that a total of 14,000 scouts made a total of 625 visits overseas in 1988, many with an adventurous purpose. There were Venture Scout expeditions to Iceland, to the Gambia, to India, to Norway and to Morocco. Certainly the most ambitious was the 'Sherpa 88' project, which involved a group of 42 Venture Scouts. To mark the 21st anniversary of Venture Scouting, the party engaged in a major community development project on behalf of the Himalayan Trust, headed by Sir Edmund Hillary. Two training weekends in Britain were the prelude to a five-week visit to Nepal, where the three groups refurbished a hospital and built an extension to a remote primary school. Subsequently all groups completed a trek to Namche Bazar. One group had time to travel to the traditional Everest Base Camp.

6.65 *The Youth Hostels Association (YHA)* and *The Scottish Youth Hostels Association* have long been a major resource for outdoor expeditions, enabling young people to journey through wild country from one hostel to the next. The YHA operates 260 hostels in England and Wales with an additional 80 in Scotland operated by the Scottish YHA, which have been established to provide for all ages, but especially for young people of limited means, the chance to gain a greater knowledge and concern for the countryside. In recent years the YHA has taken a number of new initiatives. Many of the hostels now encourage school groups and others to visit and to use the hostels as a base either for outdoor programmes, as at the Loch Morlich Youth Hostel in Scotland, or for field studies as at the Esthwaite Lodge Youth Hostel near Hawkshead in the Lake District. Many hostels have been the focus of valuable environmental work such as the creation of nature trails at Tanners Hatch. Staffed outdoor activity centres have been established at Edale and Llangollen. The YHA also encourages a hostelling group, the 'Postellers' to use hostels as a regular means of access to the countryside. The YHA provides an important low-cost resource for young people who may not be affiliated to any organisation to find Outdoor Adventure.

# Sail Training Organisations

6.66 The tradition of sail training for young people is long-established in Britain. In the last 25 years there has been substantial growth in recreational sailing, both on inland waters and at sea. The exploits of single-handed sailors, and the increasing numbers of long-distance sailing events have caught the public imagination.

6.67 In parallel with this increasing recreational involvement in sailing, there has been a notable increase in the opportunities for young people to take to the water as part of their education or in search of Outdoor Adventure. The introduction of easy-to-handle dinghies has enabled thousands of children to learn to sail in sheltered waters. At the same time there has been an expansion of opportunities to experience more adventurous voyages in larger vessels. Much of the work of the members of the *Association of Sail Training Organisations*, takes place with young people in the age-group 16 to 19 years.

6.68 The largest provider of sail training is the *Ocean Youth Club*, which takes in excess of 4,000 young people between the ages of 12 to 24 years to sea each year. Of these the majority are over 15, drawn from all walks of life. Cruises take place in waters around the British coast, aboard a fleet of ten modern ketches, a 55 ft yawl and a veteran 50 ft gaff yawl. Most cruises last for one week and may visit the Hebrides or foreign ports. The boats are big enough to cross oceans, but small enough for every person on board to have an important part to play in sailing them. Typically, each boat makes between thirty and forty cruises each year, with a crew of twelve aboard. Among the aims identified by the OYC are the following:

— To foster the spirit of adventure latent in young people,
— To inculcate a sense of responsibility among young people both for themselves and the community in which they find themselves.

6.69 The largest sail training vessels operating in Britain are those of the *Sail Training Association*, the "Sir Winston Churchill" and the "Malcolm Miller". These are three-masted topsail schooners of 150 ft overall length. Courses last for up to 13 days, and the participants are drawn from all walks of life, including the unemployed, the disabled and those on probation. The majority of the participants fall in the 16 to 19 age-group, and the normal ship's complement is thirty-nine. Courses involve voyages of between 800 and

1,000 miles, often visiting European ports and coastal waters. The prime purpose of all STA courses is to provide a personal development experience for the participants, rather than to acquire technical skills.

> *"The STA believes firmly in character development and will seek during the cruise to teach you how to overcome short-term apparent self interest where it clashes with the long-term common good. This does not mean a regimented society by any means, but the experience of high adventure will be used to show that enthusiastic co-operation under competent leadership is not only a tolerable way a dealing with life's problems, but it can be positively exhilarating. Hardship is not inflicted for its own sake, but you will be given the opportunity to overcome it in the interest of completing a co-operative adventure."*

*(A Guide to life on board a three-masted schooner with the STA)*

6.70    The *Island Sailing Club*, based in the Salcombe estuary in Devon, has eight cruising yachts and organises cruises for up to 700 young people each year. The age-group tends to be lower than in most other sail training organisations, with the majority of the participants below 16. Cruises range as far afield as Spain, the Azores and the Baltic. The emphasis is primarily upon enjoying the sport for its own sake.

6.71    The *London Sailing Project* has three vessels which provide six-day cruises for young men from London *"to acquire those attributes of a seaman, namely a sense of responsibility, resourcefulness and teamwork, which helps them throughout their lives."* An interesting feature of the organisation is the extent to which participants are encouraged and assisted to progress and develop their seamanship skills to the point where they can take up responsibility as officers on voyages. All successful trainees are invited to sail again to help others novices. Approximately 550 take advantage of these opportunities each year.

6.72    There are several other sail training organisations taking significant numbers of young people to sea. The *Shaftesbury Homes Arethusa* takes twelve young people on cruises from the River Medway. The work of the *East Coast Sail Trust* and the *Cirdan Trust* has already been mentioned (3.55, 3.56). The *Sea Cadet Association* operates Britain's only square-rigger, the brig 'Royalist', as well as three other vessels. These are normally available primarily for Sea Cadet Groups, for Scouts and for Combined Cadet Force members. *The Scout Association 'Scouts Offshore' Project* also has two boats based at

Colchester, enabling Scout and Guide groups to cruise across the North Sea. *The Dockland Scout Project* provides short-duration sailing experience as part of a range of water-based activities; of the 5,000 participants annually, about 80 per cent are below 16 and 20 per cent older.

6.73 It must be recognised that many young people are drawn individually to Outdoor Adventure activities, as a matter of personal preference and interest, and not through an established organisation or scheme of training. They may then become members of sailing, mountaineering or other outdoor clubs, and perhaps go on to organised training or leadership responsibility, through a national coaching scheme.

# CHAPTER 7
## OPPORTUNITIES AND APPROACHES

# *Access to Opportunities for Outdoor Adventure*

7.1  It is evident from the study that the opportunities available to young people for Outdoor Adventure vary greatly. On the one hand, there are sizeable youth populations where opportunities for participation are very limited (and indeed some where the very idea of doing so is foreign to the young people). There are others where Outdoor Adventure, either through participation in a national training programme such as the Duke of Edinburgh's Award or the Scouts, or family holidays (sailing, fellwalking or skiing) are the norm. This difference of take-up and expectation stems primarily from economic and cultural factors. In general, deprived youngsters from impoverished homes are less likely to engage in outdoor activity than those from more prosperous backgrounds. The family or community tradition of recreation exercises a major influence.

7.2  Within this broad generalisation, the study has revealed a great variety of provision and take-up. Many of the opportunities for Outdoor Adventure for those of school age are provided by teachers or educational institutions, and there is a wide difference of policy and provision. Some authorities have well developed outdoor education policies, backed up by impressive facilities, in many cases including residential centres or camps outside the authority's area. In some cases specialist outdoor instructors or staff are employed in advisory or leadership capacities. Other education authorities make little or no such provision and any outdoor work which takes place depends very much on the enthusiasm and interest of individual heads and teachers. The influence of the head and the enthusiasm of teachers are significant in determining whether schoolchildren participate in outdoor experiences.

7.3  In some parts of the country, it has been easier to develop outdoor experiences as part of school life, because of the easy access to suitable areas of wild country or stretches of water. The northern conurbations of Manchester and Sheffield, for instance, are fortunate in their ease of access to the cliffs and moorlands of the Peak District.

# *Opportunities in Urban Areas*

7.4   Much attention has been focused in recent years on the needs of young people in inner city areas, where there is deprivation, together with poor prospects of employment and where the immediate environment lacks social or aesthetic quality. It is generally difficult to attract young people from these areas to participate in outdoor programmes. There has tended to be a shortage of keen adult leadership in such areas, which reflects the tendency both of talented young people and the more able adult leaders and teachers to move to areas where the prospects are more hopeful. Nevertheless, it is important to recognise the large numbers of concerned adults who have involved themselves, often on a voluntary basis, to assist young people in these urban areas.

7.5   A start has been made within the deprived urban areas by government, by voluntary bodies and by charities, and in recent years there has been significant growth in the number of programmes developed in these areas. Recent government initiatives, such as the establishment of the Inner City Task Forces, the Sports Council Demonstration Project in Outdoor Activities, and the introduction of Education Support Grants in selected urban local authorities, have enabled considerable numbers of young people from these areas to engage in practical activity with includes Outdoor Adventure.

7.6   Valuable urban initiatives have been taken, either by voluntary bodies or by committed individuals, to meet the needs of young people from disadvantaged backgrounds in the urban areas. For instance, the *Liverpool Water Sports Centre* provides a wide range of water sports opportunities using the canals and docks of the Merseyside area, for young people who wish to take part. In Gateshead, the *'Way Out in Gateshead'* project enables young people and adults from the surrounding area to engage in a range of outdoor activities. This project is funded in part by the local authority and provides a large resource centre and access to a number of outdoor courses, both locally and further afield.

7.7   There are many other small initiatives and organisations operating in the urban environment, such as the *Droylsden Water Adventure Centre* in the Manchester area or the *Islington Boat Club* in north London. Many of these are jointly funded by local authorities, the Sports Council and various Trusts or Foundations. Almost all such developments rely heavily on voluntary help; the ending of the Community Programme in September 1988 created considerable difficulties of staffing supervision for some of them.

7.8    A number of national charities have established adventure programmes within urban areas, often as part of a longer term programme of development. *The Fairbridge-Drake Society*, established after the conclusion of Operation Drake, now supports 14 teams across Britain which provide a progressive series of courses and activities to enable unemployed young people to gain experience which will help them find jobs. Participants are recruited from employment centres, through careers offices or from the social services and they engage in a basic course which includes both work in the urban area and a five-day residential experience with Outdoor Adventure activity. Young people are able to progress to take part either in a residential course at the *Fairbridge-Drake Applecross Centre* in Scotland, or on their vessel *"Spirit of Merseyside".*

7.9    The *Brathay* and *Outward Bound Trusts* have also taken initiatives in urban areas. The Outward Bound Trust set up five urban projects to identify young people who might benefit from a challenging course and become involved subsequently in work with young people within their own communities. The project is funded by the Rank Foundation and other commercial or industrial companies; it enables up to 150 participants from urban areas, each year, to take part.

7.10   The *Prince of Wales Community Venture* also provides a one-year programme for unemployed young people within a number of urban areas, and during the initial team-building phase makes extensive use of Outdoor Adventure activities. There appears to be scope for increasing co-operation between some of these projects, to the mutual benefit of all, by developing more effective communication and networking, and thereby avoiding overlap or duplication.

# *Opportunities in Rural Areas*

7.11   The difficulties of young people living in rural areas are often overlooked. They have been well documented by the reports of the Development Commission (Youth Employment and Unemployment in Rural England, 1986) and the National Advisory Council for the Youth Service (Youth Work in Rural Areas, 1988). Many feel trapped by limited education and training and by the difficulties of gaining easy access to new experience, to employment or advice. There is often little choice of housing and very few jobs are available. Opportunities for social interaction in small villages or hamlets are restricted, particularly where there is a lack of personal or public transport. The more enterprising young people often leave the rural area, leaving those behind at a relatively increased disadvantage. Paradoxically, in many rural areas, where opportunities for outdoor experience are close at hand, few young people are able to take advantage of them. The physical and emotional isolation, which sometimes arises from living in the country, requires a special kind of provision of support and social opportunities, and can be as challenging as the situation in the deprived urban areas described earlier.

# *National and Regional Disparities*

7.12 In addition to the differences of opportunity and provision which the study has identified in different localities, there are also noticeable differences both of requirement and of provision between England, Scotland, Wales and Northern Ireland. Much of the study has concentrated on need and opportunity in England, where there are considerable variations in access to, or provision of, Outdoor Adventure opportunities. The study has shown that Scotland, Wales and Northern Ireland share many of the local variations which are evident in England. Each has a large rural population, whose young people are restricted by lack of social opportunities, sports facilities or transport. In each country there are also urban areas with high levels of youth unemployment.

7.13 In Scotland, there are special considerations affecting outdoor education and adventure for young people. A significant factor is the difference in post-16 education. Young people staying on at school for Higher Certificates undertake a wider range of subjects than in England. Those choosing to leave school, under the 16+ Action plan, have access to a modular education option with a strong practical emphasis. This includes a personal and social education component and may incorporate an outdoor pursuits module.

7.14 Scotland provides for its young people unusually rich and accessible possibilities for Outdoor Adventure for those with the requisite competence. Wild landscape is close at hand, and relatively free from overcrowding. The west coast provides one of the finest coastal sailing or canoeing areas in Europe. There are opportunities for serious winter mountaineering and ambitious cross-country expeditions. There is also a developing downhill and touring ski industry. Access to open country is generally unhindered except in the deerstalking or grouse-shooting seasons. However, the greater scale of Scottish mountains and rivers, and the frequent severity of weather, particularly in winter, present increased hazards to youth parties.

7.15 Parts of Scotland, particularly in the north west and the Hebrides, retain a distinctive culture which includes the Gaelic language, strong religious beliefs, and the survival in places of the crofting way of life.

7.16 The Scottish Highlands and Islands have been identified as one of Europe's finest landscapes. Owing to the growing pressures to develop certain sensitive areas, the Scottish Office has asked the Countryside Commission for Scotland to review the present system of Regional Parks with a view to upgrading their status to that of National Parks. the Loch Lomond Regional Park and the Cairngorms are under particular threat from the inroads of tourism and development.

7.17 There are also a number of special considerations which apply in Wales. It would appear from the study that in South Wales the need for outdoor recreation and other leisure provision is particularly acute because of unemployment; this is especially the case in the former coal-producing valleys such as the Rhondda; and from living conditions in such urban areas as Cardiff's dockland. A number of outdoor centres have been established, based on such areas as the Brecon Beacons and the Gower Peninsula. These are mostly operated by English authorities for the benefit of outsiders.

7.18 In the North and West, where the need is also great, there is less provision for local children. In tourist resorts along the coasts of North and West Wales and in the industrial area of Wrexham, there are local social problems and a high incidence of delinquency and juvenile crime. Provision of centres in the mountains is plentiful, but the providers are mostly English authorities; there is some antipathy, arising from Welsh culture and tradition, to the numbers of outside youth groups using these centres or making visits for educational purposes from England. One holiday camp in North Wales, for instance, caters for some 17,000 young people from outside the Principality every year. The northern Welsh authorities have been reluctant or unable to provide their own centres partly on financial grounds. Notable exceptions to the generality of English provision are Plas Menai, operated by the Sports Council for Wales, and a centre on the shores of Llyn Bala, which is run by the Urdd Gobaith Cymru (The Welsh League of Youth).

7.19 It would appear that a stronger attempt should be made to make visitors, young and old, aware of and sensitive to the tradition, language and culture of Wales, and perhaps to provide courses or experiences using existing resources for local young people and to provide opportunities for more outdoor courses or experiences for Welsh-speaking youth only, on the lines pioneered at the *Storey Arms Centre* beneath the Brecon Beacons.

7.20 In Northern Ireland the special considerations are in part linked to the social and political difficulties in the Province. Young people have sadly been involved in street violence associated with the continuing troubles, particularly in Belfast and Londonderry. These special circumstances have led local authorities, through their Library and Education Boards and the Catholic Council of Maintained Schools, to place particular value on any activity in which mixed groups from the two cultural traditions can meet and share activities together. The use of outdoor activities, particularly when allied with residential experience, is seen to be of considerable importance in bridging divisions.

7.21 A number of initiatives have been taken in the Province by voluntary or charitable groups, which have as their goal the building of contact and reconciliation and which involve Outdoor Adventure. *The Youthways Project*, the *Glen River YMCA Centre*, the *Share Centre* on Upper Lough Erne and the *Corrymeela Centre*, in Antrim all enable young people to escape the 'box' of their cultural tradition to meet others from different backgrounds. The development of the *'Education for Mutual Understanding'* initiative is also based on sharing practical activities including residential experience away from the home area. This scheme is seen as of particular importance for younger children, and is now given special funding by the Department of Education of Northern Ireland.

# The Value of Residential and Expedition Experiences

7.22 The study has examined the values of Outdoor Adventure for a wide variety of young people. Many of the activities which fall under the umbrella of outdoor sports can provide them with memorable and exciting experiences; yet of themselves they may have little enduring value. What matters is how they are used and the context in which they occur. In reading of the experiences of young people, and of adults who support them; in discussions with participants and organisers; and in examining the considerable range of opportunities available, it seems that exciting activities out-of-doors can only be transformed into a learning experience of really fundamental value when two conditions are met.

7.23 The first condition is that the participants should live together closely as a group, sharing the day-to-day tasks, the duties and the lighter moments of community living as well as the excitements of the outdoor life, over a period of time. In other words, the experience should be 'residential'. Such situations may occur on expeditions on foot, mobile adventure courses, buses, lorries, in canoes, small or large boats and canal narrow-boats, and during centre-based residential courses.

7.24 One common feature of such experiences is that they do not allow for an easy escape, either from the experience itself, since they usually involve travelling some distance from the home environment; or from involvement with the other members of the group, since they will be sharing close-quarters accommodation, be it a tent, a mess-deck or a dormitory, for lengthy periods.

7.25 Most of those consulted during the study indicated that the main purposes of Outdoor Adventure programmes for the young lie in opportunities for personal development, social development and the development of environmental understanding, usually in that order. It is increasingly recognised that, to achieve the first two of these purposes, it is necessary to have a close relationship with others, and that progress and ultimately understanding stem from experience rather than from formalised study. Therefore, the social dimension of outdoor ventures which have a 'personal development' or a 'development training' focus becomes crucial. Even where the objectives are different; for instance, on a sixth form fieldwork course, whole-hearted commitment may best be achieved in the context of a full-time residential experience.

7.26 The residential dimension allows for the full experience of shared living to be enjoyed, with all its implications; establishing appropriate rules and schedules, group responsibilities and relationships. Furthermore, there are better opportunities for recording and reviewing progress, both in the tasks confronting the group and also in the way in which the group and its individual members are functioning. There are valuable opportunities in such situations to explore ideas and myths about relationships with other individuals, the opposite sex, adults and figures of authority, or minority groups. The insight and skills of adults working with the group become very important in this situation, as does their ability to play a part directly in the enterprise.

7.27 The booklet "Residential Training in YTS" produced by the (former) Manpower Services Commission suggests three types of residential experience for trainees, which are also typical of provision generally. These are 'package', 'partnership' and 'self-programmed.' Each has certain advantages and disadvantages for YTS purposes, and are probably similar for other participants or user groups:

7.28 The 'package' type of programme is purchased from an established provider, often an outdoor centre. It is likely to be convenient, to require less preparation by participants and generally to deliver a useful and valuable experience. However, it may be expensive, poorly integrated with the requirements of the purchaser, too prescribed and inflexible and may lead to some uncertainty or even conflict over adult roles.

7.29 'Partnership' programmes use the resources of another organisation, but the visiting group and their adult supporters carry out some of the organisation and supervision. Such a programme ensures involvement of accompanying adults, creates a good structure for their relationship with the professional staff and may be cheaper and no less effective. However, the accompanying adults may be unable to exploit fully the opportunities presented by a situation which is unfamiliar to them.

7.30 The 'self-programmed' residential experience is run by the organisation or youth group itself, possibly hiring accommodation and paying for expert instructors for specialist sessions. This will probably be the cheapest alternative, and may well provide the most effective form of such experience. However, it requires a great deal of preparation and planning, and lack of experience or qualifications may cause problems, particularly where risk is involved.

7.31 Whichever type of residential experience is comtemplated, it is important to make maximum use of the situation, by establishing clear objectives, developing opportunities for sharing and interacting and providing adequate time for reflection and recording the experience. By avoiding an institutionalised approach, adults and young people can share an experience which enables both to grow in mutual understanding and confidence.

# Problem Solving and Experiential Approaches

7.32 The second condition which reinforces the impact of Outdoor Adventure experience for the young is that, as far as possible, they should be able to exercise choice, make decisions and solve problems with minimum interference from accompanying adults. It is obvious that, in any situation which involves an element of physical or psychological danger, adults have a great responsibility; the penalty for mistaken judgement can be high.

7.33 However, the study has found evidence, particularly in the work of the advisory staff in local education authorities and in the main residential centres, that increasing value is being attached to problem solving by young people in outdoor situations. This has led to changes both in the type of activities provided and in the way they are presented. Three illustrations will suffice:

7.34 One example is in the increasing use of exercises and techniques drawn from professional and therapeutic groupwork. Many Outdoor Adventure experiences now begin with light-hearted group games or 'trust' exercises, usually of short duration, which are intended to speed the process of forming relationships and becoming a team. These often involve a physical or outdoor challenge for the group to solve. Sometimes the task may require detailed organisation, or may assist with the 'settling-in' process, for instance drawing a plan of the camp, or checking the equipment. The important point is that the group should carry this out themselves, rather than have an instructor do it for them.

7.35 A second example is the introduction of extended 'adventure games' into outdoor programmes. These may involve complex problem solving tasks for the group, such as a local mountain rescue exercise, or designing and building a raft. Alternatively, they may include cross-country treasure hunts, complicated information gathering surveys or night-time journeys. These exercises usually require the use of a number of different outdoor skills, and call for a high standard of group organisation. They are normally followed by periods of reflection and discussion in order that mistakes can be identified and lessons learned. Some of these tasks are designed to illustrate specific themes, such as communication, interdependence or the need for delegation.

7.36 The third example is drawn from the recent changes instituted in the Duke of Edinburgh's Award. For the Gold expedition, candidates have to carry out a 50-mile journey according to certain clearly-defined criteria. As an alternative, an 'exploration' is now accepted as an equivalent accomplishment. Thus the group is required to plan its project, carry out preliminary research, identify problems and resources, and record the result of the venture. Exploration retains many of the characteristics of an expedition, but it is more flexible and less a purely physical undertaking, with a wider scope for learning, and a closer identification of the participants with the project.

7.37 Each of these examples illustrates the increasing adoption of a problem solving approach in the provision of Outdoor Adventure experiences. Essentially, the participant is required to discover rather than being provided with the answer. Even the task of working out for themselves how to erect their tent may have far greater learning potential for a group than simply copying a method demonstrated by an instructor.

7.38 It is widely recognised that the most potent form of learning is that which stems from practical experience. Increasingly, the term 'experiential learning' is used to describe a process which attaches value to the individual's response to, and reflection upon, his/her actual experience. A number of models have been designed to illustrate this concept, such as that presented at Brathay. ('Plan — Do — Review').

> "Experienced-based programmes reach their highest level when they contribute directly to the growth of individuals as persons by helping them to establish initiative, industry, competence and identity; and to meet the challenge of the maturing processes as they occur. At its upper register, the scale of planned, experienced-based learning merges indistinguishably with the activities of life."

*(David Hopkins; Adventure Education and Management Development, 1988)*

# Implications for Instructors and Interested Adults

7.39 Adopting a problem solving approach with young people out-of-doors, and recognising that the style of learning is experiential, will have profound effects for adults who promote or supervise such activities. It is likely that their role and their relationship with the group will be altered significantly. Indeed the title 'instructor' is misleading, for their task is to present problems, rather than provide solutions, and to examine learning processes rather than to complete tasks. The importance of teaching technical skills diminishes, although clearly some instruction is needed to ensure a satisfactory standard of safety. The instructor will have to make fine judgements as to the competence and sense of responsibility of the young people in allowing them the appropriate freedom of choice and action.

7.40 If the problem solving and experiential learning approach is to work, adults involved require appropriate awareness and skills to enable the young people to learn as much as possible from their experiences. Not only does the adult require sensitivity to the experience of the group, but he/she has also to develop skill in helping the group to identify and absorb the lessons of their experience. The goal should be to help young people to learn from all their experience, and to help in the process of their own development. The outdoor environment provides an ideal setting for this to take place.

> "When students are permitted to be in contact with real problems; when resources — both human and technical — are made psychologically available by the teacher; when the teacher is a real person in his relationships with students, and feels an acceptance of and an empathy towards his students; then an exciting kind of learning occurs. Students go through a frustrating but rewarding process in which, gradually, responsible initiative, creativity and inner freedom are released."

*(Carl Rogers; Learning to be Free, 1967)*

# Summary

(a) Opportunities available to young people for adventurous experiences out-of-doors vary greatly. (7.1)

(b) Those in deprived inner city areas are less likely to engage in such activities, partly from family or communal tradition, but also from lack of knowledge or provision. (7.1, 7.4)

(c) Provision is patchy. (7.2)

(d) The needs of young people in rural areas tend to be over looked. (7.11)

(e) Local authorities in rural areas are better placed to provide Outdoor Adventure, but not all do so. (7.3)

(f) In some urban areas appropriate small-scale projects have increased through the help of Education Support Grants (ESGs) and voluntary support. (7.5, 7.6, 7.7)

(g) There are somewhat differing needs and opportunities in different areas, e.g. Scotland, Wales and Northern Ireland. (7.12 — 7.21)

(h) Great value attaches to communal living out in the countryside, whether in residential centres or through camping, as part of Outdoor Adventure programmes. (7.22 — 7.31)

(i) Importance is also attached to encouraging young people to plan their adventures and to take decisions in the course of those activities; always subject to overall adult responsibility from considerations of safety. (7.32 — 7.38)

# CHAPTER 8
## THE NEEDS OF PARTICULAR GROUPS

## *General*

8.1 The survey has examined the Outdoor Adventure opportunities typically available for different age-groups, through formal programmes of education and training, voluntary and charitable bodies and commercial providers. However, there are some groups of young people who, through personal history or circumstances, have particular requirements. These may call for special provision, either in the context of a separate grouping, or by making a special arrangement within a normal programme. In this chapter the particular needs of different age groups, of young women, of the disabled, of ethnic minorities, of the unemployed and of young people at risk are identified, and some of the steps taken to meet those needs are illustrated.

8.2 The specific needs of every group using the outdoors environment require constant re-evaluation, in order that the experience provided is appropriate. Sir Alec Clegg, former Chief Education Officer for West Yorkshire, suggested the following useful principle;
*"You must ask yourself 'Why am I doing what I am doing with this particular group in this particular place at this particular time and in this particular way?'"*

## *Different Age-groups*

8.3 The study suggests, that in some instances, more careful attention needs to be paid to selecting appropriate experiences and approaches for different age-groups. The way in which an activity is presented or utilised can be fundamentally different, and indeed should be so if it is to match the developmental needs of the young people involved. In rock-climbing, for example, the emphasis may be on personal achievement, or on safety, supporting and safeguarding others. In bivouacing the emphasis may be on survival skills and coping with emergency situations; or it may be on teamwork. In each activity, there are many valid approaches, and it is important that the right choices are made by the instructor or teacher.

8.4    The developmental needs of human beings vary according to their age and life-experience. For instance eleven year-olds are generally much concerned with establishing their own identity, developing physical skills, finding their place in a group, and making sense of the world beyond the family. On the other hand, seventeen year-olds have a different range of concerns. These require them to achieve a satisfactory relationship with the opposite sex, develop relevant career skills, learn to take responsibility for others, and discover their place in society.

8.5    Outdoor Adventure activities can assist in meeting the needs of both age groups, and the same activity can be utilized as the learning medium, but the way in which it is presented or attempted may differ significantly. This applies equally to the reviewing or reflective process. A searching, confrontational review of an activity might provide effective learning for a group of seventeen year-old YTS trainees, but would be of little value for a group of eleven year-olds, who may be less ready to analyse their own behaviour objectively.

8.6    Often the appropriate mode or style of adventure programmes for the 8 to 11 age-group is one based on direct exploration of the activity or the environment, with plenty of variety and a strong emphasis on play and individual creativity. The role of the teacher is to present the activity in a simple way and to supervise it carefully.

8.7    The appropriate mode for the 11 to 16 age-group will usually include a greater element of project work, with more self-direction, particularly in domestic or organisational matters. The emphasis is still on enjoyment. The role of the teacher is that of problem-presenter and arbitrator. Supervision may be less close.

8.8    The appropriate 16 to 19 age-group programme usually explores activities at a number of different levels; there will be a greater emphasis on inter-personal aspects, and group issues will figure prominently. Sustained and complex field tasks or expeditions may be attempted. The tutor role will be less directive and more facilitative; the tasks themselves may be defined by the group. Supervision may be indirect.

8.9    In the case of each age-group, and equally in the case of the other groups described below, it is important for the teacher or instructor involved to engage in a three-stage preparatory process, in order that the adventure provision is appropriate; this involves:

i)   Analysis of needs
ii)  Definition of objectives
iii) Design of programme

Young people themselves may be involved in this three-stage process; the commitment to the experience will be greater if they have had a hand in defining or planning the venture.

# *Outdoor Adventure for Young Women*

8.10 The study indicates that fewer girls and young women than boys and young men take part in outdoor ventures. However it appears that certain schemes and activities may be more attractive to girls than others, and that some may be more appealing to them than to boys. This is borne out by a Sports Council survey of the extent of participation in sport (Into the 90s: A strategy for Sport, 1988 – 1993) which investigated the scale of participation by different age-groups in outdoor sports. These included walking (rambling and hiking), fishing, camping, horse-riding, sailing, field studies and climbing/potholing, as well as some of the more conventional team games. It was found that walking in some form was by far the most common outdoor activity, and that the level of female involvement here was almost as high as that of males. In the other activities investigated, women participated much less frequently than men. About 20% of males were active walkers, compared with approximately 18% of women, over the previous four years. However only 9% of the women had engaged in other outdoor activities, compared with 25% of the men. The survey indicated that participation by women in field studies and horse-riding was higher than for men. The results indicate that there has been a reduction in participation in outdoor sport by the 13 to 24 age group, for both. It seems likely that this is accounted for by the falling popularity of traditional team sports, and the reduced time given to these in maintained school curricula. It is important to note that the fall in participation was not simply a reflection of the demographic trend, but a percentage fall of 4.3% for males aged 13 to 24, and 3.5% for young women in this age-group. The level of participation by females remains roughly 19% below that of males.

8.11 The disparity between the level of participation between men and women in outdoor sport is borne out by a survey carried out into individual membership of the national bodies for sport. Only 8% of individual members of the British Mountaineering Council,

20% of British Canoe Union members, and 30% of Royal Yachting Association members are female. In contrast, 85% of members of the British Horse Society are women. The special interest shown by young women in horses and horse-riding is a remarkable feature of this survey. In total, of the major national bodies for outdoor sport surveyed, 19% of individual members were female. Even fewer of the committee members of the national bodies were female. (Source: Denis Ball; Adventure Education. Vol 3 No 2.)

8.12 The disparity between the levels of participation by girls and boys appears to be least where Outdoor Adventure is provided as part of regular education or training, and where all are expected to take part. Conversely, it is usually more marked, and girls form a smaller proportion of those involved, where participation is voluntary. One exception to this fact is the success rate among those taking part in the Duke of Edinburgh's Award. In 1988 girls received 49% of bronze awards, 43% of silver awards and 51% of gold awards.

8.13 There is substantial participation in Outdoor Adventure by some all-female organisations. For instance, the Guides encourage such activity either through their own programmes or through participation in the Duke of Edinburgh's Award. In the research exercise carried out into The Girl Guides Association by Marketing Direction Ltd, there was clear evidence of interest in outdoor activities and camping. *"Above all, the study of unit activities and the girls' reaction to them indicated one over-riding fact: that most Guides want to go to camp more often and that, in the main, the activities they enjoy the most are of the adventurous and energetic kind. Certainly more than half of the current Guides would like to do more camping, more cooking and more adventurous activities."*

8.14 The Girls' Brigade also makes use of the Award. Many of their companies each year go away to camp, which may be either under canvas, or an 'indoor camp'. Outdoor activities are a less important component of their programmes, but where skilled staff are available there may be some opportunities, particularly when Girls' Brigade members visit residential outdoor centres.

8.15 The reasons for the lower level of female participation in active pursuits have been the subject of much interest and cannot adequately be investigated in this study. It has been suggested that outdoor ventures do not reflect the needs and aspirations of young women; that they are oriented towards male needs and aspirations. Not only does this lead to frustration and often lack of involvement among female participants, but also a valuable opportunity is lost to enable young women to play an equal part in an important social and practical enterprise.

> *"At a more basic level, the notion of testing oneself physically, either against one's peers or against inanimate nature, is part and parcel of the peer group culture of adolescent males. It is not part of the culture of girls of the same age. It is still very much the peer group belief that boys have jobs and girls have husbands."*

> *Pam Lunn (Former Director, City Challenge programmes, Outward Bound Trust)*

8.16 Boys may be encouraged from an early age to go off on their own, and to develop their self-reliance, but girls may not be able so easily to develop individually and independently, and this may hinder the development of self-esteem and self-confidence. If this is true of Western girls, it is even more so in the case of some young women from different ethnic backgrounds. This is particularly the case with girls from Asian families, but is also true of many young women whose families originate from southern Europe. The question of whether it is justifiable to attempt to lower the cultural barriers which prevent girls from participating in Outdoor Adventure is debatable.

8.17 Girls achieve a greater level of success than boys for much of their early school life, but at some point in their adolescence many tend not to achieve to their full potential. An important underlying factor is that of competition with the opposite sex. The stereotypes of the active and competitive male and the supportive female still persist. Where this is contradicted, considerable stress may be experienced by both sexes. This situation is reinforced where the imagined competition takes place in a physical arena, and involves activities which traditionally have had a strongly masculine identity. To engage in the more exciting and adventurous outdoor pursuits, a girl may have to overcome a powerful pre-disposition not to take part, based on a complex web of psychological and societal pressures.

8.18 The lower participation in Outdoor Adventure by young women may be a result of the factors outlined above. At the same time it is evident that the opportunity to attempt such activities may help to develop their self-confidence, and to open up a wider range of opportunities. It has been suggested that early independence is an important factor in developing the capacity for analytic thinking. If so, by encouraging girls as well as boys to use initiative, to take responsibility and to solve problems for themselves, through

Outdoor Adventure, their effectiveness in later life may be enhanced.

8.19 Some practical obstacles to greater participation by girls are as follows:

— Reluctance of parents to allow daughters to participate in outdoor experiences;
— Difficulty in finding female friends who are equally prepared to participate;
— Too few opportunities for necessary personal privacy;
— Outdoor experiences may be too competitive;
— Outdoor experiences are seen as action-based rather than people-based, task-oriented rather than process- oriented;
— Genuine fears about activities in open country carried out alone;
— Lack of female staff.

8.20 The presence of female staff in any outdoor programme will do much to reassure both the female participants and their parents. Organisers can arrange that young women have the opportunity for privacy and for meeting in other all-female groups. Mixed groups work best when they have a roughly equal male-female composition; girls should not form a small minority. Competitive elements in the programme should be introduced with care. The purpose should be to learn from the total experience rather than to carry out physical tasks.

8.21 This may entail a departure from the prevalent male-oriented models of outdoor programmes. However, there may be substantial gains, not only in enabling and encouraging young women to participate more readily, but also for the young men in experiencing a different way of living and behaving. Both boys and girls may become more aware of their own and each other's capabilities.

> *"Boys began to recognise girls' competencies in activities which they for the most part had previously considered to be appropriate largely to boys. Both boys and girls began to recognise and accept expressions of emotions and apprehension in boys as well as girls. The forms of relationship into which girls and boys entered were indeed found generally to be different from that evidenced in schools, being frequently more collaborative and symmetrical. Girls were encouraged and enabled to participate alongside boys on equal terms."*

> *(Barbara Humberstone, Adventure Education Vol 3 No 4)*

8.22 Even this level of care in designing outdoor experiences may not be sufficient to encourage some young women to participate. The appropriate answer may be to provide an all-female outdoor experience. The value of such shared, all-female adventures can be very great. The presence of all-female staff also provides an important role-model. The experience of the Outward Bound Trust is instructive in this respect. Until the 1970s the majority of Outward Bound open courses were single sex. Later the policy of mixed participation was adopted. From 1980 onwards, however, the Trust has re-introduced some all-female courses in response to the clear preference of some young women and of some sponsoring organisations.

8.23 One organisation which has taken positive steps to redress the numerical imbalance and to develop both a philosophy and practice to meet the needs of young women is the *Water Adventure Centre* situated on the Ashton Canal at Droylsden in Manchester. In the 1978 Annual Report, the WAC identified a number of reasons why girls did not take up an equal and active part in the activities of the Centre:

– *Lack of confidence to try activities seen as 'male' sports;*
– *Intimidation by boys' bullying and taunts;*
– *Concern with appearance and keeping clothes clean;*
– *Leisure time occupied by housework or babysitting;*
– *Parental fears about daughters being attacked at night.*

8.24 A number of measures were introduced to counter these difficulties. Girls' nights, staffed by women, were introduced. Mixed activities were organised on a 50/50 male and female basis to avoid the difficulty of being in a minority. Priority was given to groups using the Centre on a 50/50 basis. Girls-only groups were encouraged. Centre staff deliberately cultivated strong links with other women working with young people in the community. Personal contacts with many parents were established. Girls were encouraged to return home in groups, or lifts were organised. Old clothing was provided at the Centre. Better indoor support facilities were provided. The role and attitude of male staff was discussed and clarified. As a result, female participation has greatly increased during the past 10 years.

> *"A considerable gap exists between the real and imagined abilities and potential of women in outdoor activities. In society at large, the image abounds that women are 'not suited' to the*

*range of potentially dangerous outdoor activities. However, within these spheres of activity, both women and men hold a higher image of women's potential."*

(Denis Ball, Adventure Education Vol 3 No 2)

*"We should be encouraging girls to have confidence in their ideas; confidence in their ability to take the initiative (not just responsibility); their ability to take the lead, including leading males; their tenacity to deal with difficulties and hardship for themselves, and not to rely on someone else to take care of them."*

(Pam Lunn, Former Director, City Challenge)

# Provision for Ethnic Minorities

*"Prejudice, it has been said, is the child of ignorance, and who better than teachers to dispel such ignorance... at the same time as they approach this task, they must examine their own practices, and make sure that they practice what they preach. Sensitivity to the needs of ethnic minority pupils is paramount."*

(The Swann Report "Education for All")

8.25 The number of members of ethnic minorities in Britain has substantially increased. Since 1945 there have been three and a half million immigrants to this country, of which one and a half million have come from the 'New Commonwealth'. It is now calculated that ethnic minorities make up 5%, or two and a half million, of the population. Over half of these are from the Indian sub-continent, and a quarter are of Afro-Caribbean background, mainly from the West Indies. Ethnic minorities tend to be concentrated in certain areas, notably in London, the Midlands and the Manchester/Yorkshire areas, although most parts of the country have some significant ethnic minority groups. Often they live in clearly defined inner-city areas; they form a majority in some schools and youth groups.

8.26 The study suggests that at present ethnic minority groups are under-represented on outdoor courses. It is difficult to produce concrete statistics to support this view, since it has not been the practice of outdoor providers, or sponsoring bodies, to record the racial or ethnic background of participants. The under-representation of minority groups may be primarily due to causes other than racial or ethnic origin. For instance, it has been shown that the cost of some outdoor experiences is a barrier to participation; insofar as black young people may be subject to economic hardship, this may be an important factor in their under-representation.

8.27 Nevertheless it remains the perception of many of those involved in the field of Outdoor Adventure that some ethnic minority groups are unable or unwilling to participate. For instance, on Merseyside it has been apparent that young people of Chinese origin do not readily engage in outdoor activities. There is also evidence that girls from the Muslim communities rarely choose to attempt such activities, particularly when they are expected to do so with boys. One inner-city youth worker wrote *"The reasons are mainly cultural. It is difficult to interest black, working-class youth in traditional outdoor activities. 'This is not for us' they say. It's not cool to be seen falling out of a canoe, climbing rocks. It's the wrong image. For many of my members it's too late. They are conditioned into another scene."*

8.28 It appears that the obstacles to participation among ethnic minority younsters are in part cultural and in part practical. Within the total education provision, there is little reason to think that any minority has fewer opportunities for participation than the majority population. However, in the informal community education sector, there may be greater difficulty of access to the minority population, due to inadequate information for parents written in their own language. There may be other practical difficulties caused by the relatively small numbers of teachers or youth workers from the minority communities with experience of outdoor activities.

8.29 It seems likely that the main obstacle to ethnic minority participation is cultural. The value of outdoor experience is not widely recognised either by parents or by young people, and may be seen as positively harmful, in that such activity may reduce the time available for academic study, or might expose young people, and particularly girls, to unacceptable physical or social risks.

8.30 Some outdoor providers have tried to address this situation, and to provide opportunities for young people, particularly from the black or Asian communities, to attempt outdoor pursuits. A very large number of respondents to the questionnaire surveys indicated their wish to attract minority participants into outdoor programmes. A number of courses have been designed specifically for minority groups. For instance, the *Windsor Fellowship* provides a general personal development training programme, spanning three years, which is primarily concerned to develop management skills of 16 to 20 year-old black students. As part of this programme they take part in a purpose-designed Outdoor Adventure course.

8.31 The number of outdoor staff drawn from the minority communities remains very small, and this is probably a factor in the take-up by young people from these communities. It may be that special steps should be taken to identify and train outdoor staff from minority communities in an effort to encourage more young people from these backgrounds to take advantage of the outdoor environment for their own personal development. At the same time, due regard must be given to the cultural distinctiveness and tradition of each group, even where this militates against participation in Outdoor Adventure.

> *"Over the centuries, Britain has evolved durable institutions and traditions, embodying a humane and tolerant philosophy. The aim must surely be to make these institutions and traditions comprehensive of the entire population, so that they continue to exert a unifying role in the national life. This unity will not survive if a large section of society is held at arm's length, as the ethnic minorities now are."*

> *(Swann Report)*

# *Outdoor Adventure for the Disabled*

> *"What of the handicapped? Is it sufficient to have to remain always on the sidelines; watching activity from the outside; never being allowed to participate? The days of mere observation are rapidly disappearing and horizons are expanding. The world of disability now seeks to merge more thoroughly into the world of ability; the handicapped person in society is not content to remain a spectator, but is looking for the opportunity to participate. All those concerned with leisure and recreation should be opening their doors to meet this demand at every level."*

> *(Mike Cotton, first warden of Churchtown Farm Centre. 'Outdoor Adventure for Handicapped People')*

8.32 The past fifteen years have seen a considerable expansion of opportunities for young people with disability to have access to the outdoor environment and to experience adventurous pursuits. This has been brought about by the wider movement to give equal opportunities to the disabled, by the development of well-designed facilities and specialised equipment, and a much more general recognition of the enthusiasm and capability of the disabled themselves. This has been reflected in the responses to the study. The questionnaire showed that a very large number of providing agencies already welcome disabled groups, and most indicate that they wish to do more in this area. A number of programmes give the disabled the opportunity to take part in adventure activity with able-bodied companions.

8.33 Young people with many different types and degrees of disability have successfully taken part in adventure activities. They may be identified under four broad headings, although some have a combination of difficulties:

— Physical disability;
— Mental handicap;
— Chronic or congenital illness;
— Emotional or behavioural difficulties.

8.34 There are a number of residential centres where the prime purpose is to cater for the needs of the disabled. *Churchtown Farm Field Studies Centre* in Cornwall, established in 1974 by the Spastics Society, was the first outdoor centre to be designed and built specifically for use by handicapped people. The centre offers three main areas of activity; outdoor pursuits, field studies and rural studies, and provides education and adventure courses for up to 1,500 people each year. The range of outdoor activities includes sailing, canoeing, camping, expeditions, initiative exercises and ropes courses, the last-named having been ingeniously designed to allow use by disabled people.

8.35 Churchtown Farm believes strongly in the value of direct experience of the outdoor environment for disabled people, who may have had little contact with plants and animals in their daily life. In addition to providing academic courses in biology, geography, environmental studies and rural studies, the centre introduces field studies to physically and mentally handicapped groups. The centre has developed its own horticultural unit, demonstration farm, nature reserve and animal house, all accessible by wheelchair. Participants can handle and learn the care of a wide range of plant and animal species, and appreciate their characteristics. There are other creative activity possibilities, such as pottery, painting and photography. In addition the surrounding area is rich with adventure and educational possibilities, including moorland, coastal and marine environments.

8.36 More recently, Churchtown Farm has evolved a more structured way of providing personal development experiences for young disabled people. This involves a progressive series of activities in physically and emotionally challenging situations.

> *"The objectives are; to come to terms with their own ability; to be part of real-life education and a deliberate planned phase of the learning process and not to be interventional or isolated; to develop generic skills that are transferable to home, work, centre or school; to concentrate on competences within the control of individuals, increasing normalisation leading to progressive development and an increasing need for self- reinforcement; to allow students to test their own abilities and to decrease dependency on prosthetics, wheelchairs and other aids."*

> *(Jonathan Chapman, Churchtown Farm tutor, Adventure Education Vol 5 No 2)*

8.37 The *Calvert Trust* operates two adventure centres for the disabled near Keswick in the Lake District and at Kielder in Northumberland. The centre at Keswick, established in 1978, provided courses in 1988 for 557 physically handicapped and 381 mentally handicapped visitors, accompanied by a total of 376 able-bodied helpers. The numbers attending have roughly doubled since the centre opened. Activities include canoeing, sailing, hill-walking, rock-climbing and abseiling (including wheelchair abseiling), archery, riding, bird-watching, angling and nature trails. More recently a self-catering bunkhouse for disabled groups has been added to the facilities. The centre has also developed an inner city enabling unit, to help inner city disabled groups to take part in courses.

8.38 Although most Calvert Trust courses are not specifically work-related, the Trust has provided some YTS courses for disabled YTS trainees. For instance Remploy, a major company employing mainly disabled people, offers a residential experience at Bassenthwaite for all its YTS trainees each year. As with all such residential courses, emphasis is placed on improving communication skills, increasing self-awareness and developing teamwork, as well as tackling outdoor challenges.

*"We recognise the problems that can exist for disabled YTS trainees, and see ourselves as a bridge between sheltered workshops and open employment. Most YTS trainees throughout Britain are given the opportunity to join a residential course and the Calvert Trust gives disabled trainees the same opportunity."*

*(Alan Rialland, Remploy Training Manager)*

8.39 The Calvert Trust *Kielder Adventure Centre* is a purpose-built holiday centre offering a similar range of activities, using the environs of Kielder Water. This 2,500 acre artificial lake allows for excellent sailing opportunities, and has a large indoor riding arena. There are also opportunities for pony-driving, orienteering and even occasionally cross-country skiing. The centre has its own renal dialysis unit, thus enabling young people with kidney failure to take part in adventure activities from the centre.

8.40 The *Bendrigg Trust*, (formerly the Northern Association for Community Care,) established in 1978, is responsible for the operation of Bendrigg Lodge, a specialised residential activities centre near Kendal in Cumbria. The establishment of the centre was to a large extent made possible by the initial support of the Home Office. In 1988 a total of 1,822 people used the centre, of which 21% were people with a physical disability and 29% were mentally handicapped. There were also significant numbers of unemployed and otherwise disadvantaged participants. Some groups were severely disabled, and this required higher staff ratios and smaller group sizes. The centre believes very strongly in the principle that activities should be shared by disabled and able-bodied participants, and this extends to the domestic routines of the centre.

8.41 An important addition to the range of adventure resources available to the disabled is the *Stackpole Home Farm* development in Pembrokeshire. Situated on a beautiful stretch of National Trust land including woods, lakes, cliffs and beaches, the centre operates on the principle that there is no branch of the arts or adventure experiences which cannot be enjoyed by disabled people accompanied by able-bodied friends. It provides a range of activities for the disabled which includes canoeing, abseiling, sand-yachting and bivouacing. In one recent year, the thousand visitors to the centre included families with disabled children, groups of mentally handicapped children, a group of young abandoned or unmarried mothers with disabled children, able-bodied and disabled participants on courses organised by Outward Bound Wales, and an international youth conference.

8.42 Another independent charitable organisation concerned primarily with the disabled is the *Share Centre* in Northern Ireland, a purpose-built residential activity centre located on Upper Lough Erne. The philosophy of the organisation is also based on the principles of sharing skills and knowledge, sharing resources, and sharing of social activities and sport between able-bodied and disabled people.

8.43 There are a large number of small companies or charities which make special provision for the young disabled, who wish to experience an adventurous course or holiday. In Scotland, the *Badaguish Centre* in Aviemore provides opportunities for canoeing, sailing, riding and camping for physically, mentally and multi-handicapped children. Sailing and water activities, often particularly appropriate for the disabled, are available through a number of sail training organisations. *The Royal Yachting Association (RYA) Seamanship Foundation* was established by the RYA in 1973 to encourage seamanship and to provide opportunities for those who would otherwise be unable to sail. The Foundation has pioneered sailing for the disabled, sponsoring the design of the Challenger trimaran for single-handed disabled sailing and each year running courses for blind sailors. More than two hundred young people each year, many from deprived backgrounds, have an introduction to coastal cruising and the experience of taking responsibility for their craft. Programmes are one week or more in length, the majority of participants are aged between 16 and 24, and the Foundation has funded or part-funded the purchase of some 300 dinghies to support this work. *The East Coast Sail Trust* welcomes partially-sighted and blind crew members aboard "Thalatta" (see 6.55). *Kings of Stratford*, a yacht charter firm, offers sailing holidays for physically and mentally handicapped young people on a six-berth yacht based at Southampton. The *Jubilee Sailing Trust* offers disabled people over 16 years of age the opportunity to become working crew members of a 400 ton square-rigged barque, the "Lord Nelson". The St. Albans based *Neighbourly Charitable Trust* operates several boats on the Grand Union Canal, one of which is fitted out to take people in wheelchairs.

8.44 Most of the major outdoor organisations make provision for disabled young people, either by integrating them with able-bodied groups or by designing experiences specifically for a disabled group. For instance, the Duke of Edinburgh's Award welcomes participation by disabled young people who can make a reasonable attempt at completing the different aspects of the scheme. Expeditions present an even greater challenge to disabled young people, but by careful choice of the expedition medium (foot, cycle, canoe etc.) according to the nature of the disability, they can reasonably expect to be successful. The exploration option, as an alternative to the traditional expedition, may in some cases have much to recommend it. The Award encourages the composition of integrated groups, able-bodied and disabled, in the belief that this adds a new dimension to the experience for all. *"Sighted participants can experience a deeper awareness of their surroundings on expedition by undertaking to describe the views in detail to blind companions."*

*("A Challenge to the Individual", Award Scheme publication.)*

8.45 The Outward Bound Trust has also made increasing provision for participation by disabled young people in their challenging outdoor courses. Such participation may take one of three forms;

— integration of disabled individuals with open courses,
— shared experiences for disabled and able-bodied groups,
— courses designed specifically for disabled groups.

The participation of disabled participants on open courses is only arranged after careful consultation between Outward Bound staff, the young people involved and the sponsoring organisations. Such factors as programme content of the courses, layout and design of the centre and access to suitable activity or expedition venues have all to be assessed.

8.46 In some cases it has been found beneficial for disabled groups to experience their own separate programme of outdoor activity, but to work in partnership with an able-bodied group. In this way, whilst remaining a part of the centre or course community, programmes can be tailored to meet the specific needs of the disabled group. *The Ullswater Outward Bound Centre* has designed a number of courses for blind participants on this basis, and the *Outward Bound Wales Centres* has done so for mentally handicapped young people.

8.47 Many courses have been tailored to the needs of disabled groups working independently. For instance at *Outward Bound Eskdale*, much work has been carried out in association with the *British Diabetic Association* to develop suitable outdoor experiences for young diabetics, with the three-fold aim of personal development, improving knowledge of diabetes and self-care, and enjoying an active outdoor holiday. These courses have been carefully monitored, both at the time and subsequently; doctors report that participants are significantly more confident, self-reliant, careful and happy in their attitudes to diabetes after their courses than before. Up to three years after their course they appear to have benefitted long-term, with increased knowledge, self-care and more positive attitudes to their diabetes. (Source: Report by Dr. Rowan Hillson, Radcliffe Infirmary, Oxford.)

8.48 Many other national associations recognise the value of adventurous experiences for young people with disability. *The British Deaf Association* encourages young people to take part in adventure courses, summer schools and youth rallies in order to increase self-confidence, and to provide activities which otherwise might be denied them. Deaf tutors are used where possible to provide 'peer group' encouragement. *The Asthma Society* sponsored sixty young people to take part in holiday activity courses in 1987, at Boreatton Park in Shropshire, Kielder Adventure Centre (Calvert Trust) in Northumbria, and at Outward Bound Eskdale. The Asthma Society arranges for specialised medical supervision on these courses. The Director of the Asthma Society has commented: *"It is generally agreed that all those who attend the courses do benefit, particularly by the development of confidence in engaging in activities which might have been thought were beyond their ability as asthmatics."* *The Royal Association for Disability and Rehabilitation (RADAR)* provides information about access to and funding for outdoor experiences for young people with disability.

8.49 One organisation which has promoted opportunities for young people with a physical disability to experience Outdoor Adventure is *PHAB*. Local PHAB groups are actively involved in two ways with the *Duke of Edinburgh's Award*; firstly by providing opportunities for many able-bodied young people to fulfil the residential or service sections; and secondly by enabling PHAB members with a physical disability to take part in various activities and levels of the Award. PHAB groups have also made frequent use of the Calvert Trust centres and of Bendrigg Lodge, and in 1988, for example, PHAB clubs in Nottinghamshire organised a range of events, including several visits to the *Holme Pierrepont National Water Sports Centre*, and week-end visits to Derbyshire for camping, rock-climbing, caving and fell-walking. Paul Hope, PHAB Director of Training, recognises the benefits of Outdoor Adventure for the disabled, and would welcome greater provision. However, he emphasises the necessity of involving adults or leaders who can cope with disabled people, and of ensuring that facilities are suitable. *"The quality of leaders has to be paramount."*

8.50 Other local initiatives for mentally handicapped young people have been taken in Sheffield and Croydon, as described in the book "Give Us the Chance" by Kay Latto. Individuals from adult training centres, *Gateway Clubs* and hospitals in Sheffield are selected and invited to join expeditions which match their own level of training and ability, or those which may expand their potential. Field studies are a part of most expeditions, and experiences and discoveries are recorded. Many of the leaders originally came from the Edale Mountain Rescue Team; there is now a systematic leader training scheme in operation. Activities have included walking, rock-climbing, caving, canoeing and pony trekking. The Croydon initiative was different, and involved the establishment of a long-term adventure centre at a scout training base, leased mid-week for six months of the year. Programmes were designed to develop social and self-help skills, communication and confidence, and participants could experience a variety of unfamiliar conditions and situations. The programme was mainly outdoor and open-air, and provided opportunities for course members to develop their sense of responsibility for themselves, their friends and the group as a whole.

> *"In most instances it was felt that by taking members away from their families, familiar surroundings, regular routine and parental supervision, they were stimulated, challenged and extended; in fact the results surpassed the highest expectations. Most demonstrated that they were able to cope with situations and activities which they had not previously encountered, and acquired skills which they had never been allowed to perform previously. Few of them had cooked a meal at home, but after patient instruction, encouragement and supervision, more than 80 per cent were able to cook their own breakfasts without supervision before the end of the course. Some trainees were apprehensive about the adventure sections of the programme, and were afraid of going into the canoes until they were assured and coaxed. These initial fears were quickly overcome, and the most timid were able to complete all the activities in the programme."*

*(Kay Latto, Project Officer, Disabled Living Foundation)*

8.51 Outdoor Adventure is also used as part of the special provision for emotionally and behaviourally disturbed young people. The aim most commonly expressed in the survey was to build self-esteem; to help young people in residential schools for emotionally and behaviourally disturbed young people to recognise that they are not worthless, and to help them "to make a fresh start". *Burrow Hill School*, a former ILEA school now part of the Wandsworth LEA provision, incorporates outdoor experiences as an important part of the curriculum. Activities include participation in the Duke of Edinburgh's Award, visits to outdoor centres such as *Calshot Activies Centre* in Hampshire or the *Tyn y Berth* and *Corris Uchaf* centres in Wales, and a three- to five-day journey each year, often on Dartmoor.

8.52 *Witherslack Hall School* for boys with emotional or behavioural difficulties is well situated in South Cumbria for providing a variety of outdoor experience. All 68 pupils are provided with a wide range of outdoor experience, including mountain activities, canoeing, caving and various team building and problem solving tasks, mainly in the Lake District. Although Outdoor Adventure is not seen as the answer to all their problems, it is hoped that such activity will reduce attention-seeking behaviour. The importance of a continuing relationship with caring members of staff is seen as a disincentive for employing temporary or voluntary staff.

8.53 Throughout the study of Outdoor Adventure opportunities for the disabled, whatever the nature of the disability, emphasis has repeatedly been placed on the importance of providing skilled staff in appropriate numbers with the necessary experience. It is evident that in this area of outdoor work, perhaps more than any other, it is not enough to have outdoor skills and enthusiasm; these must be supported by a clear and realistic understanding of the needs and expectations of the disabled, and in many cases with a specialised understanding of the particular disabling illness or condition. This suggests that a suitable partnership has to be established between the agencies that provide outdoor experience, the organisations which sponsor young people to take part, and the relevant medical authorities.

# Outdoor Adventure and the Unemployed

8.54 Several significant initiatives have been taken in recent years to provide adventurous outdoor experiences for unemployed young people. In the early 1980s, there was widespread concern about the scale of youth unemployment, particularly among those leaving school at 16. At present the combination of the significant fall in the numbers leaving school, reflecting the demographic trend, and the introduction of the Youth Training Scheme, accessible to almost all not continuing in full-time education, suggests that the level of unemployment among 16 to 18 year-olds may fall substantially. However the scale of unemployment for those over 18 remains a matter of concern. Most of the programmes described in this section are oriented primarily towards the needs of the 18 to 24 age group. The element of Outdoor Adventure is usually intended to help to build self-esteem, to extend experience, to provide a sense of achievement, and to maintain the motivation to seek employment.

8.55 *The Prince of Wales' Community Venture* is an expanding national programme which operates in five centres throughout England and Wales, with several others in the formative stages. Its main purpose is to encourage and train young adults aged 18 to 24 to give service to their community. The scheme accepts young adults from all walks of life and background, a majority of them unemployed, who after interviews and a comprehensive selection process including some outdoor exercises, commit themselves to a forty-three week programme which has the following aims:

- *To motivate young people to wish to give service to others;*
- *To train young people in the necessary skills to give that service;*
- *To provide attachment opportunities for young people to make a contribution to their community;*
- *To give personal guidance, training and counselling to the participants throughout the programme, to develop their abilities and make them better citizens;*
- *To prepare each participant for the challenge of work and community life.*

8.56 The participants work in teams of up to twelve, and the course for each team has five main phases, beginning with a period of Outdoor Adventure experience to develop self-confidence, leadership and teamwork skills. This is followed by the opportunity to become better acquainted with their local community, a two-month attachment to a local 'caring' organisation, an 'away phase' (two months in a different social and cultural environment, away from the home area) and, finally, the completion of a project within the community, identified and organised by the team. The initial adventure phase is seen to be of great importance in developing personal qualities, building the team in its early stages, and identifying and developing leadership potential. It also helps some of the participants to develop skills which will enable them to lead other young people in outdoor ventures during their course. The success of the Venture is indicated by the fact that over 70 per cent of those completing the scheme have found regular employment.

*"The majority of young people that come to us are long-term unemployed — they have spent up to three years doing virtually nothing. Our young people are attracted to the Venture by the excitement of rock-climbing and abseiling, by the idea of going away in a group. Rightly or wrongly, the Venture conjures up images of the great outdoors, and all the vigourous activities associated with that. There is nothing wrong with these reasons as long as the Venture uses them to its advantage."*

(Margaret Elliott, PoW CV leader, Sunderland)

8.57 The *Fairbridge Drake Society also works extensively with young unemployed, under the age of 25. The purpose of Fairbridge Drake is "to advance the education and physical, mental and spiritual development of young people in need or hardship, who are unemployed or otherwise in moral danger, so they may grow to full maturity and make a constructive contribution to the society in which they live, ideally by finding employment".* Within the Fairbridge Drake programme there are many opportunities for Outdoor Adventure. Outdoor pursuits are initially utilised as a means of capturing interest and building trust between individuals, recognising the importance of achieving success. There is then a ten-day basic training programme, part of which is away from base, using a wide range of outdoor activities. There may then be various follow-on projects, including expeditions, sailing voyages or conservation projects. Some of these may involve voyages aboard the schooner "Spirit of Merseyside", or visits to the Fairbridge Drake Training Centre at Applecross in the North-West Highlands.

8.58 Fairbridge Drake does not operate a selection procedure, and attracts over 3,000 participants each year. The initial training incorporating Outdoor Adventure is followed by a variety of opportunities for training for employment, training for independent living, training for involvement in community care and leadership training. The organisation is strongly committed to giving continuing support and counselling until young people are able to live and work independently.

8.59 The *Drive for Youth* programme, in contrast, has a tightly organised selection procedure, and tries to identify young unemployed who have resourcefulness and potential for leadership. The 13-week programme commences with a three-week residential in North Wales, and then allows ten weeks for the preparation and execution of a community project overseas, usually in a developing country as a guest worker. The aim is to enable over 100 young unemployed each year to develop the practical and personal skills to find employment or to continue into further education. The outdoor experience is used to develop the sense of achievement and self-esteem.

8.60 There are many other small-scale initiatives which seek to meet the needs of the young unemployed, such as the *Cop-out* programme run by the Cheshire Constabulary. This is a developmental course for local unemployed or disadvantaged youth, mainly drawn from the 16 to 20 age-range, and recruited from centres for the unemployed. Adventure activities take place in the North Wales mountains. Courses are mostly two weeks in length, and the organisers follow-up participants to check on employment progress or further involvement in adventure activities.

# Young Offenders and Those at Risk

*"The problem of locking up juvenile offenders appears to be that in so doing you remove the one thing that they must at some point learn to handle for themselves — personal responsibility."*

(Geoff Sanders, Director, Coventry Intermediate Treatment Association)

8.61 The study has revealed encouraging evidence of the value of Outdoor Adventure as a vital element in community-based initiatives to prevent crime among young people, to divert others from criminal activities, and as an alternative to custody for those found guilty in the courts.

8.62 David Faulkner, Deputy Under Secretary at the Home Office, speaking at a recent conference in Manchester organised by the Sports Council, on the theme 'Community-Based Sentencing — the use of Outdoor Challenge', said,

*"The task is to develop a more demanding and challenging range of activities which will provide offenders and potential offenders with the kind of interest, motivation and commitment to channel their energy and appetite for excitement and danger into something more worthwhile and permanently valuable than continual offending."*

He emphasised the extent of the problems of crime among young people, noting that over half the crime, which is traced to an offender, is committed by young people under 21. He went on to say,

> *"The scope for diverting young people from offending in the critical years between 14 and 21 is enormous. There are huge potential rewards if we can pull it off. This is the age group for which a programme is also most likely to have public support if it can be convincingly presented and shown to succeed."*

8.63 It is against this background that the potential of Outdoor Adventure as an agent for good in the fight against crime among young people must be considered. The survey has shown by many examples of good, imaginative practice how effective such activity can be, although as yet its use is not widely recognised. To appreciate its full potential in the complex situations through which young people pass between 10 and 21 years of age, it is necessary to identify certain stages of risk and delinquency, which although clearly recognisable merge unpredictably from one to another.

8.64 **Firstly**, at the younger end of the age range, emphasis is placed increasingly on crime prevention at neighbourhood or community level. Many young people are growing up on housing estates or in the older industrial towns, where the level of social and recreational provision is minimal. The situation is often made worse by poor housing and over-crowded living conditions in deprived areas. As the recent National Association for Care and Rehabilitation of Offenders, (NACRO) Report, "Growing up on Housing Estates", points out, in such conditions,

> *"young people can easily drift into anti-social behaviour and petty offending through boredom and limited access to more constructive activities."*

The fact that the peak age for offending in the country generally is now 15 is a further indication of the serious nature of the problem. Thus there are now many areas where a high proportion of children may be said to be at risk of offending.

8.65 It is encouraging to report many instances where in positive reaction to these problems, local adults have taken the initiative and developed projects offering a range of constructive activities. The Intermediate Treatment Fund of the Rainer Foundation has been able to support many such projects, especially with grants towards premises and equipment. Outdoor activities account for about 35 per cent of grants including projects with 'Bikes and Bangers', water sports and a variety of adventurous expeditions involving hillwalking and camping. In many cases projects are developed in close co-operation with statutory and voluntary agencies and such partnership working gives rise to cautious hope for the future.

8.66 In developing provision for social and recreational opportunities for young people there tends to be a gap between 'play' provision for younger children in adventure playgrounds and other activities and the beginnings of effective youth work provision. Some projects are therefore particularly targeted on the 12-14 age-group, who have outgrown the 'play' activities and may even disrupt them, and have not yet been drawn into youth activities. There is evidence that this particular age group reacts favourably and benefits greatly from Outdoor Adventure of the most challenging kind. This is an ideal opportunity to provide constructive outlets for children seeking adventure and excitement, and to divert them from crime.

8.67 **Secondly**, when through offending, young people up to the age of 17 enter the Juvenile Justice System, they come within the ambit of intermediate treatment. In the past decade there has been a marked change in the way offenders under 17 have been dealt with, notably an increase in the use of cautioning by the police and, in the courts, an important shift away from the use of Care Orders and custodial sentences, which had been shown to lead to a high rate of re-offending. Residential Care Orders for petty offenders have effectively disappeared from a peak of over 6,500 in 1974, while custodial sentences have almost been halved from a total of 7,700 (males 14–17 years) in 1981. Significantly, this reduction in the use of care and custody has not caused juvenile crime to rise. The developing scope and quality of intermediate treatment over this period may well have a bearing on the fall in most juvenile crime.

8.68 From small beginnings in the 1970's intermediate treatment, (IT) now offers a realistic, constructive and non-custodial way to tackle the problem of juvenile crime by:

— *maintaining young offenders within their own communities, providing them with opportunities to develop new interests, to form new relationships and to fulfil their potential;*
— *encouraging young people to think again about their futures and the consequences of offending, both for themselves and their communities, and supporting them in constructive attempts to overcome their difficulties;*
— *involving communities in finding solutions to problems through enabling concerned adults to offer their skills, knowledge and experience to encourage young people to participate actively in the community.*

8.69 This is the context in which Outdoor Adventure can play a useful part. In its early days it was virtually equated with IT; outdoor pursuits later fell into disrepute and disappeared from many programmes. There were good reasons for these initial difficulties, which arose often from too great a reliance on the therapeutic value of strenuous mountain walking and rough camping. As outdoor education developed, there emerged a more balanced and holistic approach. In this way, the quest for adventure through outdoor activities became an integral part of a group work approach, designed to foster self-knowledge, self-esteem, concern for others and awareness of the natural environment.

8.70 Whatever the factors that lead young people into crime, Outdoor Adventure provides a valuable way to work successfully with young offenders. Ian Butler, Centre Manager at Essington Lodge Childrens' Centre, Walsall, from his wide experience in this field suggests that besides the broadening of horizons and the sheer fun and excitement of participation, there are three practical advantages:

a) Opportunities for social learning. Juvenile delinquency is usually a peer group activity. Outdoor activities, despite their expression of personal motivation and the attainment of personal goals, usually involve a re-learning of social roles within a group. As such, together with other group work methods, outdoor activities often provide an intense opportunity to develop the confidence and ability to negotiate a new role within, or indeed away from, a delinquent peer group.

b) Opportunities for developing personal survival skills. Outdoor activities provide valuable compensatory experience for young people whose ambitions are limited by whatever main roads form the boundaries of their home territory. There is also an element of 'play' and even of 'theatre', from the donning of strange costumes to gaining a new vocabulary.

c) There is usually a requirement to build a relationship of trust with an adult, and a greater likelihood that this trust will be honoured, perhaps for the first time in the life of a young person.

8.71 Outdoor Adventure frequently includes opportunities for residential experience; an overnight camp, a short stay in a centre or a longer period away on an expedition. It is well established that personal and social development is greatly accelerated in the process.

8.72 In 1976-79 the *Brathay Hall Trust* and the *St. Helens Social Services Department* pioneered a three-year pilot project in which Outdoor Adventure and residential experience were built into the programmes of six intermediate treatment groups from different neighbourhoods in the borough. Each group visited the Trust's Lake District base on four occasions (11 days) during a year, with their social workers, living in self-catering accommodation on the estate. This approach, in which outdoor challenges were fully integrated into the life and experience of each small group, aroused wide interest. It led first to a research project undertaken by the Centre for Youth, Crime and Community at Lancaster University, and later to the opening in 1981 of a purpose-built centre on the estate, enabling many more intermediate treatment groups to participate. The effectiveness of this approach was well described by David Smith of Lancaster University, in a lecture on 'Helping Juvenile Offenders' given at the Policy Studies Institute in October 1982.

> *"Periods spent at Brathay have, to my knowledge, remained uniquely valued experiences in the collective life of intermediate treatment groups and in the memories of the individual offenders in them. They have also provided social workers with direct knowledge of the characteristics of offenders in their charge which they could probably not have acquired in any other setting. Social workers take risks when they share testing experiences with juvenile offenders: risks with their own authority and status, and the risk of finding out things about their clients which it would be more comfortable not to know. Extremes emerge in an unfamiliar and demanding environment which remain safely hidden in everyday contexts — extremes of destructiveness, anger or despair as well as surprising capacities and talents. Something of the reality of the juvenile's experience of himself and others may emerge which could remain hidden for ever (apart from its obscure and distorted expression in offences) in the more polite and comfortable setting of the office or the family home. This kind of explosive and undeniable revelation is not easy for either the worker or the juvenile, and it requires skill in its handling, but it does make possible a more open and potentially honest level of communication in future."*

> *(David Smith, 'Helping Juvenile Offenders', Policy Studies Institute paper)*

8.73 Since 1984, *Coventry Intermediate Treatment Association (CITA)* has made available to the courts an alternative non-custodial opportunity for young offenders to particpate in a four-month programme of 'specified' activities. The CITA aternative to custody provides an integrated programme of both indoor and outdoor activity, including a 3-week Outward Bound course. CITA seeks to take offenders beyond the constraints imposed by existing circumstances, improving their ability to function as individuals through membership of a group participating in a programme of challenging activity.

> *"The most recent CITA person on an Outward Bound course joined a group that included people from the Republic of Ireland, the USA and Norway. He was a very unlikely candidate for an Outward Bound course, being very small for his 15 years, having poor vision, unable to read or write and very quiet by nature. Other members of the group helped him out of difficulties, for example with map reading and offered him emotional support and the continuation of their friendship after the course. On his return he had significantly increased his weight and visibly grown in stature. He was more confident in self-expression and could communicate freely about his experience. His teacher was so staggered by the transformation that she contacted CITA and reported that he had become a 'model student'. Prior to this he had been described as having particularly difficult emotional problems. He has now enrolled for adult literacy classes."*

> *(Geoff Sanders, Adventure Education, Vol 3 No 2)*

8.74 Among residential centres which offer Outdoor Adventure for young offenders an outstanding example is *Parson House Farm Outdoor Pursuits Centre*, run by the Knowsley Youth Trust. This Centre, on the moors near Sheffield, has successfully pioneered challenging courses and expeditions for a variety of groups of young people at odds with the law, designing each to meet the special needs of participants.

8.75 Small converted cottages or barns in outlying hill country, unstaffed and with self-catering accommodation only, offer excellent, low-cost bases for such work with young people at risk. Examples include *Wilkin Hill Outdoor Centre*, owned by the *South Yorkshire Outdoor Pursuits Trust*, the *Rugby Mayday Trust's* cottage in Mid-Wales, *Community Action's (North Devon)* converted shepherd's cottage on Exmoor and the Newcastle-upon-Tyne *Children's Adventure Group's Ridsdale Activity Centre* in Northumberland.

8.76 The development of mobile units to provide resources for Outdoor Adventure is an important innovation and is flexible and low-cost in operation. *Grass Routes*, the Bristol based charity, was set up to achieve personal development for disadvantaged young people. The flexible approach enables the group to offer programmes suited to individual needs from short courses to longer expeditions, encompassing the full range of outdoor challenges. The pilot MOBEX unit of the Young Explorers' Trust has likewise demonstrated the value of mobile, flexible and low-cost approaches (see 6.55).

8.77 **Thirdly**, for young people aged 17-20 the offending patterns are particularly serious. As young adult offenders they are dealt with by the courts in the same way as adult offenders. In 1987, 99,700 young men and 12,300 young women aged 17-20 were sentenced by the courts. Over 20,000 young men and 600 young women in this age-group received custodial sentences. Comparative figures for those over 21 sentenced to custody are 41,000 men and 2,500 women. The Home Office Green Paper, "Punishment, Custody and the Community" (Cm424), commenting on these figures, notes that *"most young offenders grow out of crime as they become more mature and responsible"*, and goes on to say,

> *"The Government thinks it reasonable to look to a significant drop in the number of young adults sentenced to custody. But this will happen only if the courts and the public have confidence that keeping offenders in the community will be effective in preventing re-offending."*

8.78 The study has therefore looked closely at projects which offer, through the medium of Outdoor Adventure, significant contributions to programmes providing viable alternatives to custodial sentences. The Probation Service has the primary responsibility for young adult offenders and, from the evidence submitted, Outdoor Adventure activities do provide an important element in many probation programmes of supervision. There is much interesting innovation in this field, with many and varied approaches to some very difficult problems. There is also a concern, through outdoor activities, to help the most disadvantaged, the unmotivated and the apathetic drifters into crime. Of the most deprived, John Roberts, Senior Probation Officer in Greater Manchester has said,

> *"I realised that this was as a 'second childhood' for many who had never really had a 'first childhood'. Life is very serious for many of our children and 'survival' is the name of the game."*

8.79 The Merseyside Probation Service has had a long-standing commitment to outdoor activities and has its own residential outdoor centre in North Wales. The Chief Probation

Officer reported that,

> "*Our Merseyside experience demonstrates that young offenders from depressed and disadvantaged areas are not only very keen to participate in outdoor activities — but also benefit greatly!*"

*(David Mathieson, Chief Probation Officer, Merseyside Probation Service)*

The objectives of the Merseyside activities programme, which are also reflected in many other similar programmes throughout the Probation Service, are:

a) *Through challenging experiences, to influence the offender's attitudes and view of the world.*

b) *To provide basic knowledge and skills, thus counter-acting a sense of isolation, and discouraging recourse to criminal solutions to problems.*

c) *To expand the offender's awareness of socially acceptable leisure and community activities in order to improve self-esteem, provide a sense of achievement and discover ways of usefully structuring time.*

d) *To learn to co-operate with others in shared ventures which demand trust and consideration for other people, and to appreciate the effects of attitude and behaviour upon others.*

e) *To provide for a relief of tension or boredom created by the confines of the offender's environment.*

8.80 The Greater Manchester Probation Service through its Projects Unit offers many varied Outdoor Adventure activities and has its own residential centre and a canal narrowboat. It is

> "*constantly looking for opportunities to nurture, develop and promote groupwork methods as a means of working with offenders, in order to encourage crime prevention and rehabilitation.*"

8.81 The Lancashire Probation Service is similarly well organised to promote the development of outdoor pursuits. It also runs 3-week courses at Loch Grannoch Lodge in Dumfries and Galloway as a specific alternative to custody. Of special interest is the *Coldwell Inn Activities Centre* on the moors near Nelson, which specialises in courses for the disabled and the disadvantaged. The Centre is staffed by members of the probation service, who encourage offenders to participate in its servicing and maintenance, as a form of community service and means of re-integration into society.

8.82 In 1985 *Endeavour Training* obtained the approval of magistrates in Sheffield and

Nottingham to take a group of young adult offenders serving probation orders to Norway, with emphasis on Outdoor Adventure. The trip was reported as being

*"an outstanding success as the outcome was a more mutual understanding between all participants... forced to work together in some extremely rigorous terrain and inclement weather."*

8.83 *The Alternative Life Experience Course* run by the South Yorkshire Probation Service in association with the Doncaster Metropolitan Institute for Higher Education, (DMIHE), is designed for students aged 19-30 who have had one or more custodial sentences and are unemployed. Developed and run by Angela Tabrah, the course lasts 12 weeks with students attending for 20 hours each week. It is an important experiment in developing alternatives to custody within the community. Outdoor activities, including expeditions and practical projects in problem solving, are undertaken in demanding situations in which students are thrown back on their own resources. As confidence, personal skills and motivation develop, students are encouraged to feel that their learning is in their own hands and that stopping to think first does prove productive in real terms.

8.84 In Dorset and Worcestershire the Duke of Edinburgh's Award is used as the basis for supervised activities forming part of probation orders. It has also been found possible to operate the Award in some former borstals and in at least one Youth Custody Centre (Aylesbury). The enthusiasm, team spirit and self-confidence which were developed through the expedition section of the scheme made a very positive impression on the staff. It is unfortunate that overcrowding and staffing problems in HM penal establishments have severely curtailed such programmes.

## 8.85 *Summary*

(a)  The content of Outdoor Adventure programmes needs to be tailored to the different age-groups considered in this study. (8.2 — 8.10)

(b)  Fewer girls take part in Outdoor Adventure activities. But in some activities e.g. country walking (8.12) as many girls take part as boys; in others e.g. riding (8.14) many more so. The disparities are greatest when participation is voluntary. (8.15)

(c)  Certain voluntary organisations e.g. Guides, Girls' Brigade have a high level of participation in Outdoor Adventure through the Duke of Edinburgh's Award.

(d)  The reasons for a lower level of female participation are discussed. (8.18 — 8.27)

(e)  The value of all-female adventure programmes, and all-female staffing, has been demonstrated by Outward Bound and other centre-based courses. (8.28 — 8.30)

(f)  Ethnic minority groups, who are mostly concentrated in urban areas, are under-represented in outdoor programmes. (8.33 — 8.34)

(g)  There are valid reasons, mainly cultural, why many young people from these groups do not take part; but one reason is the lack of adult leaders from the ethnic minorities with experience and enthusiasm to encourage them to participate. (8.35 — 8.38)

(h)  A possible way forward is demonstrated by the Windsor Fellowship, mainly for black students aged 16-20. (8.30)

(i)  It is for consideration whether more should be done to provide training for adult leaders from this section of the community. (8.39 — 8.40)

(j)  There has been a considerable expansion of opportunities for disabled young people, whether they suffer from mental or physical handicap, to experience adventurous pursuits out-of-doors. Many organisations in both the public and private sectors, make such provision. (8.32 — 8.50)

(k)  Several significant initiatives have been taken in recent years to provide adventurous outdoor experience for unemployed young people. (8.54 — 8.60)

(l)  There is encouraging evidence of the value of Outdoor Adventure in community-based initiatives to prevent crime and as part of Court Orders imposed on juvenile and young offenders. Such activities are considered to play a useful part in intermediate treatment programmes. (8.61 — 8.83)

(m)  The Duke of Edinburgh's Award has been operated with some success in young offender custodial establishments, but over-crowding and staffing problems have been a limiting factor.

# CHAPTER 9
## ASPECTS OF DEVELOPMENT

9.1 The study indicates that a significant proportion of young people, perhaps as many as half, either do not receive or do not take the opportunity to be involved in adventurous outdoor activities. Many do not have the opportunity; others have the opportunity but do not take it. The reasons appear to be: the image of the activities; concerns about safety; inadequate information; lack of resources; cost; environmental and access factors; supply of leaders; and the extent of current legislative and organisational change. There is also a separate problem of progression - the difficulty of enabling young people to enjoy a continuity of adventurous experiences in Britain and further afield.

# *Image*

9.2 At all levels, both among adults and among young people, there is misunderstanding about the purpose and value of Outdoor Adventure. Indeed the fact that such experience may have a number of different purposes, expressed in differing language, compounds the difficulty. The dramatic, physical image of these experiences tends to mask and distort the other deeper purposes. Many parents, teachers, community leaders and employers, as well as young people themselves, are not persuaded of the relevance of these activities to everyday life. Young people may be deterred by fear of the unknown, of hardship and of risk.

9.3 Different perceptions abound: many adults see Outdoor Adventure either, on the one hand, as essentially for the better-off or, alternatively, as something which is appropriate for low-ability, underprivileged or delinquent youngsters, for whom arduous outdoor experiences may be equated with the 'short, sharp shock'. The language used in describing Outdoor Adventure is often simplistic, tending to make too strong claims. Young people frequently exaggerate the physical hardships, even when successfully overcome, and this has an off-putting effect for others. The 'masculine' image of Outdoor Adventure deters many girls from taking part. The comment of the National Association for Outdoor Education is relevant here:

*"The multi-faceted nature of outdoor education is a mixed blessing. For lay persons it projects a confusing image which probably causes them to fall back on stereotyped images so that the perceived image of outdoor education is likely to be very much out of date and misleading."*

# *Safety*

9.4    Those responsible for Outdoor Adventure programmes frequently stress the difference between the apparent risk sensed by participants and the real risk which can be measured as a result of experience elsewhere. Adventures out-of-doors often seem much more hazardous than in fact they are. There is a paradox in that the more risky a venture, the more carefully it is safeguarded; whereas inherently less hazardous activities, which have less stringent safety measures, may in practice be more dangerous. Despite a popular perception to the contrary, the great majority of outdoor programmes and experiences undertaken by young people are conducted responsibly and with a high standard of safety. Naturally, there is a serious concern for safety throughout the field, particularly among parents and other adults who may not be directly involved. Popular concern has been increased in recent years as a result of a number of well-publicised accidents on land and at sea. Some of these have occurred to parties of young people on school outings which were not properly supervised. In several cases the accidents occurred, not because of any lack of technical expertise on the part of the supervisors, but rather due to a lack of general care and common sense.

9.5    Safety standards and requirements are established by each outdoor organisation in the light of its own educational aims, area of operation, staff qualifications and experience, and the age and level of responsibility of the participants. Most of the national bodies for each sport or activity lay down suggested safety standards or procedures. It is difficult to establish a single safety framework which could apply throughout the field, in view of the great diversity of what takes place, and indeed such a national safety system would tend to inhibit some of the more adventurous approaches and initiatives. Nevertheless it is of great importance that each organisation involved should regularly review its practice in the light of developing experience. One difficulty has been that of obtaining accurate details of accidents or near-misses in Outdoor Adventure, since for obvious reasons information is not shared freely. A pilot project, the *Outdoor Education Safety Network*, has been sponsored by the Spastics' Society; this seeks to collate and analyse accident statistics and information, in order to identify patterns and trends. Such information will assist organisers of outdoor ventures when making decisions about recruiting and training staff, equipment selection and use, and curriculum content and activity. Information generated by this database will be published annually.

9.6 The matter of safety raises the difficult question of the wisdom of giving responsibility to young people to carry out their own exercises without direct supervision by adults. This is seen as the natural culmination of many adventurous programmes, but it may conflict with the requirement to provide adequate safeguards. Such difficulties may be affected by the increasing application of Health and Safety legislation to school and out-of-school activities. The requirements of accountability and the need for insurance inhibit some leaders or organisers from developing outdoor experiences for young people.

> *"In a unique way Outdoor Education has a dynamic contribution to make to the health and development of individuals. Safety in Outdoor Education is of paramount importance. Society would be the poorer if restrictive regulations were to stifle the adventurous and enquiring spirit."*

> *(Outdoor Education; Safety and Good Practice, 1988)*

# *Information*

9.7 The study has shown that there is widespread difficulty, experienced both by adults and by young people, in obtaining adequate and up-to-date information about Outdoor Adventure opportunities. A large number of national bodies are involved in outdoor education and recreation with differing aims and responsibilities. A clear and accessible rationale for the different approaches is lacking. This tends to create uncertainty and confusion in the minds of young people and some adults. There are a number of specialist sources of information, for instance from each of the commercial providers, from umbrella bodies such as the Association of Sail Training Organisations, or from the National Park authorities, but it is difficult to gain a comprehensive, overall view of opportunities for adventure out-of-doors for young people. Furthermore there has been relatively little systematic, high-quality research into the effectiveness of adventure programmes in achieving the aims which they proclaim. There is a case for the provision of a great deal more information, both centrally and locally.

# *Resources (finance, staff, equipment, transport)*

9.8　The range of organisations and resources existing in Britain to enable young people to gain experience out-of-doors is impressive. However their availability is patchy and access to them is often limited or difficult. Most individuals consulted during the study felt that shortage of money and lack of suitable staff were the main resource constraints. Several others indicated their difficulty in gaining access to suitable equipment and transport. Many organisations working in the field of outdoor activities tend to approach industrial, commercial or charitable sponsors for grants for new projects, which the sponsors have difficulty in evaluating. Claims for support from such organisations for outdoor projects also compete with increasing numbers of claims from other sectors, such as the Arts.

# *Cost*

9.9　The cost of participation in Outdoor Adventure varies greatly. A wide variety of alternative experiences is available, ranging from the professionally staffed, well resourced outdoor centres, such as the national centres at *Plas-y-Brenin* or *Glenmore Lodge*, to the largely self-financed, low cost ventures which may be encouraged by some voluntary or grant-aided bodies. In each case the direct cost to participants may differ significantly; some young people pay to participate from their own or their family resources; others are supported by charitable funds; for others the full cost may be found by employers, social work agencies or educational trusts. Local education authorities usually subsidise the cost of travel and residence in centres maintained by them.

9.10　The result is that there is no clear pattern of participation in relation to the cost of the venture, or indeed in relation to the needs of particular individuals. Often young people who obtain support to enable them to participate are those with the initiative to seek and acquire the necessary funds. This is most evidently true of overseas expeditions. For instance, to participate in the major expeditions organised by the *British Schools' Exploring Society* or by *Operation Raleigh* the applicant has to raise several hundreds, or even thousands, of pounds. While some participants are subsidised, such enterprises are enjoyed mainly by relatively well endowed and enterprising young people. A number of other organisations, of which *Endeavour Training* is an example, conduct enterprising expeditions overseas with more limited, less costly objectives.

9.11 However, there are many opportunities for young people to find adventure, in acceptable forms, at low cost. This may be in the context of a local venture, for instance in a school programme working with the local Ranger service, by using a local resource such as a nearby canal or woodland, or by taking part through one of the many urban initiatives which have been established recently, by the *Fairbridge Drake Society*, the *Prince of Wales Community Venture*, the *Outward Bound Trust* and others.

9.12 Even for those travelling away from home areas, costs can be kept to a minimum by the use of youth hostels, camping barns or tents. A beginning can be made on quite a modest budget, especially if equipment is borrowed and transport costs shared. More easily accessible information about low-cost alternatives would be helpful.

## *Access and Environment*

9.13 Problems of access to suitable open country and to waterways, or to suitable local or urban areas, have always affected the outdoor movement in Britain. Although in some respects access has improved, for instance by the designation of rights of way and by negotiating agreements with landowners and other interest groups, there are still considerable areas of difficulty, and these may increase. Access to some waterways, and in particular rivers, is fraught with difficulties. Privatisation of water may further restrict the right of public access. Changes in the patterns of farming land use have made access more difficult although availability of land for recreation through the 'set-aside' policy may help matters. The designation of areas as Nature Reserves or as sites of special scientific interest (SSSIs) can lead to conflicts of interest between their primary purpose and access for recreation, although many SSSIs are frequently used for education purposes.

9.14 There are some involved in Outdoor Adventure who are still unaware of the damage they can do to fragile environments. The scale of present use of the limited wild country landscape in England and Wales, particularly in some very heavily used areas, causes concern on environmental grounds. Some local communities feel themselves to be under pressure from groups visiting the countryside in their locality. As a result authorities in some of these areas may restrict educational use, for instance by refusing permission to establish new outdoor centres.

9.15 Responsibility for the environment lies with a number of government departments. Some of those interviewed during the study argued strongly for more effective co-ordination of all environmental interests, with a view inter alia to ensuring the greatest possible access to areas where Outdoor Adventure can be promoted. These matters are examined in more detail in Chapter 11.

# Supply of Leaders

9.16 A major obstacle in providing high-quality outdoor experiences for young people is the lack of appropriately trained and experienced leaders, whether in schools, in youth clubs or in voluntary organisations. The lack of such leaders inevitably limits the experience for young people and restricts the numbers who can participate. Many volunteers act as leaders, but opportunities to train them adequately are insufficient. It is generally recognised that training in outdoor techniques by itself is not sufficient and that leadership skills are also required for effective work to take place. The national bodies for sport are at present mainly concerned to impart technical and coaching skills. The provision of an outdoor education element in teacher training courses has been reduced. These matters are examined more closely in Chapter 10.

# Changes in Education and Training

9.17 Great changes are taking place in the fields of education and training. Despite wider recognition of the value of an educational process which includes personal and social development, education for capability, and the development of enterprise, there is widespread concern lest much of the effective work currently being undertaken in outdoor education which is closely related to these themes, may suffer, as and when the new proposals are implemented and existing resources are rationalised. The 1988 Education Reform Act makes no direct reference to outdoor education, and there is still ignorance or uncertainty about arrangements for charging for out-of-school activities. Local management of schools, and the opportunity for schools to opt out of their control, may make it increasingly difficult for local education authorities to co-ordinate the use of shared equipment resources or residential centres. The abolition of the Inner London Education Authority (ILEA) also places the future use and availability of its resources and centres in doubt. The introduction of clearly-defined teacher contracts may limit participation by teachers in informal out-of-hours outdoor work.

9.18 It remains to be seen whether compulsory competitive tendering for local authority services will impair the current development and future expansion of outdoor work in schools and in the youth service. Concern was expressed in the course of the study regarding the viability of certain residential centres as a result of this requirement in the Education Reform Act.

9.19 The targeting of financial and other resources in the inner cities is clearly welcomed, but the selective application of resources to some urban areas and not to others leads to unequal opportunities in leisure provision for young people country-wide.

# *Continuity and Progression*

9.20 Many young people have an introductory outdoor experience, but often this is not followed by further development or progression in Outdoor Adventure. Most of the young people consulted during the study were keen for additional experience, but it would seem that information about, or opportunities for, such progression are often lacking. More ambitious ventures are usually more costly, particularly in respect of travel, and this is clearly a major obstacle. Some of the organisations involved give participants clear guidance as to how they may extend their experience or progress to leadership roles.

9.21 Some organisations have been successful in building the opportunities for progression into their programmes. This is a central feature of the *Duke of Edinburgh's Award*, with its requirement for increasingly challenging expeditions or explorations at different levels. The Badge awards offered by *Scouts and Guides* present similar requirements. The increasing recognition by some local education authorities of the principle of continuing outdoor education progression through primary, secondary and community education provision is to be welcomed.

## 9.22 *Summary*

(a) A significant proportion of all young people between 8 and 19 do not receive the opportunity to take part in Outdoor Adventure. (9.1)

(b) The popular image of outdoor activities, and differing perceptions of the purpose of Outdoor Adventure, may be misleading or offputting. (9.2, 9.3)

(c) There is a proper concern for safety in the conduct of Outdoor Adventure activities, which must be related to the need to give young people meaningful adventure experiences. (9.4, 9.6)

(d) Lack of information and lack of resources are obstacles to development. There is competition between some providers for financial and other resources. (9.7, 9.8)

(e) There are many examples of low-cost ventures, limited in range and scale of activity, using local amenities and simple shelter. (9.11, 9.12)

(f) Restrictions exist on access to wilder countryside and there is concern over damage to the environment through ignorance and poor management. (9.13, 9.14)

(g) Overall co-ordination of environmental interests could assist the need for access to the countryside. (9.15)

(h) A key feature in increasing Outdoor Adventure provision is the supply of appropriately-trained leaders. (9.16)

(i) Development will depend on the wider recognition of the value of Outdoor Adventure and need for adequate provision by government, local authorities and all other bodies which have some responsibility for the education and training of young people. (9.17, 9.19)

# CHAPTER 10
## LEADERSHIP, MANAGEMENT AND ACCOUNTABILITY

## *Survey Results*

10.1    The perceived shortage of suitable leaders, tutors and instructors has been clearly identified in the survey as a factor limiting the more efficient provision and uptake of adventure activities. Most respondents to the provider questionnaire said how difficult it was to find suitable staff for their programmes. Half those responding to the third questionnaire expressed the need for more properly selected, trained, qualified and experienced leaders, and a corresponding increase in the provision for training (see 5.42, 5.46, 5.47, 5.58, 5.61).

10.2    There are believed to be sufficient potential leaders around, but they need identifying and recruiting. It was said that the quality of leadership is paramount; expansion can only come at the pace that new leaders are recruited and trained, preferably within organisations of good standing. Personal qualities, values, motivation and temperament are of crucial importance. Some respondents called for more vetting, supervision and competent training, because of the extent of unqualified, inexperienced leadership. A few wanted some kind of central control regulation or local registration; others preferred guidelines from national bodies, together with coached experience on the job.

10.3    Not surprisingly, in the light of the steady erosion over the last decade in the number of higher education institutions providing suitable courses in outdoor education, there was substantial support (30% of respondents) for more training programmes of good quality, adequately funded (especially for voluntary leaders) and perhaps leading to nationally recognised progressive qualifications, based on monitored standards of competence.

10.4    It was suggested that such arrangements should be backed up by a public policy on outdoor education and training, designed to ensure an adequate supply of trained, experienced and inspirational leaders with specific leadership skills, as well as technical outdoor skills.

10.5    Some respondents also stressed the need for first class people to be involved with the administration and organisation that is vital for expansion, and pointed to the careful planning, supervision and resource management that is needed to support, guide, assist and train those with direct responsibility for young people.

# Steps in the Provision of Competent Leaders

10.6    The study has revealed widespread concern about the *existing* arrangements for ensuring an adequate supply of properly qualified, experienced leaders — quite apart from the needs arising from *future* expansion. For employed, full-time leaders the chain of events that leads to this provision is illustrated below:

|  |  |  |
|---|---|---|
| Advertise | Job specification | Competence Appraise |
|  | Person specification | standards Accredit Certify |
| IDENTIFY |  | ENOUGH |

POTENTIAL ->ATTRACT ->SELECT ->APPOINT ->INDUCT ->DEVELOP ->COMPETENT

| LEADERS |  | LEADERS |
|---|---|---|
|  | Persuade Interview | Supervise Coach |
|  | Test | Train |
| Vet | Counsel |  |
| Individual |  | Self-improvement |
| responsibility | Provide CV | Learning for life |

———————————————>

Progressive qualifications based on competence and experience

For the unpaid voluntary leader, a less formal process usually applies, but the central chain is similar. Several of the links in this chain badly need strengthening; this report is selective rather than comprehensive in commenting on the weaknesses.

# Identification and Attraction

10.7    As a means of attracting potential leaders, advertising is less effective than personal persuasion. The young people who attend outdoor events comprise a pool in which leadership talent and potential can be found; talent-spotting is therefore an important responsibility of existing leaders. Young people need to be set alight with enthusiasm for helping to give others the kind of enriching experience they themselves have received. Many youth organisations attempt to recruit from within and offer a structured pathway to leader status.

10.8    Other people become involved because the need for voluntary help confronts them personally, for instance as parents whose children seek Outdoor Adventure, or as citizens involved in community problems. Part-time leaders can be attracted by pocket money or the chance of developing a leisure interest. Relatively few volunteer solely because of an altruistic vocation to help the young; it is better to play on their personal interests by offering the prospect of the deep personal satisfaction that accrues from Outdoor Adventure work with young people. There may also be a place for publicly funded 'taster experiences' aimed at potential leaders who are toying with the idea of taking up outdoor leadership; to redress the current imbalance, these could be targetted mainly on women and ethnic minorities.

# Selection

10.9    Although Outdoor Adventure has a great tradition of dedicated, unpaid voluntary leadership (e.g. teachers in their spare time as scout-leaders helping some of the 14,000 scouts who venture overseas each year), full-time leaders belong to a relatively ill-paid profession. Some professionals discourage voluntary workers because of their effect on pay-bargaining positions, and argue that if society wants to attract more leaders it should pay them more. In practice, however, it is most unlikely that curtailment of voluntary effort would significantly enhance material benefits for paid leaders; and even if it did, it would probably reduce the number of professionals that employers could afford. Therefore, if the scale of Outdoor Adventure is to be maintained, the arguments for attracting leaders must continue to rely heavily on the not inconsiderable intrinsic rewards that derive from outdoor work with young people.

10.10 Although most providing organisations doubtless exercise great care in selecting suitable staff, current practice is patchy, inclined to be unsystematic, and leaves too much to chance. The selection procedures advocated by such professional bodies as the Institute of Personnel Management have much to offer employing organisations, and are well established in much of industry and commerce, as well as in the uniformed services, although they are less well developed in parts of the education and youth service, and rather too formal for small voluntary organisations and groups.

10.11 The key elements in the process are:

1. A job specification, which describes the context, responsibilities and demands of the job;
2. A person specification, which describes the personal qualities, experience, knowledge and skills required to do the job;
3. Reliable information about the candidate (achievements, aptitudes, qualifications etc.)
4. A process of job application (provision of CV), short-listing, interviewing, testing, vetting (taking up references), which enables a selector to assess how far a particular candidate meets the person specification and fits the job.

Even for voluntary organisations the adoption of an informal version would help to reinforce applied common sense and guard against the appointment of unsuitable leaders.

10.12 As a backcloth to selection, no organisation should ignore the equal opportunities issue; statistically, women and ethnic minorities are noticeably under-represented in outdoor leadership positions. Expansion of youth opportunities depends in part on this imbalance being redressed.

# Responsibilities and Duties of Leaders

10.13 Each job specification will be particular to the context, but certain responsibilities are general. Any leader is responsible to:

— Young people themselves;
— Their parents, guardians or employers;
— The organisations employing the leader, or for which he/she works voluntarily;
— The guardians of the environment.

10.14 When working with those under 18, the leader is 'in loco parentis' and must legally 'take such responsibility for the care of the group as a careful parent would take of his or her children, having regard to all the circumstances'. Disregard of general principles, current good practice and the accepted standards underlying outdoor activity could constitute negligence, as could bad driving, the use of unsafe vehicles or defective equipment, lack of attention to good hygiene and to physical and emotional health. Moreover, the leader's professional responsibility is to provide a satisfying, challenging and developmental experience, conserving that ingredient of risk which is inherent in the spirit of daring, without hazarding the safety of those in their charge.

10.15 The responsibility to the parents, guardians or employers, in addition to the foregoing, is to see that they are well informed about the nature of the activities and the accompanying hazards, and to secure their written agreement to participation. Further contractual responsibilities to an employer may apply.

10.16 Leaders must follow the policies and regulations of their own organisations and work within their limits, seeking approval for any significant departure from normal practice.

10.17 So far as the environment is concerned, the leader's responsibility is to safeguard it, observing the Country Code and any other such guidance or regulations in force where the activities take place.

# Competences

10.18 'Competence' goes beyond 'capability' (possession of skills) and 'professionalism' is not to be equated with paper qualifications. Many leaders qualified only by experience are more competent at achieving results than those who have simply taken an award-bearing course. Competence can therefore be found in experienced, voluntary, unpaid leaders no less than incompetence in paid, full-time, so-called 'professionals'. To see why, it is necessary to unravel the components of competence.

10.19 The competences of a leader form part of the person specification and may be grouped into four areas:

1    The Outdoor Skills
     These include both activity skills, such as the techniques of canoeing or climbing and the environmental skills such as navigating, bivouacing, reading the weather, identifying hazards and so on.
2    The Human Skills
     These are the skills of working with groups of young people, and dealing with individuals as a counsellor or tutor.
3    Conceptual Knowledge
     This includes an understanding of learning processes, a grounding in outdoor pursuits, a knowledge of environmental matters and nature, and appreciation of the educational and social background of the young people involved.
4    Personal Qualities
     These include a positive interest in young people, self-awareness, the ability to inspire, sensitivity to people, the environment and situations, a sense of values, common sense (especially with regard to risks) and sound judgement — the glue that binds all the other components together.

# Standards of Competence and their Assessment

10.20 It is government policy to have occupational standards in place for all paid occupations by 1991; responsibility for achieving this in the field of training and development is vested in the 'lead body' for this occupational area, which was set up by the Training Agency in 1988, and which covers both vocational and non-vocational training. There is as yet no lead body for educational occupations.

10.21 The standards of competence required to work with young people in adventurous activities depend on the degree of physical and psychological risk, on the experience and maturity of the group and on whether the leader is operating alone or as part of a team (the value of having two or more staff members, both for educational and safety reasons, should not be under-estimated).

10.22 Standards and qualifications in outdoor skills have been established by the national governing bodies for each activity, affiliated to the Sports Council. Most of these bodies award coaching and proficiency certificates for instructors and leaders in mountaineering, caving, canoeing, sailing etc. The main emphasis in these qualifications is on technical knowledge and skills, including emergency procedures, but they also may include basic elements of organisation, leadership, instruction and party management. For instance, the Mountainwalking Leader Training Board provides a hillwalking leader's training scheme which incorporates an assessment of technical competence, and the British Mountaineering Council oversees a scheme of training and assessment for mountain instructors. Such schemes offer few safeguards on personal qualities, and for this reason are viewed by some organisations as being inadequate of themselves to meet their needs for work with young people. Recently the Central Council for Physical Recreation has introduced the Basic Expedition Training Award (BETA), mainly to meet the needs of voluntary workers.

10.23 The Sports Council National Centres all offer outdoor training and coaching courses in the major outdoor pursuits. Plas y Brenin (Sports Council) and Glenmore Lodge (Scottish Sports Council) cover most mountain activities, and Plas Menai (Sports Council for Wales) and Inverclyde National Sports Centre (Scottish Sports Council) specialise primarily in water-based activities. Plas y Brenin also provides a more broadly-based ten-week course for aspirant leaders and instructors and their development plan includes the proposal to train youth and community workers through links with Regional Sports Council offices. Plas y Brenin, in addition, works jointly with Plas Menai in providing a ten-week outdoor training experience covering both water and mountain activities. Both Plas Menai and Plas y Brenin also provide extended training programmes for aspirant instructors which include up to three months' intensive outdoor training and a longer period working as an assistant instructor.

10.24 Qualifications in the human skills area are offered by professional organisations such as the Institutes of Training and Development (ITD) and of Personnel Management (IPM), but in the past they have been mainly oriented towards vocational training in industry and commerce. The Royal Society of Arts (RSA) also offers qualifications, for example, in vocational preparation and counselling, and the City and Guilds offers the 924 Youth Trainers' Award which has relevance to the development of young people out-of-doors.

10.25 The ITD has recently submitted for approval to the National Council for Vocational Qualifications (NCVQ) a Certificate in the Practice and Management of Human Resource Development, which includes a development training option. This Certificate, which is probably to be piloted in 1989 and will replace the existing ITD Certificate, lists competences and performance criteria, and is accompanied by a guide to their assessment. It is intended to develop a Diploma at a more advanced level.

10.26 Another recent innovation is a competency-based qualification in education management, being developed by the RSA, and likely to be relevant to those in charge of outdoor education centres and those responsible for training, coaching, supporting and supervising other leaders (including volunteers and part-timers). It will be partly based on the assessment of a portfolio of accredited experience. The lead body in management (National Forum for Management Education and Development: i.e. the Management Charter Initiative) is also developing competency frameworks, a code of practice and qualifications, which could also prove useful to managers of outdoor adventure organisations.

10.27 In large voluntary youth organisations and the youth service, there are certificated leadership skills courses (eg the Voluntary Leader's Certificate of the National Association of Boys' Clubs), qualifying courses such as those resulting from the Bessey Report (1962), and various advanced or specialist courses which lead to a certificate. However, these were developed before the recent emphasis on 'competency frameworks' and may therefore be excessively didactic by today's standards, that is, based unduly on imparting expert information.

10.28 Standards of conceptual knowledge are mainly set by universities, polytechnics and colleges, offering certificates, diplomas and degrees. Those that specialise in the field sciences and environmental subjects, perhaps followed by a Post-graduate Certificate in Education (PGCE), and those leading to a Certificate in Youth and Community Service or of Leisure Management are favoured routes to outdoor qualifications. However, the principal value of such academic qualifications is in attesting to the body of knowledge that the holders have acquired and can reproduce in exams; they do not usually guarantee any particular level of skill in applying such knowledge in practical situations. There is therefore a real danger in managing bodies relying on the illusory safeguard of paper qualifications, without taking the skills and personality factors into account.

10.29 Several of the colleges that provide specialised Outdoor Education courses make deliberate attempts to develop practical skills and experience with young people. For instance the Charlotte Mason College in Cumbria includes within its 4-year BEd course in Outdoor and Environmental Education considerable practical outdoor and expedition experience, and also involvement with young people in the locality. Moray House in Edinburgh offers a one-year course leading to a diploma in Outdoor Education and the University College of North Wales in Bangor a one-year PGCE. Both courses arrange for 3 or 4 week secondments or teaching practice at established outdoor centres.

10.30 The weakest area covered by standards, assessment procedures and therefore, accreditation and qualifications, is that of personal qualities; yet it is probably the most important of all. Judgement, common sense, wisdom, imagination, integrity and other such qualities are notoriously difficult to assess. Despite this, it is of paramount importance that such qualities are viewed as indispensable components of competence. Although psychometric tests can be used and probably have a part to play in assessing some of these qualities objectively, it is more usual to rely on the subjective judgements of experienced peers and managers in the organisation to which the leader belongs. This approach is implicit in the recommendations in the booklet "Starting from Strengths" (National Youth Bureau, 1984) which, although directed at youth work in general, contains much valuable guidance applicable to the development and accreditation of outdoor leaders, and some sound principles for their effective training.

10.31 In order to establish a bank of information that can be used to make reliable assessments of personal qualities, and to set appropriate standards, it is important that organisations providing outdoor experiences should have systematic procedures for recording the performance of their staff and for regularly appraising them; the individual can also help by keeping a log book. This enables strengths and shortcomings to be properly identified and dealt with, either through team selection or through individual training and development.

10.32 In summary, although adequate standards and assessment and accreditation procedures have been developed for some aspects of leader competence, the general picture is patchy and incoherent. The state of progress in 1989 is that there exist a number of useful papers (mostly in, or cited in, recent issues of the journal 'Adventure Education') and reports (for example "The Competences of Development Trainers" and "The Selection and Recruitment of Development Trainers" — both sponsored by the MSC or Training Agency and undertaken by DTAG). There are several current initiatives aimed at applying these ideas and approaches to improving the present unsatisfactory situation, but much work remains to be done.

10.33 Little progress has been made in developing the corresponding competency-based standards in educational occupations. There is clearly a need for further research and development in establishing occupational standards and assessment procedures in both training and education.

# *Training and Development of Leaders*

10.34 It is only when standards of competence have been established that relevant and cost-effective training programmes can be designed to enable the leader to attain the standards required for the particular set of activities undertaken in a particular environment with the particular types of learning group with which he or she operates. Too often in the past, training has been teacher-centred, based on a deficiency model and has failed to address the real needs of the learners and to build on their strengths.

10.35 Existing provision is varied, but somewhat hit-and-miss. Different approaches to training leaders have been developed in the armed services and cadet forces, youth clubs, the LEA youth service, the uniformed youth organisations (Guides, Boys' Brigade etc.), education institutions and the major providers of Outdoor Adventure (Endeavour, Outward Bound, etc.)

10.36 Programmes of formal education and basic training leading to the qualifications already mentioned are available in a variety of educational institutions and training centres. In addition, there is a range of short (2-3 day) training events in such topics as 'Using drama in reviewing', 'Using creative techniques in development training' and 'Safe practice using ropes courses'. With the help of some pump-priming funding by the Training Agency, these are offered under the auspices of Accredited Training Centres and the various regional Associations of Residential Providers (Scotland, Wales, Cumbria, Derbyshire and soon the South and South-West).

10.37 Although the problems of co-ordination are prodigious, there may be scope for establishing a modular approach to training, in which participation in a linked series of such short courses might count towards a progressive sequence of relevant 'new-look' qualifications. Given the crucial part that practical experience plays, according to the study, in the development of leaders, the best route to a qualification probably consists of a mixture of:

1) a basic foundation course in an educational institution and/or training centre, including formal instruction in safety procedures, first aid, rescue and incident management;
2) a coherent series of short modules in specific professional skills, including refresher training for more experienced leaders;
3) accredited experience of performing in a leadership role, formally appraised within a providing institution of good standing (as in the 'teaching hospital' approach); and (perhaps as a more practicable alternative to (3) in small isolated units)
4) regular opportunities to meet in peer groups to share and review one another's practice, preferably under the guidance of a professional group leader able to maximise mutual learning by disciplined analysis and creative work; the tangible outcome from this process would be individual 'learning logs' and 'portfolios of reviewed experience'.

10.38 While experience obtained in performing the leadership role is of central importance in developing competence, learning from experience must not be left to chance, however natural it may seem. It has to be systematised in some way, so that it becomes habitual and effective. The 'experiential learning cycle' describes the process by which this is best achieved: (action -> reflection -> conceptualisation -> application -> action...).

10.39 Although individuals carry clear responsibility for their own continuing learning and professional development, the process is greatly assisted if supervisors and peers are involved. Appraisal, counselling, coaching and mentoring are all part of a development culture which it is the responsibility of the organisation (employing or voluntary) to foster, striking an appropriate balance between formality and informality. If such continuity and effective monitoring are accepted as important, then presumably the long-established and permanently-based Outdoor Adventure organisations have the advantage over seasonal, mobile or isolated operations, even of well-established national voluntary organisations.

10.40 It is implicit in the foregoing that the 'professional route' is by no means the only route to competent leaders. However, one of the most marked differences of view to emerge from the study has been the different perceptions of competence. On the one hand, there are those who maintain that in an area of physical and psychological risk, it is only justifiable to involve young people if they are professionally led; in this context, 'professional' leadership means holding a teaching or youth leadership qualification, and it follows that a 'voluntary' leader would, by implication, be less competent. On the other hand, there are those for whom voluntary and/or part-time helpers are essential to their programme, and without whom outdoor work with young people would be unable to continue.

10.41 If the first view prevails, then clearly the task of finding, training and paying large numbers of additional full-time leaders to enable more young people to venture outdoors will be impracticable. Moreover, it is by no means proven that the most competent leadership is always 'professional' in the above sense. There is ample evidence that in-service training and development, alongside experienced and able mentors, and using well-tried experiential learning methods, will enable well-selected aspirant leaders without currently recognised professional qualifications to develop sufficient competence to enable them quickly to work confidently and safely with young people, albeit at a low level at first. Models for this form of staff development are not hard to find: for instance in the work of the Scouts, who have a very carefully constructed system for the development internally of their own leaders from the young people who pass through the movement; or in Outward Bound with its long tradition of allowing new and inexperienced instructors to work alongside older and more experienced staff members who act as mentors. At the same time, those who follow the practical route to competence should be encouraged to work for relevant qualifications, based on accredited experience, so as continually to enhance their professional acceptablility and attest to the proven quality of their work.

## Systems of Management and Accountability

10.42 A key requirement for safe conduct of outdoor ventures is the existence of a clearly understood management and accountability structure. However, any system of management must be sufficiently flexible and simple to support rather than hinder; the heavy hand of bureaucracy is inappropriate.

10.43 The management superstructure may include, for example, the local education authority; the board of governors or management of a school or educational trust; the head, principal or director; a head of department; the excursion leader. Each level of management or supervision carries some responsibility for the safe and successful conduct of the overall operation, and this needs to be spelled out and communicated. The recently published booklet, "Outdoor Education Safety and Good Practice" jointly produced by the Association of Heads of Outdoor Education Centres, the National Association of Field Studies Officers and the National Association for Outdoor Education, contains useful guidelines and caveats.

10.44 Many larger organisations appoint staff members responsible for the general oversight of all Outdoor Adventure programmes; they are able to assess the appropriateness of each venture, to appraise the competence of the leaders involved and to provide further training where necessary. The Adviser for Outdoor Education in the LEA, or the Director of Training in the full-time residential centre, carry this responsibility, which provides an important check on each outdoor venture or programme.

10.45 Although most of this chapter has been concerned with the selection and development of leaders in the field, it would be foolhardy to suppose that no action is required with those who supervise them. In the words of the White Paper on Employment for the 1990s:

> *"Everybody can benefit from training. Nobody is too old, too junior or too senior or in too specialised a job."*

## 10.46 *Summary*

(a) The encouragement of recruitment and training of potential leaders, both paid and voluntary, and of the development of occupational standards of competence, should form an explicit part of public policy on education and training. (10.4, 10.33)

(b) Public funding is required to subsidise the training of voluntary leaders, by means of courses specifically designed to meet their needs, including 'taster courses' for women and ethnic minorities. (10.3, 10.8, 10.34, 10.36)

(c) Existing leaders should act as talent-spotters and personally persuade and guide young potential leaders into leadership roles. (10.7, 10.8)

(d) Selection procedures, suitably adapted, should reflect good practice elsewhere. (10.10, 10.12)

(e) Providing organisations should operate systematic procedures for appraisal and professional development, utilising and accrediting practical experience to the full. (10.31, 10.41)

(f) Award-giving bodies should develop a more coherent and comprehensive system of occupational standards, which define and assess competences and accredit experience. (10.25, 10.32)

(g) They should collectively aim to devise a progressive series of relevant qualifications that attest to all-round competence (including personal qualities); this may require funding. (10.3, 10.22 — 32)

(h) Training programmes should consist of a basic foundation course, plus a series of linked short modules plus (especially) supervised and accredited experience in an organisation of good standing and/or the opportunity to share, review and learn systematically from experience, to be recorded in a learning log or portfolio. (10.37)

(i) Responsibility for post-basic training should be shared between the individual and employing (or voluntary) organisation. (10.39)

(j) A development culture, including in-service training opportunities, should be fostered by those who manage providing institutions. (10.39, 10.45)

(k) All institutions providing Outdoor Adventure should have in place a system of management accountability.(10.42, 10.43)

# CHAPTER 11

## THE ENVIRONMENTAL IMPLICATIONS OF OUTDOOR ADVENTURE

*"The children have learned that nature possesses exquisite beauty; that she is fragile yet formidable; delicate yet omnipotent; but all the same inevitably responds to the human touch. They discovered that their horizons expand with their senses — that with feeling comes understanding. And with time comes the vital realization that there is both much to understand and much to lose. For a very small act of man can have devastating consequences."*

*(Steve van Matre, "Acclimatization", 1971)*

# *The General Background*

11.1 This chapter is primarily concerned with the environmental impact of Outdoor Adventure programmes in Britain; a parallel effect occurs overseas, when young people travel to Europe and further afield.

11.2 Outdoor Adventure programmes currently take place against a background of rapidly growing 'green' consciousness amongst the public at large, who are increasingly concerned about environmental issues, both local and global. Outdoor education programmes to some degree reflect and exemplify the wider public interest. There is a general recognition of the value of educating young people for greater environmental awareness.

11.3 UNESCO has stated the goals of environmental education as follows:

1. *To foster awareness of, and concern about, economic, social, political and ecological interdependence in urban and rural areas,*
2. *To provide every person with opportunities to acquire the knowledge, values, attitudes, commitment and skills needed to protect and improve the environment,*
3. *To create new patterns of behaviour of individuals, groups and society as a whole towards the environment.*

11.4　More recently the Department of Education and Science, in the booklet "Environmental Education from 5 to 16" (HMI Series; Curriculum Matters No. 13) has suggested there are four overlapping components for environmental education. These are:

－ *curiosity and awareness about the environment,*
－ *knowledge and understanding,*
－ *skills,*
－ *informed concern.*

11.5　The incorporation of such environmental values into Outdoor Adventure programmes is no new development. This approach was emphasised at the conference held at Dartington in 1975, where the aims of outdoor education were defined as:

*"To heighten awareness and foster respect for*
*－ Self – through the meeting of challenge (adventure)*
*－ Others – through group experience and the sharing of decisions*
*－ The natural environment – through direct experience"*

In relation to the environment, the following specific objectives were identified:

－ *To develop an affinity with, and awareness of, the natural environment;*
－ *To value natural beauty;*
－ *To observe and describe the immediate environment;*
－ *To explain natural forms and processes, including weather;*
－ *To interpret the development of the environment;*
－ *To accept the importance of conservation;*
－ *To stimulate the imagination.*

11.6　Most Outdoor Adventure programmes taking place today reflect these values and accept these objectives to some degree. However they also make some adverse impact upon the environment in which they take place. This may take one of three forms;

1)　Physical degradation of the environment by direct pressure of use.
2)　Disturbance of the ecological balance and wildlife to be found in the outdoor environment.

3) Impact upon the communities visited.

11.7    Damage to the environment caused by participants in Outdoor Adventure programmes for youth represents a small part of the total wear and tear caused by outdoor activities in general. There has been a general increase in the use of open country for outdoor recreation since 1945, made possible by increasing affluence and better means of access. The Countryside Commission, the Sports Council and other agencies have encouraged participation in outdoor sports. In the Lake District National Park alone, it has been estimated by the Special Planning Board that the number of visitors each year is between 12 and 15 million.

11.8    Many young people visit the countryside independently, often for a day visit, and some may have little knowledge of the environmental implications of their activities. However, it seems that young people taking part in well-organised schemes of Outdoor Adventure experience, with proper supervision, contribute relatively little to the total environmental degradation caused by visitors.

11.9    The study has indicated that the majority of providers of Outdoor Adventure programmes are aware of the possibility that their activities may potentially cause some impact upon the natural environment. However, although most people consulted expressed concern for the maintenance of the environment, a large proportion considered that, in the case of their own programmes, there is either little or no adverse effect, or that the net impact is positive, in that they are increasing ecological awareness and engaging in practical conservation work. Many providers and users felt that their presence in the countryside contributes to, rather than detracts from, the life of the local community. Two specific ways in which Outdoor Adventure programmes are thought to have a positive impact, are by providing employment for local people and by boosting the local economy. The greatest concern expressed by respondents to the questionnaire lay in the recognition that certain specific areas are over-used for adventure activities.

11.10   The Dartington Amenity Research Trust report "Groups in the Countryside", published in 1980, drew attention to the *"rapid and large scale growth in demand for group activity in the countryside".* The report suggested that the total scale of field studies, outdoor pursuits and other activities (including trips in the urban fringe, special interest holidays, etc.) in England and Wales was of the order of 20 million person-days each year, of which approximately 40% take place in the National Parks. It seems likely that there has been a sizeable further increase in the past 10 years, as outdoor programmes and organisations have proliferated.

# *Enhancing Awareness*

11.11 Considerable progress has been made in improving awareness of the problems caused by concentrated or excessive use of the outdoor environment by young people. Of the individuals consulted in the questionnaire, almost two-thirds already include an element of environmental or conservation work in their activities. There was some evidence of a degree of complacency, however, about the environmental impact of their own work.

11.12 Those who accepted that they make some negative impact, mentioned erosion of routes, crags and campsites, making too much noise and the practice of using fires. On the other hand, the more general view was that, by taking young people out of doors, their ecological awareness was increased, and thus further environmental damage would be lessened. One senior ranger wrote:*"a positive experience in the environment should lead to a positive response to the environment"*.

11.13 Factors which have enhanced understanding of the dangers to the outdoor environment are as follows:

a) The general development of a broader environmental awareness in the community at large, through disasters such as Chernobyl, and through increasing 'green' awareness, through the press and broadcasting media and, as a consequence of these influences, the impact on Parliament.
b) The increasing concern expressed by the national professional bodies involved in outdoor education, such as the National Association for Outdoor Education, the National Association for Environmental Education, the National Association of Field Study Officers and the Association of Heads of Outdoor Education Centres.
c) The development of campaigns and conferences such as "Watch over the National Parks" and those instituted by the "Adventure and Environmental Awareness" movement, focused primarily on work in the Lake District.
d) The establishment of schools and youth liaison services in the National Parks, working in co-operation with the Parks' Ranger Services.

e) The institution of Ranger Services by the Recreation and Leisure departments of local authorities, which include environmental education as a major element in their programmes.

f) The increasing commitment by the national governing bodies of sport to the principles of conservation, as exemplified in the appointment of Conservation Officers by the *National Caving Association* and the *Cambrian Caving Council*, and the adoption of appropriate policies by the *British Mountaineering Council.*

g) The development of codes of practice for those who use the outdoors for sport or education.

h) The growth of the 'earth awareness' movement, with the introduction of sensory awareness exercises in the natural environment.

11.14 The report entitled "Sport, Recreation and Nature Conservation", published in 1989 jointly by the Countryside Commission and the Sports Council, and launched in conjunction with the Nature Conservancy Council, investigates the extent to which the interests of nature conservation and sport and recreation are in conflict. The report concerns itself with all recreational use of the outdoors and not simply use by youth groups. It concludes that recreational disturbance and damage are relatively insignificant when compared to the major environmental threats of pollution or loss of habitat. The report nevertheless cautions that local impacts can be serious and should not be minimised; it suggests that there is much scope for co-operation between recreational and conservation interests. The Countryside Commission and the Sports Council are co-operating in a variety of strategies and actions involving land and coastal areas.

# *Differing Interests*

11.15 There are a number of other interest groups with which the Outdoor Adventure protagonist may be involved. These are the owners of land, residents in areas visited, those with a conservation interest, and other recreational or educational users.

11.16 Owners have traditionally been private landowners or syndicates gaining benefit from outdoor facilities, such as angling or shooting interests, and in Scotland the large deer-stalking estates. However there have also been disagreements with private forestry groups and in future these may occur with the privatised water authorities. The Ministry of Defence also controls and restricts access to some high quality environments otherwise suitable for outdoor recreation use.

11.17 Residents in the areas most frequently used for Outdoor Adventure sometimes tend to be inconvenienced by visiting groups. Farmers are most directly affected, but disturbance is also caused to shopkeepers and retired people living in attractive country areas. The problem is made worse when youth groups visit local public houses. In some remote areas such as the Western Isles or parts of Wales, the social and cultural norms of the residents and the visiting parties may be widely different.

11.18 Those seeking Outdoor Adventure may come into conflict, sometimes unwittingly, with the interests of nature conservation. The wisdom of allowing large-scale access to sensitive habitats is a matter of continuing concern and debate. Examples of more sensitive areas are identified later in this chapter.

11.19 Different groups of visitors to the countryside may find themselves in conflict with each other, or in competition for the same resources. The disagreements between anglers and canoeists are of long standing and are largely unresolved, despite many efforts at national level. There is a conflict between the users of trail bikes, four-wheel drive vehicles and power boats, and those who prefer a slower pace and peace and quiet. Pony-trekkers chew up the bridle-paths which others wish to walk on, and young people learning to abseil or rock-climb may have to queue for their turn on popular training crags, which may be used by several organisations simultaneously.

11.20 These problems are not easily resolved, and they have to be approached with sensitivity if young people are to have expanding opportunities to find adventures out-of-doors. Goodwill and understanding are the prerequisites, and these are directly related to responsible behaviour and good communication.

11.21 The major national bodies concerned with conservation of, and access to, the countryside, who were consulted during the study, take a positive view of the prospect of more young people visiting remote areas which are designated for protection, in the next ten years. The general opinion appears to be that there is sufficient space for more activities off the beaten tracks and that further damage can be avoided, provided that programmes include learning about the countryside and those who live there,; and provided that there is good management in exercising control and in avoiding already over-used areas. The Council for the Preservation of Rural England (CPRE), for example, believes that *"the balance of advantage lies firmly in extending and enhancing the opportunities for young people to enjoy the countryside ... through such experiences they will come to appreciate and care for the survival of our countryside."*

# Impacts on Landscapes and Seascape

11.22 The principal impacts upon the physical environment caused by youth groups are as follows:

   a)  Careless disposal of litter on land and rubbish at sea or in lakes, rivers and canals.
   b)  General erosion of sites of heavy use, e.g. footpaths, base of crags, sites for problem solving exercises.
   c)  Damage to water-edge locations caused by launching of canoes or other craft and by access for raft-building.
   d)  Damage to underground caves and mines, destruction of mineral formations, litter and graffiti, removal of artefacts.
   e)  Problems associated with camping; destruction of vegetation, ditch-digging, rock excavation, waste disposal, litter.
   f)  Impact upon woodland habitats caused by repeated use of regular orienteering courses.
   g)  Damage to areas containing special flora or physical features, particularly in Sites of Special Scientific Interest, (SSSIs), and stream ghylls.
   h)  Use of horses, mountain bikes or powered trail bikes in open country.
   i)  Competitive mass participation in cross-country events.

# Impacts upon Communities

11.23 The principal pressures imposed on local communities by visiting youth groups are as follows:

   a)  Noise, particularly at night, which may be exacerbated by drunkenness and foul language.
   b)  Litter and occasionally thoughtless or deliberate vandalism.
   c)  Fieldwork and surveys which involve questioning local people.

d) Intimidating or aggressive behaviour and theft of property.

e) Dangerous driving, either by students if they have use of their personal transport, or by staff.

f) Lack of understanding of, and respect for, the local culture or way of life such as failure to respect the Sabbath.

g) Damage to the livelihood of farmers by leaving gates open, damaging walls or fences, disturbing stock.

h) 'Wide Games' which are often carried out at night to test problem solving skills or map-reading.

i) Overcrowding of shops, inns and other local facilities.

It should be emphasised that such difficulties are not widely experienced, but they do occur where residential centres or camps are situated close to, or within, established communities, and where supervision is poor.

## *Examples of Repeated Use: Larger Areas*

11.24 Extensive areas of wild country in Britain are already under great pressure from recreational and educational use. Most of this arises from the general influx of visitors and tourists seeking active recreation, rather than from Outdoor Adventure youth groups. Nevertheless, such groups are occasionally identified as a cause of physical damage or nuisance in these areas.

11.25 In some areas, particularly National Parks which are close to urban areas, the combination of day-visitor pressure and large numbers of residential establishments leads to a heavy concentration of use for Outdoor Adventure. In the Peak District, for instance, the Castleton and Edale valley area, Dovedale, and the Kinder Scout plateau, where the start of the Pennine Way exacerbates the problem, are subject to particularly heavy use. In Snowdonia, the popular mountain massifs of Yr Wyddfa, the Glyders and the Ogwen valley are much used. In the Lake District, the Helvellyn massif, Windermere, and the Borrowdale and Langdale valleys are under considerable pressure. The summits of the Beacons are becoming very heavily eroded in the Brecon Beacons National Park.

11.26 Outside the National Parks, there is less evidence of pressure over a wide area, although individual locations are often subject to intensive use from youth groups. The establishment of Country Parks, or other accessible areas for recreation near the major cities, such as the *Lea Valley project*, has provided important additional opportunities. Some Areas of Outstanding Natural Beauty, (AONBs), such as parts of the River Wye and the Mendips, may experience comparable levels of use to the National Parks. Two areas which are significant for their potential for water recreation are the Norfolk Broads, and the Solent. The scale of recreational use in both areas has recently been the subject of study. The establishment of the Broads Authority, with a status equivalent to a National Park, and the publication of "Hampshire's Coast", a discussion document published by Hampshire County Council as part of the European Year of the Environment, reflect increasing concern to balance recreational, environmental, educational and economic interests in these areas.

11.27 In Scotland, where open spaces are on a larger scale than in England and Wales, the pressure upon open countryside from recreational use is less intense. However some Regional Parks or National Scenic Areas, such as Loch Lomond, the Glencoe and Ben Nevis areas and the Trossachs, all experience substantial and increasing numbers of visitors. The Countryside Commission for Scotland have expressed their concern about the deterioration of mountain footpaths.

11.28 The Cairngorms and, to a lesser extent, Glen Shee present special problems. As the main focus of the Scottish skiing industry, these areas have built up an extensive network of residential resources and supporting facilities, and they attract a substantial summer use. There is, therefore, an increasing opportunity for Outdoor Adventure for young people. Whilst the main focus of skiing activity is confined to a relatively small area, the subsidiary effects, both in winter and summer, are felt over a much wider area. These areas are visited increasingly by young people from all over Britain.

# *Examples of Repeated Use: Particular Areas*

11.29 Some specific popular locations show the effect of heavy use by youth groups. The following six examples are chosen to illustrate the possible effects of water recreation, underground exploration, environmental studies, group and teambuilding exercises, rock-climbing skills training and competitive cross-country events.

(a)   The River Wye at Glasbury is heavily used by a concentration of youth canoe groups. The river has a right of navigation and therefore attracts canoeists who may not be able to gain access to rivers elsewhere. The river is particularly suitable for novices encountering white water for the first time, but has limited access points. Many groups use the main pool at Glasbury bridge for skills training and also to launch for journeys downstream to Hay-on-Wye and beyond.

(b)   In South Wales, the Porth yr Ogof cave system near Ystradfellte is much used by parties of young people both from outdoor centres and from nearby schools. The cave allows a 'through trip' and also affords the chance to study a river which goes underground and later reappears. The entrance to the underground system is easily accessible by vehicle, and the cave system therefore lends itself to day or half-day trips.

(c)   Malham Tarn in Yorkshire is an upland tarn alongside a raised peat bog, situated to the north of the limestone crags at Malham Cove. It is the site of a well-known Field Studies Council centre, and is also much visited by young people on geographical field trips because of the special interest of the limestone pavement and the other natural features nearby, such as Gordale Scar. The tarn itself is environmentally and scenically unique. It presents a fragile habitat which would rapidly be destroyed under the pressure of outdoor education use if it were not protected.

(d)   Tilberthwaite Ghyll in the Lake District is a natural ravine much used by outdoor centres and other educational users as a location for ghyll-scrambling, group problem solving and environmental appreciation. The ghyll contains a wide variety of plant communities, ranging from woodland to arctic/alpine flora, which have survived because they are inaccessible to sheep. The present level of use by parties of young people presents a threat to the survival of the vegetation in the ghyll. Local residents have indicated their concern about the growing use of the ghyll, and the disturbance it causes.

(e)   Shepherds Crag in Borrowdale is another heavily used Lake District location. It offers a number of excellent rock-climbs for beginners in a relatively accessible location which is sheltered from bad weather. It is popular with climbers, and also with outdoor education parties. The beginners' routes are often crowded, and there are difficulties over vehicle parking. Not infrequently, there are problems of litter, and of noise and disturbance when several youth parties are present. Commenting on the over-use of such crags for climbing, the British Mountaineering Council

(BMC) suggests; *"wherever possible, existing urban resources should be utilised. For example, railway bridges and walls, including artificial climbing walls."*

(f) The Ten Tors expedition on Dartmoor, organised by the Army and held at Easter each year, exemplifies a different problem. Over two thousand young people set out in teams to complete an arduous walk between the Ten Tors checkpoints, with a camp en route. The intensity of use is related to the short period of time for which the event lasts rather than to the limited area involved, since the walkers spread out widely across the Moor. The safety and logistical back-up for the event and the preliminary training, as well as the numbers of participants, create a significant impact upon the Moor itself at the time of the event, and upon the surrounding communities.

# *Increasing Use of Overseas Environments*

11.30 In parallel with the growth of Outdoor Adventure in Britain, there is an increasing trend for parties of young people to travel overseas in search of adventure or for scientific and expedition purposes. Just as in Britain, such parties may cause physical damage to the environment, disturbance of the natural ecosystems and have an adverse impact upon local communities. This report is not able to assess the amount of damage caused at present, but some areas are already heavily and repeatedly used.

11.31 The River Ardeche in France is a popular venue for canoe camps and expeditions; some Alpine ski resorts are visited by hundreds of British children each winter; certain areas of Iceland, Norway and Kenya are popular youth expedition destinations. All these areas and others are used on an increasing scale by youth parties from many countries. Whilst overseas travel is much to be encouraged, the effects of such ventures need careful assessment. There is a need for accurate and up-to-date information on appropriate projects, the sensitivity of certain areas, or the cultural contrasts to be expected. The *Young Explorers' Trust* and the *Expedition Advisory Centre* of the Royal Geographical Society provide as much as their resources permit.

11.32 At the same time, there are those who believe there is an increasingly important role for expeditions, large or small, at home or overseas, to contribute through education and training to global environmental issues. If properly advised, teachers and others concerned with young people can secure a lifetime interest and commitment to the environment through the expedition experience. Furthermore there is growing interest among environmental and conservation organisations to harness the resources of school and university expeditions as a new and enthusiastic 'green task-force'

# *Future Approaches*

11.33 The development of sensitive practice in the outdoor environment will follow naturally from an understanding of the environmental considerations outlined in this chapter. The proposals set out in the report "Sport, Recreation and Nature Conservation" (Commissioned by the Sports Council and the Countryside Commission) under the heading "The Way Ahead" stress the importance of achieving improved communication, more effective self-regulation, better planning and management, and a general change of attitudes, concentrating on a creative approach. These principles seem equally appropriate in examining the future relationship of the Outdoor Adventure movement and the environment in which it operates.

11.34 There is a need to convey clearly to all those who encourage Outdoor Adventure for young people the central importance of conserving the outdoor environment and respecting local communities. The two most important concepts are the following:

**Firstly**, that of **'The finite resource'**: the outdoor resource is not unlimited,

**Secondly**, that of **'Sustainable use'**: the outdoor resource must be able to regenerate.

11.35 Even if outdoor adventure activity remains at the same level as at present, there will be considerable longer-term implications for the outdoor environment. If activity increases, those implications are even more important. It is suggested that any strategy designed to address the situation should include the following aspects:

— Understanding the developing situation
— Developing relationships
— Strategic planning
— Management considerations
— Development of practice by adults and by participants
— Corrective actions.

11.36 Understanding the developing situation requires a creative and imaginative approach which recognises the tensions arising from different uses and between different users of the outdoor environment. There is a need to accept that many of those who visit the countryside are not aware of the effect of their actions on the physical environment and on the communities which live there. There needs to be a correct understanding of the aims and values of Outdoor Adventure, and also of the vulnerability of the outdoor environment.

11.37 Relationships need to be developed between all those organisations which have an interest in the countryside, and better communication established between them. There are large numbers of organisations concerned with outdoor recreation and education, between which communication is inadequate. This should be improved, and better channels of communication established with owners, conservation bodies and those who live in communities which may be affected by the activities of visiting groups.

11.38 Strategic planning involves attempting to estimate the total demand or pressure for outdoor experience which is likely to arise, and matching it as carefully as possible to the resources; environmental, residential and tutorial, which are available. If an outdoor exercise takes place in an inappropriate environment, with an unsuitable residential or resource base and with inadequate staffing, then the environment is likely to suffer; and indeed the experience is most unlikely to be satisfactory. Serious consideration should be given to ways of spreading the environmental load, using alternative areas, and investigating less damaging approaches. Particular advantage could derive from a decision to avoid National Parks, perhaps to make greater use of the marine environment as an alternative. In all strategic planning, environmental values must be taken into account fully, as well as the needs of young people.

11.39 The management of each outdoor venture or programme requires a strong environmental consciousness — a 'green' ethic — based on the principle that the outdoor environment should remain available, in a form no less aesthetically, scientifically, as well as physically, fulfilling than at present, for future generations. This requires the formulation of clear statements of principle, policy and practice, which are understood by all leaders and young people involved. The notional 'environmental cost' of each venture should be assessed, and a corresponding 'environmental contribution' should be included in the programme.

11.40  Management will be much concerned with the three-stage process of definition of needs, aims and programmes described in Chapter 8, (8.9). The size of the group, the nature of the tasks undertaken, and the degree of supervision and control are all important management issues, which bear heavily on environmental, as well as on safety requirements.

11.41  Corrective actions are a necessary part of any successful continuing use of the outdoor environment by young people and youth organisations. As far as possible, they should be allowed for in the planning process. Such corrective actions might include the decision to avoid a given area or community, or to include a major restoration project at the site of an over-used facility. Corrective actions should be undertaken in full co-operation with the conservation or planning authorities involved; it is not always possible for young people themselves to carry out the work involved, due to lack of time or appropriate skills. It may be necessary to allow for expenditure for the required resources in the Outdoor Adventure project budget.

## 11.42  *Summary*

(a)  Outdoor Adventure activities are taking place against a background of increasing 'green' consciousness; this is reflected in many outdoor education programmes. (11.2 — 11.7)

(b)  Most providers are aware of the impact their programmes can make on the rural environment, and consider this to be positive. (11.9, 11.11, 11.21)

(c)  National bodies concerned with conservation and public access also take a positive view of increasing numbers of young people in the countryside, subject to safeguards. (11.13, 11.14)

(d)  However, there are differences of interest between visiting groups and local residents, followers of field sports and in regard to nature conservation. (11.15 — 11.20)

(e)  Outdoor Adventure activities in parts of designated areas (e.g. National Parks) and youth expeditions in remoter 'wilderness' areas overseas can create damage, as well as diminish the 'remote' quality of such areas. But the enhanced value of such wider opportunities for Outdoor Adventure are important. (11.30 — 11.32)

(f)  Outdoor Adventure activities make an impact both on the local environment and on those who live in the areas in which they take place. Not all of such impact is adverse. (11.9, 11.12, 11.22 — 11.23)

(g)    Areas under heavy pressure include parts of the National Parks and AONBs, as well as waterways such as the Broads and the Solent. There is a case for avoiding over-used parts of these designated areas. (11.25, 11.26)

(h)    In Scotland, where open spaces are on a larger scale than in England and Wales, the development of skiing as an Outdoor Adventure activity has, in certain areas, had a very damaging effect on the environment. (11.27, 11.28)

(i)    With the growth in trekking and expeditions in Europe and beyond, the adverse impact on the environment is becoming a global problem. (11.30, 11.31)

(j)    The problems of adverse impact should be tackled by better communications, especially among users and between the users of open country for Outdoor Adventure and the local planning authorities; through environmental education, leading to a greater awareness among young people; through good planning and practice by management, based on clearly-stated and commonly-agreed principles. (11.33 — 11.41)

# CHAPTER 12
## THE WAY AHEAD
## STRATEGY AND ACTION

# *General*

12.1   We preface our proposals for future action by drawing attention to the remarkable strength of conviction we have found, on the part of nearly all those consulted, as to the value to young people of Outdoor Adventure experiences. We have been impressed by the widespread and strongly-held belief in the importance of such opportunities; the belief that they may be the key to releasing the constructive energies and initiative of the young, empowering them to personal achievement; and conversely, that the lack of such opportunities may limit the potential of young people.

12.2   This conviction, expressed so widely, is the most impressive outcome of the study. Many of those consulted held that young people are no less idealistic or capable than heretofore, but that many of them are faced with changes and choices which are bewildering. They are conditioned by materialistic values and opportunities which, for many young people, provide a kind of escape from boredom and frustration. Many are living in deprived circumstances. Some display apathetic or rebellious attitudes which are signs of personal dissatisfaction and which do not serve the needs of society. Adventurous experiences out-of-doors are perceived to kindle the enthusiasm of the young, to develop their concern for others, for their community and for the environment. Such experiences provide the means of self-discovery, self-expression and enjoyment which are at once both stimulating and fulfilling. It thus emerges that, for young people and adults alike, Outdoor Adventure is perceived as a vehicle for building values and ideals, for developing creativity and enterprise, for enhancing a sense of citizenship, and for widening physical and spiritual horizons.

12.3   Notwithstanding the strength of these convictions, we recognise that adventurous experience is only one avenue of experience in the lives of young people which can benefit both themselves and society at large. We therefore believe that Outdoor Adventure should be linked with wider national initiatives designed to provide for the needs of youth, and to promote the spirit of enterprise, service in the community and environmental awareness. But we are convinced that, both because of, and despite, the wealth of initiatives already being taken in this field of Outdoor Adventure, more action is called for to extend its benefits to more young people, particularly those living in less advantaged areas: action at every level of administration, both of government and voluntary organisations.

## 12.4 *Strategy*

A strategy for action is needed; *first*, because Outdoor Adventure is a movement of great significance, as the report has revealed; *second*, because it involves such a wide range of people, interests, organisations and departments of state; and *third* because much of what is needed is about changing attitudes. The fragmented, diffuse and varied nature of adventurous activity makes it difficult to develop an overall strategy.

12.5    Experience in other fields suggests that the approach should be systematic; strategically planned and led, rather than piecemeal and haphazard. The government is using 'task forces' to spearhead innovation in a number of spheres, and a similar device will be needed to give further thrust to the the St. George's House initiative, which gave rise to this report.

12.6    The first step after the publication of this report should be the appointment and mandating of an individual or body who will carry forward the initiative and facilitate the steps needed to make further progress. The specific recommendations that follow should be a help to get this 'prime mover' off to a good start.

12.7    Task groups may have to be set up to close the gaps between how things are and how they should be; these could draw upon a range of techniques for problem solving, action planning, commitment planning and responsibility assignment, that have been found helpful in previous successful attempts at strategic change. There are, in industry and in private practice, consultants on managing change who could offer valuable advice to whatever 'steering groups' or 'task groups' are set up. We advise that their expertise should be tapped.

12.8    At some point, mandates will have to be sought: to set up local conferences, and to authorise 'prime movers' to make whatever is agreed happen. Here again, there are techniques for gaining commitment to these endeavours. If several task groups are at work, there will be a need for a local 'steering group' or some such body to orchestrate support and monitor the work, and a similar 'lead body' will be required at national level. Such a body will need a mandate from government and some administrative support.

## 12.9 *Key Strategic Questions*

In the light of our findings, the key strategic questions are: Where are we now? Where do we wish to be in five years' time? How might we get there?

## 12.10 *Where Are We Now?*

One of the main aims of this study has been to establish what is already happening as far as purposive outdoor activities for young people is concerned. Although the findings do not derive from a fully comprehensive, in-depth survey, the study has revealed widespread development of the use of the outdoors for educational, training, developmental and recreational purposes. Furthermore, there are some significant social, economic and educational trends that will encourage even greater use of the countryside for these purposes in the future than hitherto.

12.11 Many of the organisations with a long-standing involvement in Outdoor Adventure have recognised the changing needs of the times, and have re-examined and developed their purposes and practice. It is apparent too that, since the original St. George's House consultation in October 1986, a number of encouraging developments have begun to take place in both the public and voluntary sector. Local authority recreation and leisure services are beginning to take steps to provide for informal countryside and water recreation. Initiatives by national bodies such as the Sports Council, the Countryside Commission and providing agencies like the Youth Hostels Association have resulted in the provision of increasing opportunities for young people in highly imaginative ways. Some of this development may be due to the interest created by the consultation in 1986, which was followed by the circulation of the initial statement "Outdoor Adventure and the Challenge for Youth", and the discussion stimulated by this paper.

12.12 The study has also revealed a number of problems which detract from the potential benefits and which, if ignored, will impair the situation which all wish to see and lead to a situation further from the ideal. In our view, these problems need to be clearly identified and managed, so that future developments can be wisely shaped. The difficulties are exacerbated by the fragmented nature of Outdoor Adventure provision, the many approaches adopted, the great variety of sources of support, and the lack of communication and effective co-operation across the field.

The present situation, in short, is promising, but in some aspects it is not good enough.

## *Where Do We Want To Be?*

12.13 We would like to achieve, by 1995, the following objective
   **— that every young person in the United Kingdom has the opportunity to take part in adventurous outdoor activities.**

We have chosen the word 'opportunity' most carefully, believing that there should be no question of restricting the freedom of young people to choose their preferred pastimes; but that they should all be given the opportunity for this kind of adventurous activity. Many may prefer to enjoy one or more competitive kinds of sport; others may be attracted to challenges which are not physical in character.

12.14 In reaching the goal of opportunity for all, an essential exercise must be the identification of strengths to be developed and weaknesses to be overcome. It implies that the relevant statutory bodies at the national and regional level should work more closely with voluntary sector providers, and that such effort be matched by similar co-operation within the voluntary sector. Such a scenario is likely to be stimulated and accelerated by changes and new approaches resulting from the Education Reform Act, with the opportunities it offers for cross-curricular initiatives. There will also be factors in relation to the Single European Act which will doubtless have some bearing on provision and opportunity.

12.15 Difficult though it is to forecast future development, it is our hope that, provided current trends can be encouraged, strengthened, and developed, the concept of *Sport for*

*All* enunciated by the Minister for Sport, will be extended so as to give prominence to Outdoor Adventure in parallel to that which is accorded to organised games.

# How Do We Get There?

12.16 The lines of action we propose comprise five elements: improving information; enhancing quality; expanding resources; developing management and leadership; and safeguarding the environment.

## 1. *Improving Information*
### *Organisation*

1.1 Regional and district associations should be set up to develop communication at a local level, and linked to an appropriate national body.

1.2 Consideration should be given to the establishment of a national forum in which organisations with a contribution to make may meet regularly to share ideas and information.

1.3 Appropriate structures for regular communication between operators should be established.

1.4 Regional databases should be established with details of Outdoor Adventure resources. The possible value of a national database should be studied. Operators should be asked to feed information to the regional databases.

1.5 Existing sources of information such as the Regional Councils for Sport and Recreation of the Sports Council, the Council for Environmental Education and the Expedition Advisory Centre of the Royal Geographical Society, should be linked by appropriate networking arrangements. Efforts should be made to ensure that potential users know about these sources of information.

1.6 Co-ordination is required to provide access to information, equipment and skilled leadership for Outdoor Adventure and to encourage wide participation. To this end, the appointment of regional co-ordinators by the Sports Council should be extended to other regions and cities.

## *Publicity*

1.7 In view of a lack of knowledge, even among participants, about the nature, scope and benefits of Outdoor Adventure, steps should be taken to make it more widely known. Information should be available in attractive forms for potential participants, parents and the public at large. The particular value of residential experience and of expeditions should be emphasised.

1.8 The point should be made that young people seeking work are likely to be expected to provide evidence, for prospective employers, other than of technical or academic attainment. Outdoor Adventure experience is a potential asset in this regard.

1.9 An imaginative public relations programme should be embarked upon, with the backing of a supportive media group, to create an image designed to attract young people from all sections of society, making use of real-life experiences inherent in Outdoor Adventure, highlighting the achievements and endeavours of young people. To this end, a panel of media personalities should be established.

## *Research*

1.10 To overcome the lack of good and readily available research, there is a need to bring together existing material and to stimulate further research.

## 2. *Enhancing Quality*

2.1 The numerous examples of good practice illustrated in the study should be made known more widely, so as to improve the quality of all Outdoor Adventure activities.

2.2 The diverse range of activities implies a range of relevant and acceptable standards for application to particular groups. However, a code of common principles is required, taking into account such factors as safety and environmental protection. This code should be accepted by all providers of Outdoor Adventure programmes.

2.3 Whenever possible, young people should have the opportunity to progress to increasingly demanding challenges. While the basic requirement remains that of offering introductory opportunities, thought should be given to the wider provision of further opportunities for those with enterprise and desire to seek more adventurous experiences, in Britain and abroad.

## 3. *Expanding Resources*

3.1 Improved communication and co-ordination as proposed in **Section 1**, should facilitate the pooling of some resources, including residential centres and equipment.

3.2 A publicity programme, as proposed in **Section 1.7 and 1.9**, should be helpful in obtaining sponsorship and other support.

3.3 Priority in funding should be given to the recruitment and training of full-and part-time leaders, as well as volunteers.

3.4 Providers of funds for sport should bear in mind the particular value of outdoor recreation, as distinct from games and other organised sports. They should also take account of the fact that promotion of excellence in sport does not necessarily meet the needs of, nor afford opportunities for, many young people.

3.5 In funding an expanded programme of Outdoor Adventure, value for money, i.e. creating worthwhile opportunities for the maximum number of young people, should be a key consideration in approaches to future sponsors, especially in industry and commerce.

## 4. *Developing Management and Leadership*

4.1 The foundations for developing management have been suggested in **Section 1**.

4.2 The selection procedures for recruitment and the training of leaders should be developed, especially among young people who take part in Outdoor Adventure programmes.

4.3 Appropriate training programmes and qualifications should be agreed by all organisations involved in Outdoor Adventure, including programmes in courses for the training of teachers, youth leaders, the police, and prison and probation officers.

4.4 In all programmes of Outdoor Adventure, clear lines of accountability for safety should be established.

4.5 The needs of particular groups should be carefully taken into account in respect of the supervision of young people with particular handicaps and members of ethnic minorities. The needs of girls and young women should be borne in mind, in as far as these may differ from those of boys and young men. To this end, more leaders from such groups and communities should be encouraged to accept leadership roles.

## 5. *Safeguarding the Environment*

5.1 Outdoor Adventure programmes should, where appropriate, make full use of the immediate locality, including open spaces and other opportunities within, or on the fringe of, built-up areas. Some country parks may offer suitable facilities.

5.2 Careful thought should be given to the identification and management of appropriate locations, both in National Parks and elsewhere, suitable for basic training in outdoor skills and for development training exercises.

5.3 The open spaces of National Parks and other protected areas should normally be used to provide opportunities for progression to activities in which remoteness and isolation are an important part of the experience.

5.4 Communication between organisers of Outdoor Adventure programmes taking place in designated areas should be improved through the measures advocated at **Section 1** above, with a view to avoiding undue concentration of activities in particular areas.

5.5 Water-based activities, including those which can be carried out in coastal waters, have great potential for extension without detriment to the environment, and should be encouraged.

5.6 All adventure programmes should promote awareness of, and a sense of caring for, the environment. There is merit in including an element of conservation work in such programmes.

5.7 Contacts should be made with local people, especially farmers, over whose land adventure programmes are planned to take place.

5.8 Rights of free public access to areas which are suitable for Outdoor Adventure should be upheld and extended.

5.9 The development of alternative adventure opportunities in urban areas, and of expeditions in Europe and further afield should be encouraged. They help to reduce the pressure on our countryside and are a means of progression for young people.

# *Recommendations*

We recommend that:

1. The following Departments of State and other Ministries should consider in what ways they might further the promotion of outdoor adventurous activities by all young people, taking account of the strategy and lines of action proposed in this report:
The Home Department
The Ministry of Defence
The Department of Employment
The Northern Ireland Office
The Department of the Environment
The Department of Education and Science
The Scottish Office
The Department of Health
The Welsh Office

2.  The local authorities and local education authorities should likewise consider what further action they might take in the light of this report, to provide adventurous outdoor recreation for all young people.

3.  Public and national voluntary bodies which have been referred to in the report should place our findings and proposals on the agenda of their governing councils, for consideration of the parts which they might play in furtherance of the objective that all young people should have the opportunity to experience, benefit from, and make progress in, outdoor recreation.

John Hunt
John Adair
Denys Brunsden
Richard Crane
Bertie Everard
Roger Orgill
Roger Putnam
Brian Ware
Nigel Winser

# Bibliography

This is a selective bibliography giving the names of those books and reports which have been of particular assistance in the preparation of the report. It is by no means an exhaustive list of all the sources used or quoted, many of which took the form of personal communications to the Project Director.

Almost all the organisations referred to in the report have submitted much helpful material describing their objectives and their programmes. Unless this has particular historical or pedagogical interest, it has not been included in this bibliography.

In order to keep the bibliography to a reasonable length, priority has been given to material which has been recently published, and literature dating from before 1945 has been omitted. Nor have references been given to parlimentary legislation which may have a bearing on Outdoor Adventure activities.

# BIBLIOGRAPHY

| | |
|---|---|
| *author* | : Adventure and Environmental Awareness group |
| *title* | : Adventure and Environmental Awareness 1984 Conference Report |
| *publisher* | : A.E.A. group |
| *year* | : 1984 |

| | |
|---|---|
| *author* | : Adventure and Environmental Awareness group |
| *title* | : Rock-climbing and Environmental Awareness |
| *publisher* | : A.E.A group |
| *year* | : 1988 |

| | |
|---|---|
| *author* | : Adventure and Environmental Awareness group |
| *title* | : Approaches to the Environment — Towards a Common Understanding |
| *publisher* | : A.E.A. group |
| *year* | : 1989 |

| | |
|---|---|
| *author* | : Adventure Education and Outdoor Leadership |
| *title* | : Journal of the National Association for Outdoor Education |
| *publisher* | : N.A.O.E. quarterly publication |
| *year* | : |

| | |
|---|---|
| *author* | : Allcock R. |
| *title* | : Development Training — a personal view |
| *publisher* | : Endeavour Training |
| *year* | : 1988 |

| | |
|---|---|
| *author* | : Bank J. |
| *title* | : Outdoor Development for Managers |
| *publisher* | : Gower Publishing Co. Ltd |
| *year* | : 1985 |

| | |
|---|---|
| *author* | : Basic Expedition Training Award |
| *title* | : Course Directors' and Tutors' Notes |
| *publisher* | : Central Council of Physical Recreation |
| *year* | : 1988 |

# BIBLIOGRAPHY

*author*     : Blackie J.
*title*      : Inside the Primary School
*publisher*  : Dept. of Education and Science (H.M.S.O)
*year*       : 1967

*author*     : Blashford-Snell J. and Tweedy A.
*title*      : Operation Raleigh — Adventure Challenge
*publisher*  : Collins
*year*       : 1988

*author*     : British Schools Exploring Society
*title*      : Newsletters and Expedition Reports
*publisher*  : B.S.E.S.
*year*       :

*author*     : Brunsden Professor D.
*title*      : Presidential Address to the Geographical Association: "The Science of the Unknown"
*publisher*  : Geographical Association
*year*       : 1987

*author*     : Byatt D.A. (Editor)
*title*      : Kurt Hahn: An Appreciation of his Life and Work
*publisher*  : Aberdeen University Press
*year*       : 1976

*author*     : Campbell B. and Campbell M.
*title*      : Brathay: the first Twenty-Five Years 1947 – 1972
*publisher*  : The Brathay Hall Trust
*year*       : 1972

*author*     : Cheesmond J. and Yates J.
*title*      : A Report on Outdoor Education programmes in Lothian Region secondary schools
*publisher*  : Lothian Region Education Board
*year*       : 1980

| | |
|---|---|
| *author* | : Cotton M. |
| *title* | : Out of Doors with Handicapped People |
| *publisher* | : Souvenir Press |
| *year* | : 1981 |

| | |
|---|---|
| *author* | : Cotton M. |
| *title* | : Outdoor Adventure for Handicapped People |
| *publisher* | : Souvenir Press |
| *year* | : 1983 |

| | |
|---|---|
| *author* | : Countryside Commission |
| *title* | : A Compendium of Recreation Statistics 1984 – 1986 |
| *publisher* | : Countryside Commission |
| *year* | : 1987 |

| | |
|---|---|
| *author* | : Countryside Commission |
| *title* | : Policies for enjoying the Countryside |
| *publisher* | : Countryside Commission |
| *year* | : 1987 |

| | |
|---|---|
| *author* | : Cox M. |
| *title* | : Leadership: a paper presented at the MLTB Conference 1983 |
| *publisher* | : Mountainwalking Leader Training Board |
| *year* | : 1983 |

| | |
|---|---|
| *author* | : Cumbria Education Committee |
| *title* | : Outdoor Education in the Curriculum |
| *publisher* | : Cumbria County Council |
| *year* | : 1984 |

| | |
|---|---|
| *author* | : Dartington Amenity Research Trust |
| *title* | : Groups in the Countryside |
| *publisher* | : Countryside Commission |
| *year* | : 1980 |

| | |
|---|---|
| *author* | : Dept of Education and Science |
| *title* | : Environmental Education from 5 to 16 |
| | (Curriculum Matters series No 13) |
| *publisher* | : H.M.S.O. |
| *year* | : 1989 |

| | |
|---|---|
| *author* | : Dept. Of Education and Science |
| *title* | : Personal and Social Education from 5 to 16 |
| | (Curriculum Matters series No 14) |
| *publisher* | : H.M.S.O. |
| *year* | : 1989 |

| | |
|---|---|
| *author* | : Dept. of Education and Science |
| *title* | : Learning Out of Doors; |
| | An H.M.I. Survey of Outdoor Education and short-stay residential experience |
| *publisher* | : H.M.S.O. |
| *year* | : 1983 |

| | |
|---|---|
| *author* | : Dept. of Education and Science |
| *title* | : Safety in Outdoor Education |
| *publisher* | : H.M.S.O. |
| *year* | : 1989 |

| | |
|---|---|
| *author* | : Dept. of Education and Science |
| *title* | : National Curriculum: from Policy to Practice |
| *publisher* | : Dept. of Education and Science |
| *year* | : 1989 |

| | |
|---|---|
| *author* | : Dept. of the Environment, Inner Cities Directorate |
| *title* | : Developing Sport and Leisure — Good Practice in Urban Regeneration |
| *publisher* | : H.M.S.O |
| *year* | : 1989 |

| | |
|---|---|
| *author* | : Devon County Council |
| *title* | : Outdoor Education in Devon |
| *publisher* | : Devon C. C. Education Dept. |
| *year* | : 1988 |

| | |
|---|---|
| *author* | : Drasdo H. |
| *title* | : Education and the Mountain Centres |
| *publisher* | : Tyddyn Gabriel |
| *year* | : 1973 |

| | |
|---|---|
| *author* | : Keay W. Ed. Gair N. |
| *title* | : Expedition Guide |
| *publisher* | : Duke of Edinburgh's Award |
| *year* | : 1987 |

| | |
|---|---|
| *author* | : Chambers J. Ed. Gair N. |
| *title* | : A Challenge to the Individual: The Scheme and People with Special Needs |
| *publisher* | : Duke of Edinburgh's Award |
| *year* | : 1988 |

| | |
|---|---|
| *author* | : Ed. Gair N. (5th Revised Edition) |
| *title* | : Handbook |
| *publisher* | : Duke of Edinburgh's Award |
| *year* | : 1988 |

| | |
|---|---|
| *author* | : Education for Capability |
| *title* | : Newsletters and Reports |
| *publisher* | : Royal Society of Arts |
| *year* | : |

| | |
|---|---|
| *author* | : Environmental Education |
| *title* | : Journal of the National Association for Environmental Education |
| *publisher* | : N.A.E.E. twice yearly |
| *year* | : |

# BIBLIOGRAPHY

| | |
|---|---|
| *author* | : Everard K.B. |
| *title* | : Development Training — Progress and Prospects |
| *publisher* | : Development Training Advisory Group |
| *year* | : 1987 |

| | |
|---|---|
| *author* | : Fletcher B. |
| *title* | : The Challenge of Outward Bound |
| *publisher* | : William Heinemann |
| *year* | : 1971 |

| | |
|---|---|
| *author* | : Gilbert R. |
| *title* | : Young Explorers |
| *publisher* | : G.H. Smith and Son |
| *year* | : 1979 |

| | |
|---|---|
| *author* | : Greenaway R. |
| *title* | : The Training and Development of Development Trainers |
| *publisher* | : Brathay Hall Trust |
| *year* | : 1986 |

| | |
|---|---|
| *author* | : Greenaway R. and Bill C. |
| *title* | : Competences of Development Trainers |
| *publisher* | : Trainer Development Section, The Training Agency |
| *year* | : 1989 |

| | |
|---|---|
| *author* | : Grey N.E. |
| *title* | : The long-term effects of Outdoor Education; Report of a research project at Sheffield Polytechnic |
| *publisher* | : Unpublished |
| *year* | : 1987 |

| | |
|---|---|
| *author* | : H.M. Inspectorate |
| *title* | : Curriculum 11 – 16; A contribution to current debate |
| *publisher* | : Dept. of Education and Science |
| *year* | : 1977 |

| | |
|---|---|
| *author* | : H.M. Inspectorate |
| *title* | : Effective Youth Work (Education Observed 6) |
| *publisher* | : Dept. of Education and Science |
| *year* | : 1987 |

| | |
|---|---|
| *author* | : Hampshire County Council |
| *title* | : Hampshire's Coast |
| *publisher* | : Hampshire County Council |
| *year* | : 1987 |

| | |
|---|---|
| *author* | : Havinghurst R.J. |
| *title* | : Human Development and Education |
| *publisher* | : Longmans |
| *year* | : 1953 |

| | |
|---|---|
| *author* | : Hogan J.M. |
| *title* | : Impelled into Experiences: the Story of the Outward Bound Schools. |
| *publisher* | : Educational Productions Ltd. |
| *year* | : 1968 |

| | |
|---|---|
| *author* | : Hopkins D. |
| *title* | : Adventure Education and Management Development |
| *publisher* | : Bristol University School of Education |
| *year* | : 1988 |

| | |
|---|---|
| *author* | : Keay W. |
| *title* | : Land Navigation: Routefinding with Map and Compass |
| *publisher* | : Duke of Edinburgh's Award |
| *year* | : 1989 |

| | |
|---|---|
| *author* | : Keighley P.W.S. |
| *title* | : The relevance of residential and outdoor education for pupil-profiling and records of achievement |
| *publisher* | : Cumbria County Council Education Dept. |
| *year* | : 1987 |

# BIBLIOGRAPHY

*author*   : Keighley P.W.S.

*title*   : Evidence to support how a structured approach to Outdoor Education contributes to personal & social development

*publisher*   : Unpublished

*year*   : 1987


*author*   : Keighley P.W.S.

*title*   : Outdoor Education in the Curriculum — Putting the ideas into practice (Talk given at a D.E.S. Regional Course)

*publisher*   : Unpublished

*year*   : 1986


*author*   : Kolb D.A.

*title*   : Experiential Learning; Experience as the source of learning and development

*publisher*   : Prentice Hall

*year*   : 1984


*author*   : Langmuir E.

*title*   : Mountaincraft and Leadership

*publisher*   : Mountainwalking Leader Training Board

*year*   : 1984


*author*   : Latto K.

*title*   : Give us the Chance; Sport and physical recreation with the mentally handicapped

*publisher*   : The Disabled Living Foundation

*year*   : 1981


*author*   : Laycock S.R. and Munro B.C.

*title*   : Educational Psychology

*publisher*   : Pitman Educational Library, Sir Isaac Pitman and Sons Ltd.

*year*   : 1972


*author*   : Liverpool Education Authority Youth Service

*title*   : A Policy for Outdoor Education in the Youth Service

*publisher*   : Unpublished

*year*   :

| | |
|---|---|
| *author* | : Loader C.M. |
| *title* | : Cairngorm Adventure at Glenmore Lodge |
| *publisher* | : William Brown |
| *year* | : 1952 |

| | |
|---|---|
| *author* | : Lothian Region; Draft Policy Statement |
| *title* | : The Contribution of Outdoor Education to the Primary, Secondary and Tertiary Curriculum |
| *publisher* | : Lothian Education Dept. |
| *year* | : 1988 |

| | |
|---|---|
| *author* | : Lynch J. |
| *title* | : Multi-Cultural Education: Principles and Practice |
| *publisher* | : Routledge & Kegan Paul |
| *year* | : 1986 |

| | |
|---|---|
| *author* | : Manpower Services Commission Working Group |
| *title* | : Residential Training in Y.T.S. — Youth Training Scheme Manual |
| *publisher* | : Manpower Services Commission |
| *year* | : 1985 |

| | |
|---|---|
| *author* | : Mortlock C. |
| *title* | : The Adventure Alternative |
| *publisher* | : Cicerone Press |
| *year* | : 1984 |

| | |
|---|---|
| *author* | : Mortlock C. |
| *title* | : Adventure Education |
| *publisher* | : published privately |
| *year* | : 1975 |

# BIBLIOGRAPHY

| | |
|---|---|
| *author* | : N.A.C.R.O. |
| *title* | : Growing up on Housing Estates: A Report by a Crime Prevention Advisory Committee Working Group |
| *publisher* | : National Association for the Care and Rehabilitation of Offenders |
| *year* | : 1988 |

| | |
|---|---|
| *author* | : National Association for Environmental Education |
| *title* | : The Organisation of Outdoor Studies and Visits |
| *publisher* | : N.A.E.E. |
| *year* | : 1988 |

| | |
|---|---|
| *author* | : National Youth Bureau |
| *title* | : Starting from Strengths |
| *publisher* | : National Youth Bureau |
| *year* | : 1984 |

| | |
|---|---|
| *author* | : National Youth Bureau and National Council for Voluntary Youth Services |
| *title* | : D.E.S. Grants; Learning by Achievement: Guidelines to Education Support Grants, 1900 – 1991 |
| *publisher* | : N.Y.B. and N.C.V.Y.S. |
| *year* | : 1987 |

| | |
|---|---|
| *author* | : Noble P. |
| *title* | : Swamps and Crocodiles — A Study of Outdoor Education Provision |
| *publisher* | : Rotherham Education Authority |
| *year* | : 1987 |

| | |
|---|---|
| *author* | : Outdoor Education Advisers' Panel (South-west Region) |
| *title* | : Learning Outcomes for Outdoor Education — a working paper |
| *publisher* | : Unpublished |
| *year* | : 1989 |

| | |
|---|---|
| *author* | : Parker T.M. and Meldrum K.I. |
| *title* | : Outdoor Education |
| *publisher* | : J.M. Dent and Sons |
| *year* | : 1973 |

| | |
|---|---|
| *author* | : PHAB 88 |
| *title* | : The Magazine of PHAB (Physically handicapped and able-bodied) |
| *publisher* | : PHAB Publications |
| *year* | : |

| | |
|---|---|
| *author* | : Preece P. (Editor) |
| *title* | : The Venturer |
| *publisher* | : Magazine of the Prince of Wales Community Venture |
| *year* | : |

| | |
|---|---|
| *author* | : Price T. |
| *title* | : Some Aspects of Character-building |
| *publisher* | : Royal Society of Arts |
| *year* | : 1966 |

| | |
|---|---|
| *author* | : Report of the Albermarle Committee |
| *title* | : The Youth Service in England and Wales |
| *publisher* | : H.M.S.O. |
| *year* | : 1960 |

| | |
|---|---|
| *author* | : Report of the Central Advisory Council for Education (Chair; Lady Plowden) |
| *title* | : Children and their Primary Schools |
| *publisher* | : H.M.S.O. |
| *year* | : 1967 |

| | |
|---|---|
| *author* | : Report of the Central Advisory Council for Education (Chair; Newsom J.) |
| *title* | : Half our Future |
| *publisher* | : H.M.S.O. |
| *year* | : 1963 |

| | |
|---|---|
| *author* | : Report of the Dartington Conference |
| *title* | : Outdoor Education |
| *publisher* | : Dept. of Education and Science |
| *year* | : 1975 |

# BIBLIOGRAPHY

*author*   : Report of the Review Group on the Youth Service in England (Chair; Thompson A.)
*title*   : Experience and Participation
*publisher*   : H.M.S.O.
*year*   : 1982

*author*   : Report of the Study Group on Education and Field Biology
*title*   : Teaching Science Out of Doors
*publisher*   : Longmans
*year*   : 1963

*author*   : Roberts K. White G. and Parker M.
*title*   : The Character Training Industry — Adventure Training Schemes in Britain
*publisher*   : David and Charles
*year*   : 1974

*author*   : Rogers C.
*title*   : Learning to be Free; in Person to Person by Rogers C. & Stevens B.
*publisher*   : Souvenir Press
*year*   : 1967

*author*   : Scarf M.
*title*   : Unfinished Business: pressure points in the lives of women
*publisher*   : Fontana
*year*   : 1981

*author*   : School Curriculum Development Committee
*title*   : Out and About; a teacher's guide to safe practice out of school
*publisher*   : Methuen
*year*   : 1987

*author*   : Scottish Education Dept. Consultative Committee on the Curriculum
*title*   : The Structure of the Curriculum in the 3rd and 4th years of the Scottish Secondary School (The Munn Report)
*publisher*   : H.M.S.O.
*year*   : 1977

| | |
|---|---|
| *author* | : Sharpe S. |
| *title* | : Just like a girl — How girls learn to be women |
| *publisher* | : Penguin |
| *year* | : 1973 |

| | |
|---|---|
| *author* | : Sidaway R. |
| *title* | : Sport, Recreation and Nature Conservation |
| *publisher* | : The Sports Council |
| *year* | : 1988 |

| | |
|---|---|
| *author* | : Skidelsky R. |
| *title* | : English Progressive Schools |
| *publisher* | : Penguin Books |
| *year* | : 1969 |

| | |
|---|---|
| *author* | : Smith D. |
| *title* | : Helping Juvenile Offenders |
| *publisher* | : Policy Studies: the Journal of the Policy Studies Institute, Vol 4, Part 1 |
| *year* | : 1983 |

| | |
|---|---|
| *author* | : Sports Council |
| *title* | : Into the 90s; A Strategy for Sport 1988 – 1993 |
| *publisher* | : Sports Council |
| *year* | : 1988 |

| | |
|---|---|
| *author* | : Sports Council (North West Region) |
| *title* | : Community-based sentencing — the Use of Outdoor Challenge (Conference Report) |
| *publisher* | : Sports Council (North West Region) |
| *year* | : 1987 |

| | |
|---|---|
| *author* | : Standing Committee, A.H.O.E.C., N.A.O.E., N.A.F.S.O., O.E.A.P., S.P.A.O.E. |
| *title* | : Outdoor Education and the National Curriculum |
| *publisher* | : Duke of Edinburgh's Award |
| *year* | : 1989 |

# BIBLIOGRAPHY

*author*    : Standing Committee, A.H.O.E.C., N.A.O.E., N.A.F.S.O., S.P.A.O.E. and O.E.A.P.
*title*     : Outdoor Education, safety and good practice; Guidelines for Guidelines
*publisher* : Duke of Edinburgh's Award
*year*      : 1988

*author*    : Stead D. and Swain G. (Editors)
*title*     : Youth Work and Sport
*publisher* : National Youth Bureau
*year*      : 1987

*author*    : Stern E. and Turbin J.
*title*     : Youth Employment and Unemployment in Rural England
*publisher* : The Development Commission
*year*      : 1986

*author*    : Swan (Lord)
*title*     : Education for All; a guide to the Swann Report into the education of children from
              ethnic minority groups
*publisher* : H.M.S.O.
*year*      : 1985

*author*    : The Cookham Group
*title*     : Headlines 2000: The world as we see it
*publisher* : Hay Management Consultants Ltd.
*year*      : 1988

*author*    : Van Matre S.
*title*     : Acclimatization — A sensory and conceptual approach to ecological involvement
*publisher* : American Camping Association
*year*      : 1972

*author*    : Which? magazine
*title*     : Which? January 1986: Children's Activity Holidays
*publisher* : Consumers' Association
*year*      : 1986

| | |
|---|---|
| *author* | :Winser N. and Winser S. |
| *title* | : Expedition Planners' Handbook and Directory, 1986/1987 |
| *publisher* | : Expedition Advisory Centre (Royal Geographical Society) |
| *year* | : |

| | |
|---|---|
| *author* | : YETMAG |
| *title* | : The magazine of the Young Explorers' Trust |
| *publisher* | : Young Explorers' Trust Bi-monthly |
| *year* | : |

| | |
|---|---|
| *author* | : Yorkshire & Humberside Regional Examinations Board |
| *title* | : Records of Achievement; Recording Residential Experience |
| *publisher* | : Northern Partnership for Records of Achievement |
| *year* | : 1987 |

# INDEX

(Numbers refer to paragraphs and P to Preface)

## A

British Nuclear Fuels 4.61
British Orienteering Federation 6.31
British Rail 4.63
British Schools' Exploring Society 1.17, 3.17, 4.21, 5.66, 6.57ff, 9.10
British Trust for Conservation Volunteers 3,17, 4.40, 5.66, 6.34
British Waterways Board 6.15f
Brown, Hamish 1.47
BTEC National Diploma 4.29, 4.31
Burrow Hill School 8.51
Butler, Ian 8.70

# C

Calshot Activities Centre 8.51
Calvert Trust 8.37ff
Cambridge University Explorers' and Travellers' Club 4.79
Camley Street Natural Park 2.6
Camp schools 1.15
Carnoch Outdoor Centre 6.53
Castle Park Primary School 2.15
Cawston College 3.33
Central Council for Physical Recreation 1.30, 6.32
Certificate of Pre-Vocational Education (CPVE) 1.51, 4.10, 4.26
Chapman, Jonathan 8.36
Character training P, 1.23
Charlotte Mason College 2.18, 4.82, 10.29
Cheshire County Council 2.19
Chichester, Francis 1.36
Christian Mountain Centre 6.53
Churchtown Farm Field Studies Centre 8.34ff
Cirdan Trust 3.56, 6.72
City Challenge programme 6.45
Clegg, Sir Alec 1.43, 8.2
Clients 5.16
Clubs 1.20

# D

# E

Gilbert, Richard 1.47, 4.24
Girl Guides (Association) 1.10, 2.16, 3.48ff, 5.66, 8.13, 9.21
Girls' Brigade 3.53 8.14
Gittins, John 2.19
Glen River YMCA Centre 6.48, 7.21
Glenmore Lodge 1.29, 9.9, 10.23
Gloucestershire Youth and Community Service 4.38
Gordonstoun School 1.18, 3.30
Grass Routes 8.76
Greater Manchester Probation Service 8.80
Groundwork Trusts 4.40, 6.35

# H

HMI Survey, 'Learning out of Doors' 2.13
Hadow Report 1.13
Hahn, Kurt 1.18f, 3.30
Havinghurst, R.J. 3.2
Hazards 3.16
Highland Fieldcraft Training Centre 1.21
Hillend Ski Centre 1.44
Hogan, J.M. 1.23, 1.43
Holme Pierrepoint National Watersports Centre 8.49
Holt, Laurence 1.23
Hopkins, David 7.38
Hughes, Dillon 4.42
Human development 4.1ff, 8.4: see also Adolescent, Human, Personal development
Humberstone, Barbara 8.21
Hutchings, G.A.

# I

ILEA 9.17
Image 9.2f

# *M*

Norfolk Youth and Community Service 3.43
Northern Ireland 7.20f
Norwich Union 4.9
Nursing, UK Central Council for 4.9

# O

Oakham School 4.24
Oaklands LEA Centre 3.23
Ocean Youth Club 1.45, 4.20, 6.68
Offenders: see Young Offenders
Operation Drake 1.47
Operation Innervator 3.58
Operation Raleigh 1.47, 3.17, 4.21, 4.49, 5.66, 6.61, 9.10
Organisation of Scottish Providers of Residential Education (OSPRE) 6.42
Organisations, awareness of 5.66
Outcomes of outdoor adventure 4.87, 5.22, 5.41, 5.53, 7.22ff, 12.1ff
Outdoor Education Safety Network 9.5
Outdoor adventure P
Outdoor education P
Outdoor pursuits P
Outdoor (pursuits) centres 1.15, 1.42
Outward Bound (Trust) 1.23, 1.27, 1.39, 3.17f, 3.47, 4.14, 4.49, 4.66, 4.86, 5.66, 6.45f, 7.9, 8.22, 8.45ff, 9.11
Overseas travel/expeditions 4.14, 4.21ff: see also Expeditions

# P

Parson House Outdoor Pursuits Centre 8.74
Personal and social (spiritual) development P, 3.20, 4.1, 4.10, 4.53: see also Human, Adolescent development
Pestalozzi 1.9
PGCE 4.84, 10.28f
PGL 2.25, 3.61

Ranger Service: see Country Ranger Service
Rank Education Services 2.24
Rank Foundation 7.9
Rannoch School 3.31
Records of achievement 3.8
Recreation in countryside 1.11
Recruitment of leaders, staff 5.47, 10.1f 10.7f
Research 12.16
Residential experience P, 3.16, 3.36, 4.54, 4.59, 7.26ff
Resources 9.8, 12.16
Responsibilities of leaders: see Duties
Reviewing 3.16, 5.35, 8.5
Rhos-y-Gwaliau 5.66
Rialland, Alan 8.38
River Dart Country Park 6.52
Roberts, John, 8.78
Robinson, Don 4.23
Rogers, Carl 7.40
Romantic movement 1.6
Roose School 2.11
Royal Association for Disability and Rehabilitation (RADAR) 8.48
Royal Geographical Society 6.54
Royal Society for Nature Conservation 2.20, 6.33
Royal Society of Arts 4.11, 10.24
Royal Ulster Constabulary 3.59
Royal Yachting Association 6.31, 8.43
Runcie, Dr.Robert 2.22
Rural areas 7.11

# S

Safety 9.4ff, 10.43
Sahara Expedition 3.29
Sail Training Association 1.45, 4.14, 6.69
Sail training 1.23

# *Y*